Kayal
The Syrian-
Lebanese in
America

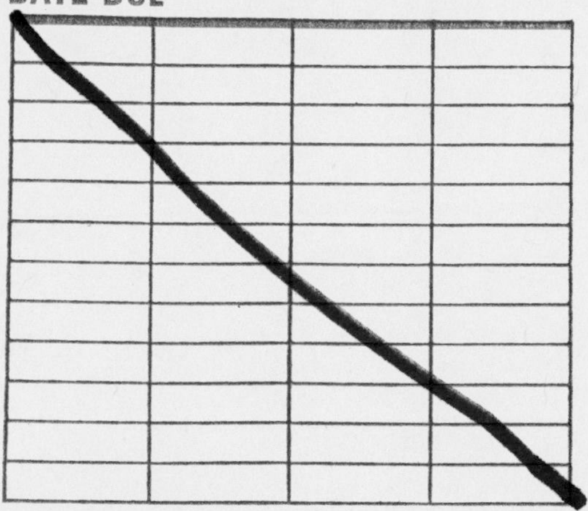

THE IMMIGRANT HERITAGE OF AMERICA SERIES

Cecyle S. Neidle, Editor

The Syrian–Lebanese in America

A Study in Religion and Assimilation

By PHILIP M. KAYAL and JOSEPH M. KAYAL

Foreword by MICHAEL NOVAK

TWAYNE PUBLISHERS

A DIVISION OF G. K. HALL & CO., BOSTON

Library of Congress Cataloging in Publication Data

Kayal, Philip M 1943–
The Syrian-Lebanese in America.

(The Immigrant heritage of American series)
Bibliography: p. 250-57.
1. Syrians in the United States. 2. Lebanese in the United States. I. Kayal, Joseph M., 1942– joint author. II. Title.
E184.S98K33 917.3'06'9275691 74-18424
ISBN 0-8057-8412-8

MANUFACTURED IN THE UNITED STATES OF AMERICA

Patricia

Michele
Matthew
Justin

Contents

About the Authors

Philip M. Kayal was born in Brooklyn of an immigrant father from Aleppo, Syria and an American-born mother. He attended Fordham University and was awarded the Master of Arts degree in 1966 and the Ph.d. in 1970.

Dr. Kayal is a member of the American Sociological Association and the Association of Arab-American University Graduates. He has lectured at the School of Education, Fordham University and Richmond College. After a period at Notre Dame College of Staten Island, he served as Chairman of the Department of Sociology at Seton Hall University.

He has read papers on Religion and Assimilation before the Association for the Sociology of Religion and is a member of the Center for Migration Studies and the editorial board of the *International Migration Review* which has published his recent monograph on Syrians in the United States. Another article, entitled, "Religion in the Christian Syrian-American Community," was published in *Arabic-Speaking American Communities*, edited by Dr. Barbara Aswad of Wayne State University. Dr. Kayal is presently Associate Professor of Sociology in the Department of Sociology and Anthropology, Seton Hall University.

Born in Brooklyn, Joseph M. Kayal did undergraduate work in history and earned a Master of Arts degree in sociology at Fordham University. As Instructor in Sociology at Fordham and at Herbert H. Lehman College he taught courses on the social structure of the United States and comparative anthropology. He has also lectured on criminology and deviant behavior at Hofstra University.

Mr. Kayal is presently associated with the New York Telephone Company as supervisor of educational services. His professional affiliations include membership in the American Association for the Advancement of Science, the American Sociological Association, The Center for the Study of Democratic Institutions. He is also an elected member of the board of education of South Huntington, New York.

Note to the Reader

The ideas of *Lebanon* and the *Lebanese* people are fairly recent POLITICAL constructs.

Historically and politically, Lebanon was an integral constitutent of Syrian society and its people almost indistinguishable participants in its socio-cultural dynamics.

Since this text deals with the religious rather than geo-political phenomena whereby various groups in the Syrian population came to identify themselves, the terms Syrian and Lebanese will be used interchangeably throughout this text.

Acknowledgements

This text could not have been completed without the inspiration and guidance rendered by our parents, Mitchell and Alice Kayal, who spent untold hours educating the authors in the traditions and history of the East and the difficulties faced by the Syrian immigrants in New York.

The bibliographic guide included at the end of the text could not have been written without the assistance of Dr. Barbara Aswad of Wayne State University and Dr. Stewart McHenry of the University of Vermont.

We are also indebted to the editorial assistance given us by Mr. Michael Wallace of Staten Island Community College and Dr. Adele Younis of Salem State College in Massachusetts.

Special thanks is also given to Dr. Cecyle Neidle for her patient review and critique of the manuscript.

Typing assistance was rendered by Mrs. Florence Taras, secretary of the Department of Sociology, Seton Hall University, South Orange, New Jersey.

Foreword

Among the nations on this planet, the United States is in a fortunate position. Our peoples reach out to virtually every other culture with bonds of family, memory, and shared tradition. An event can hardly happen at any place upon this planet without profoundly affecting some part of the American population. A revolt in Cambodia, a tidal wave in Pakistan, terrorism in the Middle East, civil war in Ireland, invasion on Cyprus, revolution in Ethiopia, insurrection in the Dominican Republic—each such event is for some Americans a family event, and each touches some part of the American people with sympathy, sorrow, outrage, or concern. We are in fact—but not in consciousness—the most multicultural people on this earth.

A century ago, nativists feared that immigrants from some cultures might not be able to be "assimilated" into Anglo-American traditions. In this inverted way, they were suggesting that Anglo-American traditions had a certain narrow human range. Perhaps their cultural traditions were too insular; in any case, they feared pluralism. Such fears had some plausibility, since the nation did need unity. Yet there are many strategies for obtaining unity, without imposing homogeneity. Fear of diversity led to a costly social error.

Emotional, intellectual, familial, and behavioral norms were expected to be internalized as quickly as possible. These norms may have been imposed unconsciously rather than consciously; few Anglo-Americans seemed to recognize the hurdles they asked others to jump. Those who seemed foreign, different, out of step with American ways, not American in appearance and style, or not sufficiently cognizant of American superiority found it difficult to become accepted fully. Anglo-Americans did respect success, but economic success did not always mean equivalent success in status, prestige, and cultural respect. Strait was the gate, narrow the way. Millions came to feel gratitude toward America, and appreciation for its social system, but anger toward and resentment of WASP pretenses. Confidence in WASP leadership rested on a fragile base. "The best and the brightest" could very quickly fall in general esteem.

The nativist strategy was a costly mistake in a second way: it wastefully promoted cultural amnesia. Frugal in material things, the nativist was prodigal with cultural resources, emptying them out upon the ground. Those citizens who possessed a second language were not praised, encouraged, and rewarded; they were made to feel ashamed. In the schools, connections with a second culture—through poetry, fiction, drama, dance, music, history, and social studies—were not encouraged. In the curriculum, many of the world's cultures were deliberately and systematically ignored. No great efforts were made to revise the curriculum to maintain the life and power of the cultures the immigrants brought with them.

The national policy was narrow, insular, even chauvinist. Being more American than others was a matter for boastfulness. Other cultures of this planet were treated as though they were inferior.

Now that the United States is the most central and powerful of all nations, we pay the serious penalty of this early chauvinism. Now that we need a clear understanding of other cultures on this planet, now that we need a kind of internal sympathy with every other culture, we are embarrassed by our national ignorance, *gaucherie*, and imperceptiveness. Instead of gaining a reputation as the culture most sympathetic to all the world's peoples, we have won a reputation for being somewhat innocent, somewhat arrogant, and culturally naive.

The Anglo-American treatment of non-English-speaking immigrants and the flawed foreign policies of the United States have a common source: the same lack of interest in others, the same sense of superiority.

Studies of American immigrant groups are not, then, a mere luxury; they are essential to the nation's social health and intellectual honesty. Such studies provide a living connection to the other cultures of this planet. If Americans would come to full self-knowledge—to knowledge of all its own participant peoples—it would discover in itself vital links to every other culture. It would possess resources for understanding the complexities and subtleties of human perception and aspiration everywhere.

Thus, while Joseph and Philip Kayal shed light on the extraordinary pattern of Syrian-Lebanese acculturation in the United States these last hundred years, they also shed unusually helpful light on the currents of cultural and political life in the present Middle East. And by describing the experience of Syrian-Lebanese in the United States, they often shed fascinating light, from a new angle of vision, on the character of Anglo-American culture. For the Syrian-Lebanese experience differs from the Jewish experience, the Irish experience, the Italian experience, and other group experiences. Only when the stories of *all* the peoples of America have been told will we have a full, rounded view of a marvelous and unparalleled phenomenon: the multi-sided American character.

Moreover, the Kayals have shown that even the fundamental tools of analysis in such matters need revision. The Syrian-Lebanese are not exactly an "ethnic group" in the same way as the Irish, the Latinos, or the Poles, or others may be. Distinctions between cultures, religions, national states, linguistic families, and disparate social institutions need to be carefully drawn, if we are not to impose models derived from certain ethnic groups upon all the others. We know far less about such matters than we need to know.

The insistance of these two young authors on distinctive notes in the Syrian-Lebanese self-consciousness is both intellectually sound and highly significant. On the one hand, they insist, self-consciousness in Syrian-Lebanese experience is primarily religious rather than national; moreover, they add, the distinction between religion and nationality is drawn rather differently in the Arabic-speaking world. On the other hand, they also insist, the relatively recent emergence of an independent Syria and an independent Lebanon has caused Americans of Syrian-Lebanese background to experience several different currents of self-identification.

The spectacular cultural and financial successes of Syrian-Lebanese in America—Ralph Nader, William Blatty, Michael DeBakey, Philip Habib, Danny Thomas, Senator James Abourezk, Najeeb Halaby, the Haddad family, Farah, Hagar and others may stand for their approximately one million fellow Americans—suggest a type of cultural preparation best suited to success in America. The remarkable tendency of the Syrian-Lebanese to spread out thinly all over the United States, while retaining cultural control at long distance, contrasts sharply with the pattern of other immigrant groups.

Given the low estate of translation from Arabic texts into English (a low estate shared by virtually all immigrant literatures except perhaps French and German), the authors did not and could not explore the more subtle psychological connections between the Syrian-Lebanese Americans and the historical world of Arabic culture. It would be surprising, indeed, if rhythms of Arab passion, emotion, intuition, and sensibility had wholly disappeared in a short three or four generations. And yet without an Arabic-American literature—without poetry, plays, novels, histories, dramas, philosophies—such matters remain unconscious or deeply buried. They find, in the objective world of public discourse no mirror, no echo, no flash of recognition. Thus, like many other immigrants, many Syrian-Lebanese possess no conscious articulation of the inner music of their own souls. To this extent, they may appear to be more "assimilated" than they are. Their consciousness is furnished with English and American literature, German and French philosophy, Irish-Latin theology, and the other Western appurtenances of a sound education. In all these resources there are, to be sure, universal elements, helpful and illuminating to all. Yet creative writers, great artists, and original thinkers of all sorts must eventually dig into the soil of their own deepest identity, and discover materials not possessed by others but solely their own. Therein lies their distinctiveness, their originality—which is always as much social as personal.

The Syrian-Lebanese are in the process of re-possessing their own history and re-establishing contact with the cultures of their own land. Thus we may expect soon new and penetrating self-revelations, which will shed fresh light on the identities of the rest of us. Each American who discovers himself or herself illuminates from a new angle every other.

I must add in concluding this brief preface my singular pleasure in being able to repay some personal debts. In Johnstown, Pa., where I grew up, a friend of my family and a highly respected surgeon represented in my earliest consciousness the Syrian-Lebanese experience. During my college years, Joseph Skaff and Ferris Kleem were among my closest circle of friends, and introduced me to magnificent Lebanese dinners, a belly dance or two, and worship in the Maronite rite. I learned from them a sense for Arab intensity, wide emotional range, wit, laughter, and expressive family warmth that remains exceedingly vivid. Finally, my younger brother Dick, a priest of Holy Cross, spent two idyllic weeks in the hills of Lebanon, visiting the Skaff family abroad, on his way to studies in Arabic at the University of Dacca. His untimely death a year later prevented the fruition of his studies in Arabic culture, which he loved, and so even in this brief word of introduction I feel as though I am gesturing in a direction he would have taken. That this book, too, is a collaboration between two brothers strikes me as a poignant symbol.

MICHAEL NOVAK

Preface

It is the general consensus of contemporary sociology that the concept of America's ethnic past and future as a great "melting pot" is somewhat less than accurate. In its magazine,[1] The Center for the Study of Democratic Institutions discussed the dynamic nature of "the new ethnicity" in personalized and popular terms.[2] Jimmy Breslin, social gladfly and columnist makes part of his living helping Americans feel comfortable with ethnicity and campaigning politicians deliberately apply their knowledge of its regional character in their efforts to appeal to local sensitivities.

In America's large cities one usually thinks mainly of Irish, Italians, Poles, Jews, Germans, and other Europeans when enumerating ethnic groups. It was not until fairly recently that America's popular conception of ethnicity became sophisticated and expansive enough to include the people from the Middle East. Until a short time ago only one scholarly text was available to students of the Syrian (Lebanese) migration and assimilation experience in this country. Our study attempts to organize the literature on Syrian–Lebanese Americans and to examine their Americanization. More particularly, our concern will be with the function of religion in the assimilation of Eastern rite Catholics (Melkites and Maronites) of Syrian (Lebanese) ancestry. The transformation of identities and the rise of ethnic consciousness among these Christian Arabs was a consequence of the external relationships the collectivity's religious institutions have established with their American counterparts.

To a lesser extent, the text will also deal with the Americanization of Eastern Orthodox Syrians and their relationship to their coreligionists of Greek, Russian and Ukrainian origin. This phenomenon affected the nature of their social intercourse with the Catholic Syrians. Eventually an American Orthodox Church will be formed and take its place beside the American Protestant,

Catholic and Jewish establishments.[3] Undoubtedly, this will affect the Syrian American community.

American interest in the Middle East was generated in 1819 by the arrival there of Presbyterian missionaries who generally failed to attract converts because they were steadily resisted by both the native Moslem and Christian communities. The missionaries then moved into more practical projects, such as the establishing of schools and hospitals which were the beginning of a long tradition of American philanthropy in the area. American foreign aid eventually made the United States the most trusted of all foreign nations to the peoples of the Middle East. American schools, foremost among them the American University of Beirut and Robert College (Istanbul), not only imparted knowledge to their students but also instilled in them a resourceful and creative attitude and style.

It was the spontaneous and nonsectarian generosity of America which helped inspire the original migration from the Middle East to these shores, and the outpouring of American concern for the civilian victims of war and famine during World War II gained added stature for the United States.

Unfortunately, America's reputation in the region for fairness and integrity was shaken by its unilateral support of Israel after 1948. The Arabs claimed some 750,000 Palestinians were left landless, were blocked from returning home and were left without a viable means of supporting themselves because of partisan American policy. They felt it unjust for Arabs to be made the scapegoat of European or Christian barbarism especially when Jews and Arabs had lived together in the area for centuries in relative peace.

Whatever the merits of the Arab argument, America's preoccupation with securing peace in the area actually reflects this country's ethnocentric evaluation of the so-called Middle East "dilemma." Idealistic conceptions of our own history led us to favor Israel because of the supposed parallels affecting the founding of the two nations. Consequently, Arabs and Arabic-speaking people, wherever they are, have fallen into disrepute. The Nixon administration even attempted to infiltrate long-established Arab American social groups because they were assumed to be pushing the Arab position and were trying to gather information that could be used against Israel.[4]

Middle East peace must be predicated on assumptions and perceptions other than those commonly used in the West. Peace in the Middle East must be based on more than territorial guarantees, the stockpiling of armaments, or the mere absence of conflict. Cultural integration of the region must be encouraged and an honest history of the area should be promulgated, understood and accepted by everyone. There must be concurrence on racial, nationalistic, and religious conceptions before international political decisions can be made.

It is the presence in this country of Christian Arabs which may increase our knowledge of the Arab East and alter our relationship to that area. Americans are generally surprised to learn that millions of Arabic-speaking people are in fact Christian with hundreds of thousands of them peacefully and prosperously residing in the New World. Yet, these Oriental Christians (whether Roman Catholic or Eastern Orthodox) are torn between loyalty to their particular country of origin (and now country of residence), loyalty to their religion, and the conflicting plea for Arab unity.

Americans assume that Syrian and/or Lebanese Americans are members of ethnic groups which are similar in structure and function to all other American ethnic groups. They forget that from the very beginning of the migration Middle Easterners were improperly identified in terms of their origins and cultural ancestry and as such perception of their structure and function as an integrated ethnic community has always been conventional rather than accurate.

Accordingly, there are no accurate statistics available on their numbers here. Moreover, confusion in identity also existed among the Christian immigrants themselves who traditionally identified themselves by their "millet." This was a form of organization which grouped the various Christian denominations into separate and distinct civil societies predicated on sect (rite) and religion. It was imposed by the Turkish government and became the immigrants' "nation." This identity, as will be demonstrated, and the nature and role of their religious heritage became transformed by their desire to be known as "Americans," and by the pressure of living in an ethnically and religiously pluralistic America. In time, they resolved these tensions by becoming Americans of Syrian and, eventually, Lebanese ancestry.

To some observers not familiar with the Middle East or its his-

tory, there is a real nationality difference between Syrian and Lebanese Americans. At the same time many publicly perceive and collectively treat them as Arabs and Moslems. Strangely enough, these Middle Easterners do not really identify strongly with any of these categories. This situation is partially due to our tendency to view and interpret reality on and in our own terms. We think that the people we are observing should view themselves as we view ourselves—as secularly oriented with geographical boundaries and visible governments. Christian Arabic-speaking Americans do not, in fact, come out of this tradition or rationale. Thus, when we speak of Syrian or Lebanese Americans in nationalistic terms we are referring to a phenomenon born out of the need to have a relevant identity in western terms.

In this light it is religion as a dynamic social institution which is the key to understanding Arab-American history. It is religion as theology and religion as social interaction which has guided the development of nationalistic identities in the Middle East and especially ethnic identities in America.

As a result of the belief of the dominant American Latin (Western) rite Roman Catholics that the Oriental Catholics were disrupting America's melting pot thrust toward cultural and religious uniformity, attempts were made to absorb them by depriving them of their historic rights and traditions and by "latinizing" them. The latter strategy reduced them to nothing more than Catholic ethnics who would maintain a separate, but only temporary, social and cultural existence. As another Catholic ethnic group without their own hierarchy, however, they faced wholesale absorption into the general Catholic American population. The Eastern Orthodox Syrians, of course, being even more bedeviled had to ward off both Protestant and Catholic attempts to proselytize them.

Three different schools of thought and patterns of response emerged within these Oriental Christian communities: churches could support and accentuate a ghetto existence based on the maintenance of certain American "Syrianisms"; churches could become ritually devoid of ethnicity, but socially or informally remain ethnic; churches could dispense with ethnicity completely. In light of the general level of acculturation reached by the community, the last alternative eventually emerged as the most feasible. Being highly middle class in value orientation, financially successful, greatly dispersed and not institutionally inclusive, Syrian-Lebanese Americans quite early, of necessity, temporarily transformed their cultural heritage into something relevant and functional and by so doing maintained a separate social life which helped reduce the threat of total absorption into American society. They became acculturated but not assimilated and linked themselves to American society through their religious faiths.

Since they customarily did not think in broad social categories, they failed to develop viable institutions to maintain the in-group homogeneity they desired. Frequency of out-marriage was persistently high and their churches soon discovered that the ethnic group they were maintaining was essentially American in composition and character. Their continued reliance on ethnicity, however, meant that when the ethnic group disappeared as a cultural form then the institutional churches which supported it would also be threatened. As such, the merely ritualistic religious traditions of the Syrian immigrants could become the only ethnic legacy left to the United States once assimilation was accomplished.

Our study of the Syrians and Lebanese in America, then, will be socio historical in nature since sociology offers us the means of investigating how religion affects social behavior and how religious behavior is socially determined. There can be no understanding of the assimilation of the Syrians and Lebanese into American society without an appreciation of the function of religion in the development of their psychosocial and cultural identity. It was at the root of their rather successful entrance into the American way of life.

CHAPTER I

The Phenomenon of Arab Christianity

MOST WESTERNERS ARE UNAWARE AND OFTEN STARTLED TO learn that there are over 9,000,000 Christians living in the Arab World. Americans, being generally unfamiliar with the politics, social structure, culture, and religious history of the Middle East, are especially prone to view all Arabic-speaking people as long-robed, desert-dwelling, wandering Bedouins. Any acknowledged Arabic-speaking Christians are assumed to be converts to Protestant Christianity from Islam and not members of congregations who have a continuity in faith dating from apostolic times.

The majority of the Arab East is Islamic in religion and the largest proportion is of the Sunni sect. Christians constitute barely 5 percent of the population. Lebanon, which has a slight Christian majority, is the sole national exception. Relations between Moslems and Christians have not always been easy especially in the area of human and civil rights. As Arabic-speaking people the Christians have been torn between loyalty to their country and the conflicting plea for Arab unity which they feel would lead to the subjugation of their national and religious identities.

The problems created by the presence of competitive religious systems are compounded when we consider the unique place of ethnicity, religion, nationality, and locality in the life of the East. Unlike most modern nations, Arab society has traditionally been fragmented by religion, which is at the root of each individual's social identity. In spite of socioreligious heterogeneity, the region is culturally unified. It is Arabic in language and its life-style is derived from the social traditions of the Arab conquerors of the seventh century. It is, nonetheless, pluralistic in social organization even though a common language and an ancient and complete pattern of living pervade the land. A person is classified as an "Arab" if he participates in the cultural style of the Middle East and not because he is racially or genetically an "Arab." It is the general consensus that anyone who speaks Arabic is an Arab if he resides in the Middle East. This definition is plausible if we accept the fact that "Arab" defines not a nationality, religion, or a people, but rather a cultural style of living.

Consequently, Middle Eastern civilization is considered "Arabo-Islamic," since most of its mores are derived from Islam, and its folkways from the desert. After the Islamic movement left the Arabian peninsula it changed its orientation toward the native populations. Eventually, it learned to tolerate and honor all people of "the Book"—Judaic and Christian—and achieved its cultural ascendency by replacing Aramaic with Arabic as the language of the land. Moreover, the Arab converts to Islam gave the traditional society of the Middle East its dominant creed, moral code, and political organization. Arab civilization has its roots in Islam and has developed its political and social system accordingly. Islam, nevertheless, began as a sectarian movement dominated in many ways by Moslem sheiks or statesmen. Every sphere of activity became regulated by a system of generally accepted principles that were drawn from the "theology" of Mohammed in the Holy Koran.

Arab language, literature, art and music, images of heroism and human grandeur dominated the Middle East. Social organization was based upon the prerogatives of the clan and the tribe or collection of clans held together by blood relationship and regulated by customary law. As in many early societies law was dispensed by chieftains who owed their position to a combination of birth and ability.

Arabic Culture

Psychologically, Arabic-speaking people perceive and conceptualize reality differently than those of the West. They are oriented toward the mysterious and the spiritual rather than the pragmatic, manipulative, man-centered, and man-controlled world view of Westerners. They are usually "otherworld" directed and not overly concerned with "this-world" objectives

—especially those that would separate them from their blood relatives. Social systems that are impersonal and goal oriented do not attract them because they have difficulty perceiving the world of ideas as distinct from the bearer of the idea. Thus, they remain unresponsive to pressures stressing social change that damage the fabric of the community. In most of the small cities and villages of the Near East, personal security is to a great extent still bound to "community" integrity and survival. Beirut, Lebanon, being highly urbanized and Westernized, is the only major exception to this cultural modality.

It was the nature of religious belief and organization that promulgated this form of social-communal consciousness throughout the area. Even the historical Jewish desire for a separate communal life was usually honored by the ruling classes, The Christians likewise organized themselves according to the particular tradition (rite) or sect they followed. Since religion descended in and through the family, very homogeneous and tight-knit social units were formed between families of the same religious tradition. The Ottoman Turks eventually capitalized on this situation by incorporating each religious sect separately into the state. This is called the "millet" system of government.

The typical Middle Easterner sees his family as an extension of himself, and his religious grouping becomes the demarcation point between himself (family) and the world outside. The members of one's family are almost always of the same faith and tradition, and consequently it is his religion which locates and identifies a person in time and space. His coreligionists are "his people" and act as his extended family. It is a collective individualism of sorts: he may belong to a particular faith, but all his coreligionists are treated in the same fashion and expect the same response from any "outsider." Of this situation, ethnographer Lewis Gaston Leary writes:

> The ecclesiastical bodies of Syria are numerous, jealous and extremely fanatical. In striking contrast to the awkward reticence of the West regarding religious matters, every Syrian not only counts himself an adherent of the faith into which he was born, but he thrusts that fact upon your attention and, on the slightest provocation, is ready to fight for his belief. A man's ancestors, descendants and home may be cursed with all the wealth of Oriental vituperation, and he will probably accept this as a

mere emphatic conversational embellishment. But let the single word DINAK! "thy religion!" be spoken with a curseful intonation to a follower of a different faith, and the spirit of murder is let loose.[1]

The culture of the Moslem Arabs was the common unifying force of the Middle East and the North African continent. Still, the sharing of a common language, world view, and pattern of living, until very recently, failed to endear the various local populations to one another. Civic pride was channeled into religious separatism and jealousy which changed one's fellow nationals into enemies unless, of course, they were of the same faith and sect. Though the cultural background was universally the same, the social consciousness of each group remained limited to a narrow base.

To some extent this is true even today. Religious ideologies still reinforce this type of social consciousness and tend to foster isolation from the mainstream political movements of any given state on the assumption that they are not intended for the universal good of all the citizenry but just the religious group that sponsors the program. Yet no religious tradition separates its members completely from the national society. Rather, it limits the scope of activities of its members through either informal pressure or socially enforced proscriptions. In recent times, the Lebanese Maronite Catholics have actually modified the socioreligious barriers between themselves, the Moslems and the Eastern Orthodox Christians resident in Lebanon.

Because of this social pattern, it becomes difficult to view the Arabic-speaking people in America as members of an "ethnic" group—similar in structure and function to all other American ethnic groups. If anything, the story of Arab Christians in America is a reflection of their ancient and modern experiences in the Middle East—a region traditionally dominated by political intrigue, religious sectarianism, and communal jealousies. Although the Middle Easterners began arriving in the United States in large numbers at the turn of the century, misconceptions in the host society and the political situation in the Orient caused them to be defined not in terms of their country of origin but rather as "Turks" (since the Ottomans controlled the area) or as "Arabs" (because they spoke Arabic). Actually, most are Semitic Christians from Mount Lebanon, which at the time of the migration was part of the modern Syrian nation.

The presence and function of religion, the role of nation-states, perceptions of race and nationalistic identities all have different meanings for the Middle Easterner. Yet, because Westerners are people with a geographic referrent, they are conditioned to think that all groups should collectively consider themselves secular nationals with governments recognizable by and acceptable to everyone. But nationalism as a political and social reality in the Middle East has only been successful since 1923, when the British control over Egypt was relinquished.

Syria and Lebanon's independent history began in 1941 and actually paralleled the development of similar identities among their emigrants in the United States. Except for the Lebanese Catholics, the establishment of such independent and separate states, and hence identities, was not the goal of many of the peoples of the region—especially the Christians. Christians feared being absorbed into dominant Moslem states. Moreover, "nationalism," as we understand the term, always had and will always imply and mean something different for Arabic-speaking people.

The idea of belonging to a nation-state and of developing national sentiments requires the cultivation of wider loyalties and a growth of consciousness. The establishment of an integrated political order for a group of people on the basis of a common culture and a land was, and may still be, beyond the Arab's comprehension and range of experience.

Christianity in the East

Eastern Christianity developed in regional and rather isolated cultures and is composed principally of Eastern Orthodox Christians (since 1054 A.D. outside Roman Catholic union) and Roman Catholics of the Eastern rites (Melkites, Maronites and others).[2] To a lesser extent certain heretical groups, such as the Monophysites, the Nestorians and the Jacobites, who were not in communion with Rome, the capital city of Western Christianity, or with Byzantium (Constantinople), its Eastern equivalent, can also be counted. At one time, there was a universal Christian Church throughout the East and West. In the fifth and sixth centuries these "heretical" groups separated from the Christian Church, and in

1054 the entire Church split apart. The Christian Church in the West became known as the Roman Catholic Church, and in the East it was called the Eastern or Greek Orthodox Church.

Because the East underwent a different sociocultural experience from the West, geographic locality became a major force in religious development. The isolated character of the various populations contributed to this development. In the West, where Christianity more or less inherited the Holy Roman Empire, one single religious tradition developed and unified the area. In the East, however, plurality characterized the Christian experience. The symbiosis between religion and culture finally resulted in the formation of local Christian communities that developed their own liturgical expression of their faith. This is what is commonly meant by the term "rite." It is an entire way of life that is spiritually and liturgically unique. The very nature of these rites allowed them to be eventually organized into religious "nations," or "millets."

Indeed, all the ruling powers in the East, whether Moslem, Turkish, or European, capitalized on this unique situation and treated each sect or rite as a separate "nationality." The Ottoman Turks formalized this custom into the socio-political reality known as the "millet," which was really a church organized into a nationality as well as a nationality organized into a church. The millet system of control and political integration originated in the very nature of Eastern Christianity long before the establishment of the Ottoman Empire and preserved not only self-respect and a sense of community among the religious minorities but also created bitterness and suspicion.

Noted Catholic historian Yves Congar tells us that because of the isolation of each Christian community in the early Church, the various churches were free to choose their own liturgical forms, traditions, and theologies.[3] Everywhere in Christendom, however, it was understood that these local organizations of the Christian Church had validity only as they remained in organic connection with the "Church Universal." Moreover, in the great centers of Christianity, a process of synthesis set in and patterns of uniformity began to appear. These spread slowly to neighboring regions, demonstrating that the "rites" of the Church did not evolve from unity to diversity but from diversity to a certain degree of unity. By the fifth century the entire Christian population of the Eastern and Western Empires was organized under the authority of five apostolic cities: Jerusalem, Rome, Antioch, Byzantium (Constantinople), and Alexandria. Most Arab-Americans use the rites of Antioch or Constantinople.

Each group of believers who elected to follow the traditions of one particular city became organized across geographic boundaries with others of the same mind. Since populations were constantly shifting, each rite had to have a bishop in each city. Moreover, there were minor variations in the practice of each rite as it developed in the diaspora. In Syria, followers of the Byzantine rite were called Melkites, and in Lebanon, where the Antiochian rite dominated, followers of this tradition were called Maronites. In time, the patriarchs, or spiritual chiefs of each major city, took upon themselves the administration of their own rite regardless of its particular location. Thus, the Byzantine patriarch became, in title, the spiritual head of all Byzantines in Jerusalem, Antioch, and all the Orient. He was the patriarch of all the Byzantines in those cities and wherever they lived.

In the West, even though there were several rites, the Latin became preeminent because it was the rite and language of Rome—the sociopolitical capital of Christianity. Western Catholics still think their traditions, which are really only localisms, are the only truly Catholic ones and the most original and authentic. As a result, they tend to view the Catholic Church as monolithic and uniform, whereas there are many Catholic traditions that collectively make up the "Church." Roman Catholicism is a worldwide religion that is often confused with the customs and history of the Latin or Western rite, even though there are millions of Roman Catholics who are known as Eastern-rite Catholics, or "Uniates." However, they are Easterners for more than geographic reasons. They are members of spiritually unique traditions which take their inspiration from non-Western sources.

In terms of numbers and influence, the dominant religious-cultural style of all Eastern Christianity was that of Byzantium, whose missionaries converted Russia, the Ukraine, Greece, and the Slavic countries. When the Great Schism of 1054 effectively severed Eastern, or Byzantine, Christianity from Western, Latin Christianity, Eastern Christianity became known as Eastern or "Greek" Orthodoxy, since Constantinople was becoming the "new Rome." In the Arab East the Orthodox are called Syrian Orthodox because they follow the Byzantine rite, live mostly in Syria, and are not in communion with Rome.

Splinter groups known as "Uniates" subsequently broke off from this Orthodox mother church and rejoined Roman Catholicism centuries later. In Russia, they are known as Russian- or Ukrainian-rite Catholics. Similar events took place in the Slavic countries giving us Ruthenian-rite Catholics. The Melkites, one of the largest and most important groups who use the Byzantine rite, are Middle Eastern Arab (Syrian and Lebanese) Uniates. Since the Melkite reunion with Rome in 1724 they have been known as Roman Catholics of the Byzantine-Melkite rite, or Greek-Catholics. They now number approximately 450,000 faithful. This left their schismatic mother church, the Syrian-Antiochian Orthodox, with 700,000. Together these two groups constitute a substantial proportion of the Arab emigration to America.

The Maronites of Lebanon, another Eastern-rite Catholic group who have emigrated to the United States in exceptionally large numbers, constitute the largest single Arab Christian group in America. Unlike the Melkites and Syrian Orthodox they take their inspiration, religious style, and theology from the early Christian community at Antioch. Like the Melkites, they owe allegiance to the Pope of Rome, but they differ dramatically in their rituals, fidelity to the Roman bureaucracy, and relationship to their fellow Arab nationals.

In spite of the differences in style and theology between the Eastern and Western Catholic Church, there are numerous similarities between them. Their doctrines are essentially the same, the main difference being one of emphasis rather than substance. When placed together, the totality of early Christian (Catholic) faith emerges. The word "Catholic," which means universal and not uniform, is technically a misnomer when applied to the Roman Church or rite of the West since it ignores the other traditions or rites which, when taken collectively, constitute the totality of Catholic Christian history.

Within the Arabic-speaking Eastern Catholic Church, we have both Melkites and Maronites who have fascinating and important histories which must be noted since they are the foundations upon which the Syrian-American community is built.

The Syrian-Orthodox Church, the mother church of the Melkite community, constitutes the third major Arab Christian migratory group to arrive in the United States at the turn of the century. Because they are not Catholic, however, the Syrian-Orthodox had a slightly different social reality to deal with. They had to disengage themselves from both Protestant and Catholic attempts to proselytize and label them. After all, American society had little experience with the Eastern Christian Orthodox church and is only now beginning to recognize the religious legitimacy of Russian, Ukrainian, Syrian, and Greek Orthodoxy in the United States.

The Catholic Syrians, on the other hand, had to deal primarily with an uninformed American Catholic population which would not recognize the legitimacy of their Eastern patrimony. The story, then, of Syrian Christian Americans is one of conflict between the Catholic segments of the community, i.e., Melkites and Maronites and the American Catholic Church, as well as the relationship of these two sects to their Syrian-Orthodox compatriots. Ironically, being Catholic did not necessarily endear the Maronites and Melkites to one another. While they both have suffered for and are today loyal to the Roman Catholic Church, they differ significantly from one another in their attitude toward the Latin Catholic Church of the West and the Western style of life in general. Their experience of each other in the Middle East made them skeptical of each other's honesty and intentions. The Syrian Orthodox essentially disliked both groups because they are Catholic, more Western oriented and politically, at least in Lebanon, more secure.

The Melkites

The Melkites have survived because of their ability to accommodate and adjust to a changing sociohistorical environment without losing sight of their religious roots and ties to the Arab and Byzantine religious-cultural tradition.

At the very dawn of Christian history they were part of the Apostolic Church of Antioch founded in that city by Saint Peter before he journeyed to Rome. The Church rapidly grew in strength and stature among the communities of the Christian world, and at the Ecumenical Council of Nicea (325 A.D.), it was decreed that Antioch should rank third among the churches of the world, preceded only by Rome and Alexandria.

In the fifth century the Monophysite heresy arose in the Antiochian Church asserting that Christ could not be truly God and truly man as well. Its proponents would not accept the Church's teaching as confirmed by the Ecumenical Council of Chalcedon in 451 A.D. Their following increased in the Middle East, and today they form the Jacobite Church of Syria, the Coptic Church of Egypt, and the Gregorian Armenian Church. These religions are not usually considered part of either the Eastern Orthodox or the Catholic Churches. They arose centuries before the Great Schism of 1054 and are considered "heretical" by most Christian bodies.

Despite pressure, many Christians in Antioch accepted the teachings of the Chalcedon Council and kept themselves in communion with the other Christian bishoprics. Those Syrians who followed the lead of the emperor in staying faithful to the Church were dubbed Melkites, or "kings men," from the Syriac word for king (*Melko*). From the seventh century onward, however, the city of Antioch was a place of contention in the Middle East. Successive hosts of Persians, Arabs, Crusaders, and Turks struggled for control of the territory. Most of these invaders persecuted the Melkites because of their Christian faith as well as their close ties with the Byzantine emperor, who had become their protector. The persecutions, of course, brought the Melkites in closer touch with and made them more dependent on Byzantium (Constantinople). As the persecutions increased, the Melkite patriarchs were forced to live in exile, usually in the imperial city itself, and their followers eventually adopted the city's Byzantine religious style.

As a result of the geographic separation between Rome and Constantinople, the disastrous Crusades, and the schism of 1054, communion between the Melkites and the Catholic West was disrupted. When the Turks conquered the Byzantine Empire in 1453 and established their own capital in Constantinople, the Melkites' identification with the city was further intensified to the point where religious and civil life blended together. For the conquerors Turk and Muslim were identical, and they viewed the Christians not only as members of a different faith but of a different nation as well. Christian-Islamic differences eventually became stabilized by the institution of the millet—the union of religious rite and civil power and status which gave religious leaders or patriarchs wide civil jurisdiction over the members of their communities.

According to Werner Cahnman:

> . . . the millet may be defined as the peculiar political organization which gave to non-Moslem subjects of the Ottoman Empire the right to organize into communities possessing delegated political power under their own ecclesiastical chiefs. In matters affecting the community, the government treated it as a whole unit dealing with its leaders rather than individual members. The head of the millet was directly responsible to the state for the administration of all his subjects. Although the millet lacked territorial cohesion and military power and had, therefore, to be protected by the ruling warrior class, it formed in many respects an autonomous unit within the state. Yet, the members of the millet were limited in their general citizenship by virtue of the very fact that the laws of personal statute were based upon religious sanctions.[4]

This form of political organization is beyond the Western ideas of states and nationalities. The Syrian Christians eventually internalized the Turkish definition of the situation and began to consider their religion or rite as their nationality.

By the time of the Turkish conquest, the Melkites were already sociopsychologically within the Orthodox Byzantine orbit. For this reason the Turks numbered them among the Eastern Orthodox ("Roum") or Greek millet and made them subject to the schismatic Ecumenical patriarch of Constantinople. This situation persisted for many years and would have remained static were it not for later contact with the West. From 1625, Western Roman Catholic missionaries entered the Middle East under the patronage of the French consulates. Movements toward union with Rome, which these missionaries engendered, culminated in the separation of some Melkite bishops from their schismatic Orthodox mother church. By 1724 two Melkite hierarchies or power structures developed: the Catholic followers of Cyril, who was elected patriarch of the rite and then moved toward Roman unity, and the followers of Patriarch Sylvester, who was consequently elected in opposition.

The Turkish government upheld the decision of the Ecumenical patriarch of Constantinople, whom they already controlled, because he would naturally favor Sylvester—who would be faithful to him—as leader of the entire "Roum" millet. For the next hundred years the Roman-oriented Catholic Melkites were in constant conflict with the Turkish authorities, who would not recognize them as a separate millet, as well as with the Greek hierarchy, who tried to force them back into "orthodoxy." It was some time before the jurisdictional dispute between these large Christian sects was resolved. Not until 1848 did Catholic Melkites receive their civil emancipation. Most hostilities between the Melkites and their Syrian-Orthodox brothers, which flare up even today, can be traced back to this basic jurisdictional quarrel.

The Maronites

The Maronites, on the other hand, have their own ecclesiastical history. While their roots are essentially Syrian and Antiochian, they have proceeded to develop along Western lines to a degree resented by other Eastern Christians.

Late in the fourth century, a Syrian monk called Maron (350-433 A.D.) and a group of followers living near Antioch escaped persecution by hostile neighbors by fleeing to the Orontes River valley, where they transformed an abandoned temple into a place of Christian homage. This community became a monastery known today as Beit Maron, or the House of Maron, since he became its first abbot. The monastery flourished and its members defended the faith against the prevailing heresies. Highly lauded for their loyalty to the Roman Catholic pontiffs, the descendants of Saint Maron have become a distinct rite of the Catholic Church with their own hierarchy and canon law.

In 694 the Maronites came to inhabit "the Lebanon." Seeking refuge in these mountains of Syria near the Cedars, the Maronites converted much of the population. Their continuing loyalty to Catholicism made them an island of Christianity in an ocean of Islam and won for them the praise and assistance of many of the Roman popes.

By the time of the Crusades the Lebanese mountains became the permanent home of the Maronites. Because of their large numbers and their desperate struggle for survival, they became guardians of the land they occupied. Fighting for Maronite civil security and autonomy became synonymous with freedom for the land. Their Christian faith brought them to the side of the Crusaders and consequently they became more vulnerable to

Western sociopolitical ideals and, more important, to Western theology and spirituality—a source of dispute between them, the Melkite Catholics, and the Syrian Orthodox.

In addition to their religious-political squabbles, another problem area was the overall reaction of the Maronites to the French Latins and Western Protestants who introduced, albeit indirectly, more than Western spirituality. Being the first to arrive, the French did not meet with the same reception as the Protestants who came to proselytize in the early nineteenth century. For political, social, and religious reasons the French became highly valued friends of the Orient, giving it a basis for its nationalism and modernization. Being Catholics, they had their greatest influence on the Lebanese Christians. Hitti mentions that "of the contacts established by the Latins with the peoples of the Near East, those with the Maronites proved to be the most fruitful, the most enduring."[5]

The outcome of the French influence was the intertwining of the fate of the Maronites with that of the state of Lebanon. The "cause" of one became the "cause" of the other, making the history of the contemporary Maronites the history of Lebanon as well. It is significant that the Maronite patriarch, with a staff of bishops, went to the Paris Peace Conference of 1919 to voice the national aspirations and political sentiments of the Christian Lebanese.

Today, the Maronite patriarch is a highly respected and esteemed politico-religious figure in the national life of that country. The nearly 750,000 Maronites in Lebanon still dictate that the national religion remain Christian. Because they are the largest Christian community in Lebanon, the Maronites have a very strong identification with the land and a strong sense of nationalism which they insist on tracing back to the pre-Arab Phoenician presence in that area.

As we have indicated, since the Lebanese Maronites were the first Middle Easterners in modern times to establish significant relations with the West, they eventually became responsible for the Western-style development of the country. So close are their bonds with their national state that for all practical purposes they constitute the "national church" of Lebanon even though they have become dispersed throughout the Mediterranean and the New World as a result of migration. Yet the tie with Lebanon is hardly broken. Indeed, its people talk of two Lebanons: "Lebanon the resident" (*al-muqim*), and "Lebanon the emigrant" (*al-mugtarib*), literally "the resident abroad."

Basically, the Maronites are Syrians living chiefly in "the Lebanon," and are of the same cultural and racial origins as the Melkite Catholics. Their existence as a "separate nation" is due chiefly to their ecclesiastical origins, which resulted in a strong group consciousness nurtured by persecution. Attachment to the Roman See has been a cornerstone of Maronite tradition and invariably a source of suffering for them. Their staunch Catholicism has also impeded their relations with Moslem Easterners as well as their fellow Christians, who feel that the Maronites have become too latinized and consequently cannot be "true" to their Eastern patrimony.

Religion and Intragroup Conflict

Even though a rite is based on customs conditioned by history, geography, and tradition, and varies with the national background of the people, it is supposed to be adaptable to any social environment and culture in a kind of symbiotic way. It is not a closed, historic artifact. Nor is it merely a ritual. According to Jesuit scholar Yves Congar, a rite "encompasses the totality of forms and symbols by which a community gives complete expression to, and lives its Christian faith."[6] The Roman (Western) Catholic Church historically has failed to understand this principle. This is why it insisted that Latin be the universal language of the whole Church. The Eastern Christians almost immediately adopt the local language of the community they are residing in or administering to. This means using English in the United States and Spanish or Portuguese in Latin America.

Theoretically, it should be possible to separate from the intrinsic nature of Christianity what is essential and what is accidental or secondary. Failure to understand this is at the root of both Melkite-Maronite discord and Orthodox fear of these Catholic "uniate groups." It also explains why Roman Catholics had so much difficulty dealing with the growing American Eastern Catholic population, which was characterized by a multitude of liturgical languages, a married clergy, a different sacramental life and religious calendar, an elective form of church government, and a spirituality that stressed contemplation over action.

Whether in the United States or in the Orient, Eastern Catholics feel that the Latin Church of the West has organized itself as if it were *the* Catholic Church without consideration for the traditions and mentalities of others. For the East, the "catholicity" of a church is seen not so much in the number or color of her people, but in her power to adapt to all people at all times and maintain unity in multiplicity. The Eastern Catholic churches feel that Romanism and Catholicism are not synonymous and that Catholicism must remain open to every form of organization compatible with a unity of faith.

Herein lies the source of Syrian-Orthodox distrust of Melkites and Maronites. History has brought both these latter groups into Catholic unity, but because of Roman pressure it seems almost impossible to remain Eastern and Catholic at the same time. In the view of the Orthodox, Roman imperialism and paternalism have disfigured all the Eastern churches leaving them impotent and directionless. The Orthodox consider them anathema. For them, "Catholic" has come to mean not only Latin but anti-Oriental as well. They consider the Uniates nothing more than schismatic Orthodox who have become Catholic at the expense of their own Eastern heritage.

While the Latin Church of the West represents a threat to all forms of Eastern Christianity, there are other historical forces that are responsible for the perpetual conflicts between Melkites, Maronites, and the Syrian Orthodox. These are the same conflicts that presently affect both the rise of Arab nationalism, which has persistently been confronted with the problem of neutralizing potentially competitive religious identities, and the emergence of an integrated Syrian-American community.

A Syrian Christian's identification with his rite is so emotionally intense that for many persons religious and sectarian fidelity often replaces nationality. It is frequently possible, for example, on asking an Arab to what country he belongs to receive the answer, "I am a Christian."

While it is true that for Christians and Moslems alike consciousness of belonging to a religious community was the basis for political and social obligations, it would be premature to conclude that the Christians acted consistently as a unit. Consciousness of not belonging to each other's communities led to suspicion and dislike, and this was true of every Christian sect in its relations with the others. Differences of sect were no less important an element in the common consciousness than differences of religion.

Probably no part of the Christian Church has been so subjected to ecclesiastical quarrels, jurisdictional disputes, clashing of personalities over doctrines and their interpretations than the East. So severe have these internecine conflicts been that one author writes:

> The vital spirit of Christian love and fellowship failed to assert itself in the midst of those whose prudence and competent erudition otherwise left little to be desired. When finally construed, the settlements were not the outcome of calm inquiry and mature judgment. They came out of a frenzied arena where cleric quarreled with cleric and where the loosing of religious passion had transpired in a series of clashes between metropolitans, bishops and patriarchs. The overtones soon became rivalries and rifts, estrangement between ecclesiastical prelates, noisy councils, imperial edicts, exiles, riots and schisms.[7]

These conflicts undoubtedly stemmed from the ecclesiology of the East, which encouraged diversity and local autonomy. More important, however, were the reactions of the various groups to the political intentions of the French, English, and Turks—all of whom were more than happy to see the Christians fighting among themselves. The English and French, especially attempted to gain a foothold in the national life of the area by supporting a millet that would become their ally.

The other Western powers with any influence in the East were Russia and Austria, but since France and Austria were Catholic countries that pursued a policy of support for Catholic leaders and rites, especially the Maronites, they further aggravated and divided an already splintered and hostile East. The same was true of the Russians, who supported the Syrian Orthodox. These powers became in effect patrons of the respective millets as a matter of official policy. Meanwhile, the British had no millet to support until 1850, after the Melkites gained their independence from the Orthodox. Often they supported the Druse as well.

It was several decades before the Christians themselves solved the problem of millet jurisdictions. The Grec-Catholiques or Melkites were under the sole jurisdiction of the Orthodox patriarchate (their mother church) until 1830. Their emancipation is attributed to Maximos III Mazloum, who reigned as Catholic Melkite Patriarch from 1833 to 1855. For the Turks, religion was a form of "nationhood." When the division in hierarchies between the Melkites and the Orthodox became evident, it made no difference to a Turk because both were part of the same Byzantine tradition; he still looked on them as one nation. The Melkites were put at a disadvantage since the government took the side of the Orthodox Patriarchs who had civil jurisdiction over them and since they appeared more loyal to the Turkish overlords.

This state of affairs became intolerable to the Melkites, for the Orthodox used their authority to vex, annoy, and persecute them whenever possible. They even insisted that the Melkites change their style of dress to make them feel like strangers who were "Latins" in disguise. It was not until 1830 that the Sultan freed all Uniates from dependence on their rivals by putting all of them under the civil jurisdiction of the Armenian Patriarch, who represented the largest and best-known group of Catholic Easterners. The Turks were again acting narrowly. They erroneously thought that all Catholic Easterners were the same. They were insensitive to distinctions of rite.

Maximos III, after enormous labors, at last obtained the repeal of this law and the complete civil autonomy of the Melkites under their own patriarch. He also obtained his own appointment as agent (*murakhkhas*) of the Armenian Patriarch for the Melkites. But there was a general movement in favor of complete separation from the Armenian patriarch among all the other Uniates. The Syriac- and Chaldean-rite Catholics demanded the same thing as the Melkites, but with less success. In 1846, after long negotiations, Maximos persuaded the government to recognize the Melkites as a distinctly separate nation under himself and his successors. From that time the Melkite patriarch has received a *berat* (commission) from the Porte giving him this authority.

There were also some Melkite-Maronite antagonisms present, and they reached their height in the early 1700's when the Maronite patriarch, on the strength of an ancient Roman constitution authorizing him to receive heretics and schismatics into the Church, began turning Melkites (who were Orthodox at one time) into Maronites. The Melkites retaliated by calling the Maronites heretics, and publicly destroyed pictures of their national hero, Saint John Maron. The Pope intervened and severely reprimanded both sides.

Contemporary differences between the Melkites and Maronites

stem from the Melkites pro-Eastern approach to theology and culture and the Maronites pro-Western orientation and eager adaptation of "Westernisms." But these historic differences became less significant in the United States, since America has traditionally stressed and supported religious separation and toleration. In America these groups had to learn to coexist with the Syrian-Orthodox and the relatively few and new Presbyterian Syrians in their midst. But it was no easy task for them to overcome their own conflict-ridden history. Nor did they completely or successfully do so. Their communal life in America today still reflects some of these ancient divisions, but they have achieved a working unity which has begun to replace religious differences with a community of ethnicity. The difficulties they experienced in accomplishing this can be traced back to the peculiar form of Christian nationalism that permeated the Arab world—especially among the Maronites of Lebanon.

Christian "Nationalism"

The development of rite as nation stemmed from the confusion in the Turkish mind between religion and race. The Turks thought that differences of religion or rite in their empire could be explained by the "fact" that each group descended from a people who once held that particular religious tradition. Since civil law applications and the state of each subject in temporal matters depend on the religious body to which one belongs, it is not surprising that the Christians themselves began to look upon themselves as different nations in the ordinary sense of the word. The Maronites of Lebanon typically identify themselves as such.

This is encouraged by the fact that it has always been extremely difficult for a man in the Turkish Empire to change his religion. Each man is, in religion, what his fathers were before him: he marries a woman in the same church, and it is assumed that a different blood type develops for each group. Even the Christians have succumbed to this way of thinking. They speak of their "nation," meaning their church, without realizing this is a purely artificial use of the word introduced by the Moslems because they had no other way of classifying the Christians.

Furthermore, all Maronites are Roman Catholics, i.e., they are an Eastern rite in full communion with Rome. All other Eastern-rite Catholics such as the Melkites are composed of former members and partial segments of the Eastern Orthodox Church. Consequently, if one asks a Maronite if he is a Catholic, he says, "No, I am a Maronite." To him, Catholic means Catholic Melkites or Uniates. To be a Maronite is ipso facto, to be Catholic, if not super-Catholic.

What the Maronite reaction reveals here is the historical sensitivity of the Easterners to being lumped together as "Syrian-Christians." A Syrian traditionally divides the principal Christian doctrines into "Roum Orthodox" and "Roum Catholique," and then he speaks of Maronites, Latins, Syriacs, Armenians, and others. Of the half-dozen Catholic rites represented in Syria, Palestine, and Egypt, the Melkites are hierarchically the authentic local Catholics. The present Syriac and Maronite Catholic communities are the result of historical-cultural transitions, while the Armenian-rite Catholics of Syria are considered refugees. The Latin-rite Syrians are seen as a foreign importation.

In addition, the Maronite nation is non-Byzantine in usage and history. Its inspiration and style comes from the Antiochian tradition. The Melkites and Syrian Orthodox, on the other hand, are both Byzantine and have a common and broad heritage. Because of this, they are both universal and international churches by their very nature, that is, they include many groups and nationalities, while the Maronite development has been greatly limited to Lebanon.

To complicate the situation further, the Maronites have come to rely quite heavily on the liturgical practices of the Western, or Latin, Church. The civil, religious, and political upheavals in Islam in the Middle Ages and the arrival of the French under Louis IX mark the beginning of both the indebtedness of the Lebanese to France and their initiation into Latinisms or the religious style of the West. It was with the Crusades that latinization of the Maronite rite began. The process, once introduced, accelerated rapidly so that by the fifteenth century, in token of their obedience to Rome, they were following the customs and rites of the Latins almost completely. Von Suchem, who sojourned in the Holy Land from 1336 to 1341, saw many Maronite bishops consecrated by Latin archbishops.[8] It is certain that "ever since its affiliation with Rome, the Maronite Church has followed a course of adaptation, often useless and servile, to Roman usages."[9]

The Maronite savants, mostly graduates of the Maronite College of Rome, established in 1584 by Gregory XIII, were instrumental in effecting the "disfiguration." In 1736, Clement XII delegated the eminent scholar Joseph Simeon Assemani (Al-Sim'ani) to the Luwayzah Council of the Lebanon to put the finishing touches to the romanizing process started six centuries earlier.

For the Maronites, then, the adoption of "Latinisms" showed not only their attachment to the Roman See but their idealization of Western culture as well. It was in America that latinization reached its height and affected the type of accommodation these Arab-Christians would make with American society. The Melkites, on the other hand, view latinization only in religious terms and do not see it as a necessary corollary to Lebanon's or Syria's socio-political advancement. Since they have always been able to separate their Byzantine heritage or rite from reliance on any one particular culture or nationality, they have come to resist latinizing in the United States for the sake of facilitating acceptance. Rather, they now prefer to bring an authentic Eastern witness to America by making only necessary adjustments in their exterior life to American society and culture. In their essentials they attempt to stay faithful to the Eastern patrimony. Whether in the Middle East or the United States, they attempt to participate in viable political and social institutions without having to become overwhelmed or totally committed to all Western institutional forms. The same is true for the Syrian Orthodox, who also use the cosmopolitan and international Byzantine tradition.

The Protestant Syrians

Despite the differences within and between the Eastern Catholic and Eastern Orthodox sects, their reaction to the arrival of the Protestant missionaries from the West was uniformly hostile. The Moslems, who had appeared in the East after Christianity and who considered themselves its successors, viewed their presence differently than their Christian counterparts. For them, the Protestants were non-Moslem as well as non-Arab. At least the local Christians were indigenous and Eastern or Arab to a degree. But now the curse of "Levantism" would be upon them completely and directly. As John Badeau expresses it:

In practice, Western Christian faith has influenced the Muslim Middle East at many points. It has been the bearer of modern education and social ideas. The Protestant . . . missionary was never simply a Christian; he was always a Western Christian carrying with him the fresh and modern outlook of the Western world as well as the Gospel. . . . The missionary identified his kind of Christianity with progress and social concern—the two things that Eastern religion, both Muslim and Christian, seldom included.[10]

The original intention of the missionaries was to work among the Moslems and Jews, but they soon found that as far as the former were concerned the door was closed, for under Islamic law as applied in the Ottoman Empire and Persia, apostasy from Islam meant death! Consequently, they were forced into contact with the existing Christian communities, some of whom eventually overcame their suspicions, welcomed them, and invited them to preach in their churches. However, this cordiality ended after the wide divergence of faith and practice became obvious. The fact that converts to Protestantism had to come from other smaller Christian sects undoubtedly added to the tension.

The Protestants represented, then, more than a theological threat to the Easterners. The entrance of another religious sect into the social system would seriously challenge and upset the established patterns and lead to changes in the traditional social organization of the rural population. Moreover, the Syrian's fear of the institutional church as represented by Protestantism was, according to Hitti, based on the assumption that "its chief interest in them consists in cutting them off from their traditional past and relating them to an entirely new and alien institution."[11]

The Syrian Orthodox were especially fearful because the attraction of either the Protestant or Catholic (French) school system could entail the loss of their laity. Since their work among the Moslems was frustrated, potential converts had to come from those upwardly mobile Christians who sought to gain from the educational and economic advantages offered. Isolation and alienation from the community was solved by having whole families change faiths to the point where one could tell the precise religion or rite of a fellow Syrian by his last name. Hostility was high and opposition by the Maronites, who more than typified the East's reaction, was intense:

The Maronite Patriarch in Syria pronounced anathema on the missionaries and their converts. Maronites were "not to visit or employ them or do them a favor, give them a salutation, or converse with them in any form or manner, but let them be avoided as a putrid member and a hellish dragon." Native Christians who turned Protestant were persecuted. Their shops were boycotted, native teachers and ministers were banished, men and women were stoned in the streets, hung up by their thumbs, spat upon and struck in the face, tortured with the bastinado, and imprisoned without charge or trial.[12]

The most important conclusion to be drawn thus far regarding the role of religion in Arabic culture is that the traditional categories of historical analysis such as nationality, statehood, and ethnic group must be reconceptualized if we are to understand the basic dynamics of Middle Eastern life. Even the word "Arab" is a misnomer. Racially and ethnically they are a small if not an extinct minority. Yet, the "Arab cause" in the Middle East is supposedly transnational and assumes the awareness of being "*Arab*" first and Jordanian, Syrian, Lebanese, Moroccan, Egyptian, second. Moreover, full "Arabness" is historically a monopoly of the Moslems.

Syria has changed geographic boundaries constantly since the time of Christ. Once it included nearly all the Middle East; today it is an off-and-on partner of Egypt in the United Arab Republic. Lebanon is a distinct national republic. Yet, socially, a Lebanese Maronite Catholic has more affiliation and sense of relationship with a Maronite from Aleppo, Syria, than with a Lebanese Moslem or Greek Catholic, even though their secular fates are determined by the same political authority.

Arab nationalism constantly confronts the dual problem of the Middle Easterner's general inability to think broadly, abstractly, and objectively and his limited definition of social responsibility. It seems doubtful that a movement like "Arab nationalism" will ever overcome more traditional forms of nationalism linking state with religious identity.

Interestingly, the present conflict with the Zionist state of Israel has led Westerners to believe that there are "Arabs" united together somewhere "out there" who are going to attack Israel. This is a false perspective. Even the Palestinians had to learn that their own homeland would have to be reclaimed by no one but themselves. Why? Ultimately, Lebanon is concerned with maintaining her own national identity, which is only thirty years old. Syria focuses on its relationship to Egypt, which it uses to distract the attention of its people from the real problems of economic development; Jordan insists on controlling its own internal politics and in maintaining its national integrity.

Egypt, a late comer to the Arab nationalist movement, is really interested in controlling the whole area for its own aggrandizement because of its historical position as the strongest and largest of the Arabic-speaking nations. Moreover, for hundreds of years Egypt has been robbed of its valuable resources by constant invasions. Its own economic health might necessitate that it now control the area. Culturally it is the preferred leader, and every nation in the area has populations resident in Egypt because it is a familiar refuge in time of trouble. Egypt today is threatened by Israel, which is considered a totally foreign nation-state.

Ironically, Israel's interference with and effect on local Arab politics might indeed cause a pan-Arab movement to develop, and Israel's militant disposition might sustain it. It was the desire to remove the Turkish domination which led to the rise of Arab nationalism in the first place. Zionist expansion may generate the same response—only now Arab internationalism would have to compete with a newly emerging nationalism on the local state level. Modernization is affecting the Middle East on all levels of life and continued turmoil can be expected.

Not surprisingly, the Arabic-speaking people in the Americas reflect their history in their attitude toward the various national states they now live in. The organization of their communities, their cultural orientations, and their general social adjustment to North and South American society are also rooted in their centuries-old past. Their acculturation and adjustment to American society is a predictable continuation of their historic ability to acculturate without assimilating to the point of becoming nonentities. As a result of the cultural shock they experienced upon arrival in the United States, the Christian Syrians altered their cultural heritage and communal structures to the extent required for entrance into the mainstream of American life. At the same time they held on to what they considered culturally distinctive and socially important and that which would allow a modified form of communal life to persist.

Survival for people of Arabic-speaking ancestry means the sustaining of their community, traditions, and way of life. Accommodation, the mutual adjustment of groups that still allows them to retain their own identities and interests, though risky, was the means by which this was accomplished. If an outside threat to his community is political in nature, the Arab will accept the "new order" or state and incorporate himself into the structure of the government. Rarely, if ever, would he challenge the legitimate government or take it over. Governmental laissez-faire is more to his liking. If the threat is ideological, he will resist it, especially if it strikes at the root of his community, or he will alter it until it is nonthreatening.

This helps explain the Arabs' general dislike for social forces and movements like Protestantism and urbanization. How could a religious tradition and an industrial movement that are Western and that stress the prerogatives of the individual be accepted by a society that is essentially communal? Lebanon represents one possible resolution for that politically and economically progressive nation of like-minded groups dominated by the Maronite Catholics. Each group contributes only what is necessary for the national society to exist and remains separate in the matters that are essential: social and communal life. But how Arab is Lebanon?

The geographic position of the Middle East has forced its occupants to deal with cultural diversity in a tolerant fashion. People from the region, especially from the large cities and trading centers, are not unfamiliar with the life-styles of other people. Centuries of exposure to the various cultural and military invasions of the West have served as a preparation for accommodation to the social milieu of both North and South America. The following examination of the Christian Syrian-Lebanese migration to America will further reveal the Arabs' continuing capacity to survive and adapt to a society and culture that are basically predicated on assumptions foreign to them.

CHAPTER II

The Middle East in History Syria and Lebanon

WHEN THE ARAB CHRISTIAN IMMIGRANTS ARRIVED IN THE Americas from the Middle East they were generally unfamiliar with their own history and related to only a small segment of it when they were forced to identify themselves as "Arabs" or "Orientals." While they came from the area usually referred to as the Levant or the Orient, the immigrants were not accustomed to identifying themselves in either of these terms or any specific national ones. When they were made to do so, they invariably used the word "Syrian" to mean their "nationality," but since this nation-state only became definable in modern terms after the Second World War, they did not use the word in the contemporary sense.

Since the whole Orient lies east of the Mediterranean and has only recently come to consist of the modern states of Syria, Lebanon, Jordan, Egypt, Yemen, Saudi Arabia, Israel, and other smaller principalities, it is not surprising that the immigrants used the referent "Syria" loosely. In the past, the appellation "Suriya," or Syria, was used to describe the whole Arabian peninsula including all the above-mentioned nations except Egypt. Historically, Syria was an all-inclusive territory, not a modern, independent political unit, until it was dissolved in 1919. Its boundaries varied throughout the long course of history. At one time "Syria" included the entire area between Asia Minor and Egypt, and at another, the region stretching from the Taurus Mountains in the north to the Sinai Peninsula in the south, and from the Mediterranean on the west to the Eastern Syrian desert.

In many ways the region constitutes a single geographic unit. But its inhabitants are derived from numerous settlers and invaders who conquered and eventually assimilated the cultural style of the area. Consequently, everyone speaks the same language and observes the same social traditions. Since World War I European conceptions of nationalism have become incorporated into Near Eastern political thought. Previously, national consciousness based on territory was the least likely way for the Middle Easterner to find his political identity and sense of belonging.

At the turn of this century, when the migration to the United States increased,[1] Syria was a land of plains, valleys, rivers, and mountains. Its great trading centers of Beirut, Damascus, Aleppo, and Tripoli lay on the line of least resistance between Europe, Asia, and Africa and consequently provided the ancient, and to a large extent the medieval world, with its battlefields and marketplaces. "Nowhere else has so much human achievement been squeezed into so narrow a space,"[2] comments Philip K. Hitti, a noted Arab historian.

In earlier times, the Egyptians, Assyrians, and Babylonians held sway over the country and left an indelible impression upon the people. Both the Egyptians and the Assyrians developed and advanced ideas of mercantilism and public administration that influenced Europe centuries later. The Babylonians gave the world its basis for astronomy, mathematics, and law. The Macedonian invasion of 332 B.C. under Alexander the Great began the politico-cultural unification of the area and brought Syria under Greek control until Pompey wrested it from the Seleucidae and added it to the Roman world in 63 B.C. After the rise of Islam (634-640 A.D.) the Arabic language pervaded the region, and Syria became the seat of the ruling Umayyad dynasty (661-750 A.D.) who transferred the area's knowledge to Spain where it blossomed during the Renaissance.

For the next three centuries, greater Syria served as a battleground for conquerors from Africa, Asia, and Europe, and became the field of decision between the Cross and the Crescent. European expansionism also increased in the nineteenth century and eventually undermined the Ottoman expansion in North Africa, which by 1516 had overtaken the Egyptian Mameluks. The Turks continued their domination there until the English, on the pretext of need of a water passage, marched through Jordan and the Esdraelon plains in the second decade of the twentieth century with their own expansionist ideas.

For centuries the history of Syria was rooted in the ambitions and designs of outsiders who tossed the country about like a pawn. Even its modern history is a litany of successive domination by both Western and Eastern political and religious forces. Some semblance of security and stability was achieved when the English and the French assumed mandated power after World War I. Through secret treaty, the northern area was subdivided into several political units which were given the collective name of the "Levant States." Between 1925 and 1936, there were four such states: Syria, Greater Lebanon, Latakia (known originally as the "state of Alawis") and Jebel Druze. The latter were annexed to Syria in 1947, making it and Lebanon independent sociopolitical entities.

Until 1919 all Syrians were Turkish citizens. The reshuffling and creation of Syrian-Lebanese political boundaries took place after 1915 when the bulk of emigration to the New World had ended. The forebears of today's "Lebanese-Americans" arrived in the United States with Syrian passports even though Lebanon was given only nominal independence in 1861. More important, these "Lebanese" owed their primary allegiance not to a secular state, region, or culture but to their people, who were defined not as fellow nationals but as other Lebanese Christians of the same rite. This phenomenon is understandable when we become familiar with the historical relationship between religion, nationality, and Arabic culture and its effects on ethnic solidarity, nationalism, and social identity.

Within the national boundaries of the Middle East, then, can be found numerous subcommunities that live more or less independently of each other though they occupy the same land. Bedouins, for example, have no political boundaries and roam across the region freely. Most Lebanese Christians are tied ecclesiastically, socially, and psychologically to a national church that has members outside geographic Lebanon. In this text, therefore, when we speak of emigration from the Middle East we will be referring to a very select group of emigrants, *not* representative of all the people of the region. The emigrants of which we write are Christians from the cities and towns of Syria and from the mountain area known at one time as "the Lebanon" or "white capped mountains" of Western Syria. Nearly 90 percent of all Arabic-speaking immigrants to the Americas at the turn of the century came from this region.

Religion and Social Structure in the Middle East

Since religion defines the limits and objectives of one's community, the interaction of religion and culture is basic to an understanding of Arab history and politics. For this reason we have probed the religious history of the Middle East in some depth. Non-Arabs, especially Westerners, often have difficulty understanding the social and political structures of the Middle East because they have never experienced the relationships between religion and social life common to the area. The millet, for example, the uniquely Middle Eastern politico-religious institution which has been described, is beyond the historical Western idea of states and nations. All the region's present political, economic, military, and international affairs are a function of the past and present intertwining of religion with these institutions. Needless to say, in America the assimilation process experienced by these immigrants perpetuated the patterns of their religious-cultural history.

The pervasiveness of religious values and a religiously based world view in the Middle East require all individuals to subordinate their actions to a God who rewards or punishes them after death on the basis of their behavior in this life. The specific differences in religious belief among Jews, Christians, and Moslems are not so important as the status and social definition inherent in being a member of a particular group.

To the Westerner, it is the ideological differences between these groups which are falsely taken to be the crucial differentiating forces in determining social boundaries. Actually, the theological differences have become translated into social and structural realities with each community becoming socially separate from the others. What the people believe is not so important as the fact that people who believe similarly are considered to belong to some social order qualitatively different from that of the rest. Since religion deals with things of primary importance, a different religious persuasion turns others into members of a somewhat distinct society or "nation."

But a common culture can be shared despite religious differences. The sharing of a common language and land mass is important to a common life. Secondary or impersonal social relations can exist across religious lines without threatening the intensive primary, intracommunal social life necessary for the community to survive. What is crucial to the Arabs is a shared community life to support them—a place to return home to where intensive social intercourse can be carried on. From whom you buy your bread is not important as long as the more serious matters of life and love are taken care of in approved fashion in your own legitimate community.

The Moslem Presence

The force for unity in the Middle East has to come from an overall subscription to a common way of life and this was supplied by Islam. The faith of Mohammed has no organized church structure and, therefore, imposes no distinction between church and state or the kingdoms of God and man. An Islamic state is no more than an association of believers gathered together for the purpose of living in accordance with the tenets of their religion. In short, as A. H. Hourani notes,

> The Islamic community as it has traditionally been conceived is to its members all and more than all that the nation is to the modern Western man. Islam in its great days was a nation, transcending distinctions of race and colour. Although an Arabic-speaking Moslem might take a special pride in the peculiar relation of the Arabs to Islam . . . it is safe to say that normally he did not distinguish his being an Arab from his being a Moslem, and even when he did . . . it was the latter which was foremost in his thoughts and life.[3]

The more important Muslim sects are the Sunni and Shi'ah, which are also called "Metawileh," especially in Lebanon. The Sunni Moslems claim to be the practioners of the original and unadulterated Islamic orthodoxy as formulated in the Holy Koran. The Shi'ah sect started immediately after the death of the Prophet Mohammed and its appearance marked the first schism in Islam. Deciding the question of who had the right to succeed the Prophet was the root problem. The differences between the Sunni and Shi'ah religious practices are mainly confined to minor details of ritual, yet there is no mixing or intermarriage between them.

The Shi'ah, moreover, draw their strength from local nationals who are less rigid in their religious beliefs and who are more likely to opt for commitments to national political goals than to international religious ideology. A question of religious belief produced another schism out of which the *Druses,* the *Nusairiyah, Assassins,* and *Isma'iliyah* sects emerged.

The religion of Nusairiyh, although Islamic in inspiration, seems to bear a close affinity, in its general principles, to that of the Druses, a remnant of some pre-Islamic groups who sought refuge in the southern part of the Syrian mountains. They have always retained a certain degree of independence and primitiveness. They were never fully integrated into either Islam or Christianity, although they prefer to identify themselves as Moslems. At one time the Druse seriously threatened the security of Lebanon by battling the native Christians (Maronites) there for control of the Syrian coast. The Nusairiyh are closely related to the Druse in belief and practice, but are basically a syncretism of the Isma'ili Moslem tradition, the pre-Christian worship of nature, and the ancient heathenism of the Hauran district of Syria.

The Arab Moslems became conscious of America around 1890 while their Christian counterparts had become aware of it some twenty years earlier. Although migration and travel are nothing new to Moslems, the reason that the Moslems were later than the Christians in emigrating to America lay, according to Abdo Elkholy, in the religious differences. "The fear of losing their religion in the unbelieving country was the main factor delaying the Moslems a quarter of a century in their immigration in groups to America."[4]

Today the distribution of the Arab Moslems in America is still unknown since there is no census taken there by religion. Estimates range from 30,000 to 80,000 with some 30,000 additional Moslems of nationality other than Arab, such as Indians, Albanians, Yugoslavians, and Turks.[5]

Christianity and Lebanon

Since its population is about 50 percent Christian, Lebanon is considered the only "Christian nation" in the Middle East. The total population of the Near East is roughly 125,000,000 people, of whom not more than 7 percent or 9,000,000 are Christian. The Copts of Egypt, whose development was influenced by Saint Mark the Evangelist, form the largest single Christian (though non-Catholic) group, with approximately 7,000,000 followers. They constitute a distinct minority of the total population of the country and yet are considered full and committed Egyptian nationals. Estimates of the Christian population of Syria range from 3 percent to 15 percent of a total population of 6,000,000. The ratio of Christians to non-Christians in Lebanon, however, is roughly even, with a slight preponderance of Christians. Outside Egypt, Syria, and Lebanon, the indigenous Christians constitute even smaller minorites. Moreover, the number of Western Catholics and Protestants in the Middle East barely reaches 75,000. The overwhelming majority of the Christians of the Near East (excluding Egypt) are Roman Catholics of the Maronite and Melkite rites. The next largest group is comprised of the Eastern Orthodox bodies of Byzantine, Syriac, and Armenian origins.[6]

Some Christian sects, like the *Nestorians* and *Jacobites* who historically have been considered "heretical," are in communion with neither Eastern Orthodoxy nor Roman Catholicism. These two faiths are in a schismatic relationship to each other—the most serious difference between them being the former's refusal to assent to papal and Western supremacy as it is presently understood.

The government of Lebanon takes pains to remind the West that it is a Christian nation and hence worthy of special recognition and treatment. Historically, the hills of "the Lebanon" have served as a haven for all persecuted minorities. Even the French Crusaders relied on the Lebanese mountain folk for protection and succor. Not that the various Moslem minorities there have no political power or rights—they certainly do. But the character and political organization of the country were created by the Catholic Maronites and are derived from Christian rather than Islamic sources. Lebanon is Arab in language, culture, and custom, but is Western in outlook, multilingual (French and increasingly English are additional languages), and least Arab in orientation because of the historic predilection of the Maronites for Western thought and life-styles. To Christian Westerners and Easterners, Arab means Moslem!

Social order, stability, and continuity, then, in the Middle East depend upon the ability of any particular government to integrate a religiously heterogeneous population. Former President Nasser of Egypt, for example, asserted at the cornerstone laying for the new Saint Mark's Cathedral in Cairo on July 14, 1964, that "we are all Egyptians; Islam recognizes Christians as brothers in religion and brothers in God. . . . I pray God that love and brotherhood may prevail in our land and that He may help us all."[7]

The following New Year's Day, Lebanon's President Helou, a Christian, gave similar reassurance to his Muslim constitutents: "We have chosen," he averred, "to live and die on this narrow stretch of land, according to laws inspired by a pact of brotherhood. With the help of the one God in whom we all believe, we are achieving a national community, a human synthesis, a universal society."[8] These statements were not simply the occasional rhetoric of support-seeking politicians. Such feelings are also common, though by no means universal, among both the intelligentsia and the general public. The delicate balance between religions is critical for both national and regional security and now international peace.

It is for this reason that the very constitutional structure of the state of Lebanon reflects the religious distribution of her population: only a Maronite Catholic can be president and a Sunnite Moslem must be given the prime ministership. In a less formalized fashion, the national governments of Syria, Jordan, and Egypt exist by consent of the various religious subcommunities within them as long as the national government does not interfere with the legitimately constituted prerogatives of any particular one.

The "modern" Western state of Israel (created by the West and reflective of many of its values), carved out of the authentically Arab community of Palestine, is considered the only Middle Eastern country that violates this traditional approach to coexistence in a religiously pluralistic region. Israel has not been able to come to grips with the problem of coexistence with the various socioreligious minorities present in and around it, and this same plurality and segmentation have made it difficult for the Arabs to form a united front. Israel's strength, consequently, lies not so much in its superior economy, Western political forms, or military might, but in the overall inability of Arabic culture to unite its members in a pragmatic, singular effort to reclaim Palestine. Sociologically, the goal of reclamation is beyond their range of historical experience and is a real problem for the localized Arabic-speaking population (Palestinians). Ironically, the unified and theocratically organized Israelis, and now the Palestinian refugees, seem to understand this better than the Arabs themselves.

What is important in the Arab world, then, is the position of one's group vis-à-vis all other socially distinct groups. This is so because everyone belonging to a community becomes identifiable through it and is thus equal in his rights and privileges to everyone else in the national society. There is no overt discrimination or legal restriction on the communal life-styles of Christians, Moslems, Jews, Druse, and others—at least not in Syria, Lebanon, Egypt, and Jordan. All are equal before the law and all share the same cultural heritage. But all remain structurally distinct from each other though tolerant of each other's distinctiveness.

This became especially evident with the advent of Moslem rule in the seventh century. Even Jews, as "people of the Book," were not exempt from the Moslem purview. Dr. Merlin Swartz of the Near East School of Theology in Beirut, Lebanon, writes:

> For Jews in the Near East, North Africa and Spain, the Arab conquest marked the dawn of a new era. Those forces that had led to the progressive isolation and disruption of Jewish life were not only checked, they were dramatically reversed.[9]

Contrary to popular Western thought, neither Christians nor Jews were coerced into becoming Moslem.[10] Indeed, the image of Moslem armies forcing conversion at the point of the sword in the manner of the Conquistadores is a blatant distortion that has its roots in Crusader propaganda. How does one explain the continued existence and growth of numerous Christian and Jewish communities after the Moslem takeover and the Quar'anic injunction that there was to be no compulsion in matters of religion?

Moreover, Islamic law generally made no distinction between Jews and other minority faiths. Together with Christians and Zoroastrians, Jews formed part of a much larger class of "protected persons" (*Ahl al-dhima*; *dhimmis*). Nor was it a temporary sufferance. Jews both individually and collectively were granted a permanent positive legal status in the emerging Moslem Empire which often became a haven when persecutions erupted in Europe.

> Based in part on precedents established by Muhummad in the constitu-

tion of Medina and in part also on pre-Islamic tradition, the right of Jews to life, property, protection, and the free exercise of their faith (so long as it did not prove offensive to Muslims) was guaranteed by Islamic law. In the spheres of religious practice and personal life, Jews were to be governed by their own law. Only in their relations with the larger non-Jewish community were they to come under the jurisdiction of the law of the state. On the other hand, individual Jews could always have recourse to Islamic law if they preferred. And from the sources we know that occasionally, at least, they did avail themselves of this privilege.[11]

In light of this, Arab governments have often regarded reinforcement of collective pluralism as one of their particular responsibilities. From the Western perspective this is unfortunate because a person's identity becomes unchangeable, is not freely chosen, and becomes an impediment to individual mobility. But the system has redeeming features: individuals remain secure in their identities, they have a community to support and to sustain them, and real pluralism is maintained without infringing on the rights of any single group. More important, the Middle Easterner does not view the situation as one causing problems.

In Arabic society, the individual has traditionally been considered secondary in importance to the family, clan, religious association, and townsfolk. This is his accepted position. All have a common heritage and hence a common future and all rise and fall at the same time. Even in the Americas, it was the immigrant families, not isolated individuals, who were the successful units of mobility and social consciousness.

Individuals in the Middle East can raise themselves in stature by migrating to another town and prospering economically. But to a great degree, they still remain clan members and their allegiance belongs to the family. They are neither free to nor desirous of constructing a world that is immune to communal responsibilities and that merely serves the individual. They are not interested in selecting and choosing options that accentuate personal independence and responsibility. If their individualism becomes too obvious or distinctive, they are dropped by the community and they cease to be recognizable. In a sense, the person suffers sociological death. One does not exist for the perfection of self but for the benefit of the community. This concept is expressed in the theology of the Eastern mystic Saint Basil the Great to the effect: "If you live alone whose feet shall you wash?"

At the root of this contemporary "communalism" lies the generally low degree of urbanization and industrialization. These worldwide forces have yet to make the same impression or impact on Arab life that they have made elsewhere. Modernization is a recent phenomenon in the Middle East and even where it has taken root successfully (Egypt and Lebanon), it has not caused the traditional breakdown of cultural norms, style, and meanings characteristic of its presence. This might be due to the fact that Middle Easterners have always been familiar with some type of urban living. Damascus, Syria, is reputed to be the oldest continuously populated city in the world. Moreover, Syrians have always been traders and Lebanon and Syria are at the crossroads of three continents. Possibly the cultural sophistication of the residents, developed over centuries by trading and exposure to competing world views, may have helped insulate them against rapid social change and disintegration. The Arabs seem to have mastered urban living and the integration of cultures and peoples centuries ago.

While Arab influences were brought to the area by successive waves of Bedouin invaders, Lebanon, which harbored most of the Christians, remained attached to the West through its Catholicism and through the establishment of the American University of Beirut and other educational enterprises. It is in Lebanon, therefore, that we have a microcosm of the Arab world and its dilemmas. It is Arab in culture, yet splintered religiously, a democracy of socially isolated groups, a Western-oriented nation within an area of strong Russian influence.

A strange type of "soul" is often formed under such conditions. The term "Levantine" has been aptly used to describe it.

> To be a Levantine is to live in two worlds or more at once, without belonging to either; to be able to go through the external forms which indicate the possession of a certain nationality, religion or culture, without actually possessing it. It is no longer to have a standard of values of one's own, not to be able to create but only able to imitate; and so not even to imitate correctly, since that also needs a certain originality. It is to belong to no community and to possess nothing of one's own. It reveals itself in lostness, pretentiousness, cynicism and despair.[12]

The problem of Westernizing while remaining genuinely Arab

is difficult for all Lebanese. Generally, the Moslems see Westernization as de-Arabization rather than synthesis, and point to Israel as an example of the consequences of such a trend. The Christians, on the other hand, remain conscious of their minority status, which for them is twofold: they are Christians in a sea of Islam and oftentimes Eastern Catholics in a sea of Roman Catholicism. Former president of the United Nations General Assembly Charles Habib Malik writes:

> The Lebanese Christians . . . when they mentally set themselves politically within the context of the larger Muslim world of the Near East to which they belong, automatically fall into the strange unauthentic workings of the minority mind. The Christians of the Near East develop a dual soul, with a terrific inner tension, often also exceedingly comic, and they suffer under a pathetic sense of insecurity. They will not let go their Christianity, but at the same time they must do nothing that will offend their Muslim world. They do not want to betray their Christian heritage, but neither do they want to prove traitorous to the Muslim world to which they belong economically, socially and politically.[13]

If Christian/Moslem differences discouraged their emigration, the reverse was true for the Catholic and Eastern Orthodox "Arabs." The Syrian Christians were quick to respond to the new opportunities afforded them by the decline and eventual collapse of the dominant feudal sociopolitical order established by the Turks. An area with inhospitable soil, such as Lebanon, was always threatened with famine and overpopulation, and the strife between the Druses and the Christians set a precedent for the latter to leave the area. Moreover, the opening of the Suez Canal in 1869 gave the Syrian traders, a disproportionately large number of whom were Christians, a staggering blow. While the Canal improved communication between the Occident and the "land of the rising sun," it also created strong competition with Japan over control of the silk industry, the products of which are a staple of Syrian export. "Syria," writes Hitti, "then began to present the spectacle of an agrarian economy of the primitive type dislocated by the competition of modern industry."[14]

Syrian Christians, then, increased their migration to the United States toward the end of the nineteenth century.[15] It is believed that the first Syrian to enter the United States was a Lebanese named Antonious Al-Bishallany who landed in Boston and who came here to study. He was influenced by the American missions who wanted him to return home as a missionary-educator. Unfortunately, he died in 1856 of tuberculosis and is buried in Brooklyn's Greenwood Cemetery. He was born and educated a Maronite Catholic but apparently died a Congregationalist. Among the more prominent Syrian families to enter the United States was that of Joseph Arbeely of Damascus which arrived here in the spring of 1879. While the name indicates Eastern Orthodox Christian parentage, the family was joined by other emigrants of all the Arab Christian traditions. In the early 1880's, a considerable emigration occurred from the city of Zahleh, which has always been a haven for all the Christian Arab sects.

For the first time in its history, the United States was absorbing increasing numbers of Eastern Mediterranean people who were Arab in culture yet Christian in religion. However, they were not Western Christians, and the Americans' ignorance of the traditions and history of these long-time Christians created the sociocultural setting for their assimilation story. Who these Arab-Christians are is asked even today!

CHAPTER III

To America: The Land of Freedom

THE TERM "SYRIAN" AS USED IN THIS TEXT INCLUDES THE PRESENT Lebanese nationality. Most Arabic-speaking Americans are descendants of migrants from the part of Syria that became Lebanon in 1947. The use of "Syrian" springs from a desire for historical-statistical accuracy, since many of the migration statistics previously compiled have been misleading. Lebanon was a province within Syria and both were part of the Ottoman nation.

The problem of accurately identifying the Syrian immigrants is not unique to North America. Such data from Argentina, Brazil, and other Latin American countries have also been difficult to decipher because of the presence of "passport Turks" who in reality are Syrians. Argentina, for example, lists as "Turks" some 18,000 immigrants by 1915 as against the United States' 71,000. An accurate investigation of their background would probably reveal them to be either Syrians, Lebanese, Greeks, Armenians, or other nationals under the Ottoman rule. Another complicating factor in the demographic data is that a number of Syrian-Lebanese Christians migrated into the Americas from Egypt and elsewhere in the Middle East.

Because of its broadness, we shall avoid using the term "Arab" to describe these people. If and when "Arab" is used it will refer only to Christians of "Syrian" ancestry. Biologically, culturally, and socially, few Arabic-speaking people are exactly the same. Syrians belong to both the Islamic and Christian faiths and are considered Semites. The modern Lebanese assert that they descend from the Phoenicians, but like the Syrians are Arabic in culture. There is also a sizable Arabic-speaking Jewish population (Syrian-Jews) in the United States that was part of the original Syrian migration here, but which is now integrated into the

American Jewish community. Since the religions of the Middle East were all structurally and socially separate from one another, the Jewish community and the immigrant Moslem and Christian communities continued this pattern of separation in the United States. Today, for all practical purposes, we have in this country three basically distinct social groups with little or no contact among them: Syrian Christians, Syrian Jews, and Arab Moslems from Syria, Lebanon, and other Middle Eastern states.

Causes of the Migration

A distinctive feature of the Syrian migration to the United States was its continuity as part of an age-long movement that earlier brought them into Europe, Africa and Asia. Almost at the center of the countries that formed the seat of Western civilization, it is no surprise that its citizens used the Mediterranean to become its traditional merchants and traders.

Contact with non-Arab civilization has been commonplace for the Syrians throughout history and their colonies have been established throughout the Mediterranean and the New World for centuries. As such, the great recent migration to the United States had substantial historical precedent. For example, in 1283 the first and one of the largest migrations of the Maronite Catholics of Lebanon took place because of the Ottoman oppression. Possibly as many as 80,000 Maronites fled to Cyprus so that by 1340 it became necessary to establish a bishopric on the island for them.

The earliest contact between the Middle East and the New World seems also to have had a religious character. Immediately before the era of mass emigrations to the United States a Catholic Melkite-rite bishop made the long journey across the Atlantic in 1849 to solicit funds to reconstruct Saint John's Monastery in Khonshara, Syria (Lebanon). In Latin America, Fr. Pedro Raful reportedly was the first known immigrant to enter the Aztec country in modern times. His superior, the Maronite patriarch, was defying the Ottomans—refusing their jurisdiction—when Padre Raful arrived in 1879 to lay the foundation for today's "Colonia Libanese" in Mexico's Federal District. The Ottomans were unmerciful to any national group attempting to secede from the empire. The Maronite patriarch was trying to find a suitable refuge for his people. who suffered at the hands of the Ottomans for decades and especially around the mid-nineteenth century.

The Syrians and Lebanese had little realization of the powerful influence of England and France in the area. The English supported the sovereign claims of the Druse to Southern Lebanon and the French supported the Maronites. The Turks, indifferent to local squabbles, let the Druse massacre the Maronites in 1860. This event was particularly brutal and swept from Beirut to Damascus. An eyewitness wrote: "Even now I find it difficult to recall the scenes and events . . . without a shudder. Every event was so brandished into my memory that it seems but yesterday that this beautiful land was grimed with fire, and sword, pillage and carnage."[1]

The Turkish army, believers in the principle of "divide and conquer," stood aside and permitted the atrocities. The Maronite abbot of Deir al Kamar was flayed alive, and his twenty monks poleaxed, while in the space of twenty-two days 7,771 persons were murdered, 360 villages were destroyed, 560 churches overthrown, 43 monasteries burned, and 28 schools destroyed.

A personalized version of the massacre was collected by Morris Zelditch[2] from another survivor:

> We had suffered from the Turks all our lives and had come to accept their methods of taking everything from us and giving us nothing in return but harsh words and more taxes. In 1860, however, there was a climax. The Druses hated us Christians and used to raid us every once in a while. That year the Turks urged them on us. The Druses and the Mohammedian Syrians, backed up and helped by the Turks themselves attacked us. For three days the men and women of our village fought back. My husband shot and killed two of them and I was loading guns. They killed a good many of our neighbors before we fled. I had six young children by that time, but I was determined that if I ever got the chance to leave this place I would do so.[3]

The rivalry between Maronites and Druses over economic and social control of "the Lebanon" had other important sources besides religious differences. For many years, Maronite peasants slowly spread southward into the Druse territory, replacing the local Druse peasants on the farms. Often the local authorities gave their land directly to the Maronites, who prospered considerably. Both Moslem and Christian landlords preferred the

Maronites because of their more efficient farming techniques. The Druse who were forced out migrated to the Hua'ran districts of Syria, but those who remained felt insecure about their political, religious, and economic position. Eventually widespread fighting began. Inevitably, the Maronites were supported by the French, who wished to gain an entrance into the country, as did the English, who supported the Druse. In a sense, political factions became identified by their religious base. The Christians, therefore, often brought persecution on themselves because of their successful yet apparently threatening economic-political activities and not just because they were Christians as such.

Moreover, the Christian Lebanese were nationalistically motivated and consequently when their attempts to break away from the Turkish empire were resisted became the largest emigrant group to leave the region.

Yet, it was not the United States that first attracted Syrian emigrants: it was Egypt, which was then the "promised land." Though overpopulated itself, the Nile region urgently needed educated personnel to fulfill the modernization plans begun by the Khedive Ismael (1862–1879), who opened the Suez Canal. Apparently, the better-educated Christians proved successful in their new homeland. By 1907 their wealth had risen to an estimated one-tenth of the entire nation's wealth, and their numbers in Egypt increased to about 30,000.[4]

For the Syrians of Mount Lebanon, population pressures could be eased and occupational goals more easily fulfilled by migration to Egypt. Up to the time of the present regime (1880), a number of educated Syrians, "the intellectual cream of the Near East,"[5] held positions of eminence and responsibility in Egypt, the Sudan, and other regions. By 1882, however, the Turkish yoke had again tightened in Egypt when Arabi Pasha attempted to liberate his country from Ottoman control. By 1890, the movement of Syrians *out* of Egypt actually developed into a mass migration.

The second and most substantial emigration to America occurred between 1890 and 1914 as a result of renewed Turkish oppression brought about by the political designs of the English and French and their Christian sympathizers in Syria and Mount Lebanon. This reached its height during Jamal Pasha's reign of terror when Turkey entered World War I in October of 1914. Christians would not wait around for wholesale conscription into the Turkish army, especially in view of the low esteem in which they were held by the Turks.

Emigration was an evasion tactic, as the Turkish government also demanded that the people provide food and services for the troops. Anyone suspected of sympathy with the Allies was arrested, and consequently many of the Christians, Druse, and Arab nationalists were put to death, banished, or imprisoned. To curb her nationalistic fervor, Lebanon's semiautonomy was also temporarily abolished. Between 1900 and 1914 the population of Mount Lebanon is said to have been diminished by one-fourth or 100,000 through emigration to the four corners of the globe.

Turkey was very conscious of the designs of both England and France on the "Arab" countries within its empire. The Europeans would support any movement leading to Turkey's disintegration. The plots against Turkey's lands had to be resisted, and this often meant oppressing its own Christian subjects who erroneously felt that they would never be politically, socially, religiously, and economically free if they stayed within the empire. England and France naturally fed these fears. While the harsh reaction of the Turks cannot be underestimated, they have been somewhat overdramatized by Western historians who ignored the fact that the Turks also respected the Christians as "people of the Book" and actually sought to revitalize the economy of their Arab subjects through loans from Germany. None of this sat well with the English and French, who chronicled Turkey's presence thus:

> The Turk has heaped up great evils by his economic neglect and fiscal oppression. Save for some sporadic efforts, he has been wanting in all for which government exists—justice and security, the development of national resources, the organization of public utilities, the encouragement of industry and trade—not to speak of education, in which his endeavors have been limited to a meager number of primary schools, and a supply of fanatical instructors in the Moslem religion. Upon the social desert into which he has turned nine-tenths of the country, the only cases are some hospitals, a few centers of higher education, the revival here and there of ancient water supplies, a couple of good roads and a railroad or two with some examples of scientific and successful agriculture. But all these are due to other influences or inspired by other faiths than his own.[6]

Another writer offers the following evaluation of Turkish rule in 1913:

Today, Turkey has no government, no real institutions, and her leaders are suicidally sealing up the sources whence these pressing wants might be supplied. . . . Among the complex problems, Armenia and Syria stand for the most urgent and dangerous. . . . All the elements of the population are in effervescences and the only sedative that can take effect upon them is adequate reform. . . . It [Syria] is a land which might have become the wealthiest in Asia if the natural forces at work had been allowed free play. But they have been paralyzed systematically by the masters of the country, who are the Turks, and whose steady aim has been to drain the land of its resources and use them for their State. . . .[7]

Regardless of causality, Lebanon experienced the most systematic persecution in the Middle East. Those who did not flee to the interior in quest of sustenance joined the ever-increasing army of beggars in the cities. Among these were some with enough energy to roam the streets and knock at doors or ransack garbage heaps in search of food. Others would lie down at the side of the street with outstretched arms and await succor or death. By 1918, the lower classes were practically wiped out and the fledgling middle class began to replace them.

To intensify the suffering, an army of locusts attacked the country already beset by such diseases as typhoid, typhus, malaria, dysentery, and bubonic plague. Lebanon had lost 100,000 people and would have lost more had it not been for the remittances of its emigrants, reaching $259,000,000 in the First World War, and American philanthropy initiated by Cleveland H. Dodge. Thousands of Iranian and Armenian refugees from Turkey also flocked into Lebanon. In its camps, Beirut had 15,000 while its environs received an equal number. One coastal town, Batrun, began the war with a population of 5,000 and ended it with 2,000. An American survey showed that in Southern Lebanon and Sidon, of 182 villages with 10,000 dwellings and 77,000 inhabitants, 2,500 dwellings went to ruin in the four years of war and 33,000 people perished, leaving 44,000 (of whom 16,400 were paupers and 2,600 orphans).[8]

In addition to war-induced poverty, the Syrian economy was experiencing serious changes and challenges. The opening of the Suez Canal undermined the Syrian silk industry, while its form of agriculture remained ineffective because of the poor quality of the land. Many of the Christians, who were particularly affected by these unfortunate economic conditions, held that the religious factor took precedence over the economic in provoking the emigration. The English and French encouraged them to think along these lines. In reality, because of conditions in the Turkish Empire, religious, economic, and political considerations were all intermingled, making it impossible to isolate one variable as causal.

Yet, the American Industrial Commission reported that Syrians of all persuasions were unanimous in ascribing their wholesale expatriation to the rapacity and misrule of the Turkish government. The Syrian newspapers of the time were generally unanimous in their anti-Turkish policy and a glance through them reveals that great emphasis was laid on the political and economic causes of the emigration. Only the Maronite Lebanese insist on the primacy of the religious factor and they do so in order to further their own nationalistic goals, which means keeping Lebanon Christian—implying that there can be no other haven for Christians in the Middle East.

In this region, it is religion which in fact does ultimately separate men from one another. It is the chief means of locating and identifying individuals and groups of people. Consequently, economic and political status is related to and often stems from one's religious identity. For example, one can trace the economic "superiority" of the Christians to the fear of the Turks of arming them. Being freed from service in the military, out of religious apprehension they became economically successful, giving rise to the jealousy of the Druse and Moslems. Religion precipitated social fragmentation and became the basis for discriminatory treatment.

Historically, the Ottoman administrators recognized religion as both a divisive and a cohesive factor in their provinces. They held the various Christian religious leaders responsible for the civil activity of their people. But it was not until 1848 that the Melkite-rite Catholic patriarch obtained formal civil jurisdiction over his own people. Previously the Armenian Catholic patriarch was the civil head of all the Eastern Catholics in the Turkish Empire except the Maronites.

In contrast to the rule applying to other rites, the Maronite patriarch in Lebanon was not obliged to solicit his *firman*, or sign of investiture, from the Turkish Sultan or Porte. He was understood to be the civil head of his rite or nation, and needed no agent at the court of the Sublime Porte. The Maronites were, together with the other Arab Eastern Catholic communities, represented by the vicar of the Latin Catholics, who acted as intermediary between the Western and Turkish powers and the Eastern Christians. Unlike the others, however, the Maronites were socially, economically, and politically tied to the Lebanese nation, making them a nationality as well as a religious rite. Persecution of them as Christians or as Lebanese nationals led to the same result: emigration.

Emigration was also spurred by the American Expositions and various money lenders and steamship agents who capitalized on the generally depressing situation. "Good news" of the United States was also spread by the pen and/or by returning emigrants themselves. Equally important were the fantasies that American Protestant missionaries working in the East spurred. They told of the wealth, generosity, and apparent respect for religious diversity which characterize the United States. The cultured life-styles of these missionaries, their democratic ideals, and their relative wealth and health told of the opportunities America offered to discontented Syrians. A reporter in the March, 1903, issue of *Harper's* magazine summarized it thus:

> It was said that the ignorant Italian dreams of digging great channels of gold from the streets of New York, but the Christian Syrian when the Mohammedan oppression falls heavily upon him says "it is the land of liberty! Let us arise and go to that place." That is why he comes. He is interested in the freedom rather than the dollars of the land.[9]

In the main, the Syrians' desire for freedom was economic, political, and religious and their failure to achieve it in their native land led to emigration to the New World.

Demographic Characteristics of the Migration

While no statistics are available for the years immediately after 1882, it can be taken for granted that there was some emigration of Syrians at that time. Although Table I describes the emigration as Turkish, it is known that a significant number of these people came from Syria. Eighteen ninety-nine marks the first year Syria was specifically cited as an emigration source; the data are shown in Table II. Once they had discovered North America, the Syrians came yearly in ever-increasing numbers, the emigration rising to nearly 6,000 in 1907. The peak years exceeding 9,000 immigrants were reached in 1913 and 1914.

The war years saw a steady drop. In 1918 only 210 Syrians entered the United States. With the war's end, emigration picked up somewhat and reached a high of 5,105 in 1921. Emigration gained momentum in the 1890's and increased steadily until the outbreak of World War I. Between 1900 and 1914, one fourth of the region known as Mount Lebanon emigrated—a total of 100,000—with the United States as their destination. In one single eighteen month period, 2,000 out of the 18,000 inhabitants of the Lebanese community of Zahle migrated, most of them young men.

Yet, in the overall immigration picture, they were a small minority. Between 1900 and 1915 total immigration to the United States was running from 800,000 to more than one million each year. In that entire period, about 85,000 Syrian-Lebanese immigrants arrived.

After this date, the reduced figure can be accounted for by the restrictions imposed by the United States on the admittance of aliens especially those from Eastern and Southern Europe. Entrance into the United States became regulated by the Quota Limit Act of May, 1921, which set Syria's quota at 882. The act expired by limitation on June 30, 1924, and Congress passed the Immigration Act of 1924, generally known as the "Quota Law," which reduced Syria's quota to 100. Some Syrians entered over the quota as the wives and children of naturalized Syrians who had returned to the homeland to either find mates or bring over their families.

Tables I and II also indicate that until 1895 few Syrian women entered the United States, the ratio of males to females often being four to one. The number of male Syrians has always remained higher than the number of females in this country. By 1920, out of the estimated total of 51,901 foreign-born Syrians there were 31,341 males and 20,660 females, creating a sex ratio of 151. In 1930, out of a total of 57,227 foreign-born Syrians 32,510 were male and 24,717 were female, for a sex ratio of 131.[10]

The early male immigrants had as their goal the amassing of as much wealth as possible in the shortest time and then returning to Syria to enjoy it in peace and quiet. But World War I and the establishment of families interfered with this plan. However, of the older Syrians interviewed by Zelditch in 1932, eight out of

TABLE I

Number of arrivals in the United States from Turkey in Asia, by sea, 1869-98

Year	Males	Females	Total
1869	2	0	0
1870	0	0	0
1871	2	2	4
1872	0	0	0
1873	3	0	3
1874	2	4	6
1875	1	0	1
1876	5	3	8
1877	3	0	3
1879	19	12	31
1880	1	3	4
1881	5	0	5
1882	0	0	0
1883	0	0	0
1884	0	0	0
1885	0	0	0
1886	14	1	15
1887	184	24	208
1888	230	43	273
1889	499	94	593
1890	841	285	1126
1891	1774	714	2488
1892	n.a.	n.a.	n.a.
1893	n.a.	n.a.	n.a.
1894	n.a.	n.a.	n.a.
1895	n.a.	n.a.	2767
1896	2915	1224	4139
1897	3203	1529	4732
1898	2651	1624	4275
TOTAL:	12, 356	5,565	20,690

Source: *International Migration Statistics*, Vol. 1, National Bureau of Economic Research, Inc., 1925, Table II-a "Distribution of Immigrant Aliens by Sex and country of Origin," 1869-98, pp. 418-31.

TABLE II

Number of arrivals from Syria in United States by Sex, 1899 to 1924

Year	Males	Females	Total
1899	2446	1262	3708
1900	1813	1107	2920
1901	2729	1335	4034
1902	3337	1645	4932
1903	3749	1802	5551
1904	2480	1173	3653
1905	3248	1574	4822
1906	4100	1724	5824
1907	4276	1604	5880
1908	3926	1594	5520
1909	2383	1285	3668
1910	4148	2169	6317
1911	3609	1835	5444
1912	3646	1879	5525
1913	6177	3033	9210
1914	6391	2632	9023
1915	1174	593	1767
1916	474	202	676
1917	690	286	976
1918	143	67	210
1919	157	74	231
1920	1915	1132	3047
1921	2783	2322	5105
1922	685	649	1334
1923	605	601	1207
1924	801	794	1595
1925	205	245	450
1926	184	304	488
1927	302	382	684
1928	226	387	613
1929	245	387	632
1930	249	388	637
1931	103	241	344
1932	114	170	284
TOTAL:	69,514	36,877	106,391

Source: *International Migration Statistics,* Table X, pp. 432-43, for data to 1925. Data from 1925 on is found in *Annual Reports of Commissioner General of Immigration,* 1926 to 1933, Table(s) VIII, "Immigrant Aliens admitted fiscal year ending June 30 by race or people, sex and age."

ten had intended to return after they had earned sufficient money to permit them to live comfortably according to Syrian standards. Of the eight, four made return trips, but none remained in Syria more than two years. A representative attitude is presented by one such immigrant:

> Naturally when I left Syria I did not plan to stay permanently. I hoped to make enough money to live comfortably, then return . . . perhaps to Tripoli. Well, I did return in two years time, carrying $10,000 back with me. But I stayed only ten months in Syria. My family and all the people in my town were so admiring and so excited about my good fortune that they insisted I must return with them and show them how such fortunes were to be obtained. I also found that living in Syria was as hard as ever, and I had begun to enjoy some of the American luxuries such as good sanitation and freedom of movement. So, accompanied by my three brothers, and fifteen of our neighbors, I returned. It was not long afterward that I met my wife in Brooklyn. She too was Syrian. My business prospered and soon we began to raise our children. Then I realized I had no reason to return to Syria. This was my home here. It was then that I became a citizen.[11]

Likewise, many of the Syrian-Americans who had planned to return to their natal places changed their minds in time, and of the few who did return many came back to America.

The wives of the Syrians did not start arriving until the men discovered that in the United States women were an economic asset rather than a liability. Consequently, of the 9,188 immigrants admitted in the years 1908 to 1909, 8,725 or 95 percent, declared that they were coming to join relatives and friends, making the emigration to the United States in its later years essentially a family movement. The proportion of women emigrating was higher among the Syrians (32.1 percent) than among the Armenians (23.5), Bulgarians and Serbians (4.3), and Greeks (4.9). The average female percentage of immigrant groups to America was 30.5.

The promised "return to Syria movement" simply did not materialize. The birth of their children, the arrival of spouses, and the wedding of the Syrians politically, socially, and economically to the United States militated against their returning to a land devasted by years of war. In addition, return was limited because of the Syrians' uncertainty concerning the political destiny of their country, which was being partitioned by three contending Western powers and torn asunder by a general paralysis of the means of livelihood. Also, travel by boat at the time was not pleasant, and Syria represented the farthest distance one could travel by steamship. Of course, Syrians could not be sure of their status when they did return, since the Turkish government considered naturalized Syrians to still be Turkish citizens.

A considerable proportion of the immigrants came from the urban centers of the Middle East—Damascus, Aleppo, and Homs in Syria, and Beirut and Zahleh in Lebanon—and their settlement in the United States retains this urban dimension. But while Melkites and Orthodox Christians were citified, the least urbanized group in the Levant were the Maronites of Mount Lebanon who traditionally were rural people. Though the immigrants to the United States were predominantly Lebanese and therefore rural, most of these immigrants came from villages dense enough to have an active social life. As such most of them were not isolated farmers or "rural folk" in the sense understood by Americans, but were quite familiar with urban life. This familiarity with urban living affected their adjustment to American society and culture in a positive way.

CHAPTER IV

The Immigrants Arrive

IN 1947, *Life* MAGAZINE PUBLISHED A SERIES ON "THE PEOPLE of New York," which made reference to the "American Arab." The caption under the picture of an austere-looking immigrant read: "Mohammed Abdullah works as a house painter and lives near New York's rapidly diminishing Syrian colony. Like other Arabs, Mohammed was named after the prophet."[1]

This characterization was not really descriptive of the Syrian immigrant in America, and in some respects underscored the fundamental problem of the Syrian Christians in America: identification.

The Problem of Origins–Who Are They?

Americans in general, and apparently New Yorkers in particular, mistook the early Syrian immigrants for "Turks," "Arab-Moslems," or "Assyrians." Philip K. Hitti, who became the ranking American scholar on Arabist studies, recounts a revealing anecdote:

> My first day in New York. I met a lady who said to me; "You are the first 'Assyrian' I have ever seen." I explained to her that the kingdom of the Assyrians was destroyed in 606 B.C., and so I could hardly claim any connection with them.[2]

The confusion in identity was augmented by the classificatory terminology used by the immigration authorities who did not differentiate between "native Syrians," "Turks," and "Armenians," all of whom were considered as coming from "the Turkish Empire." It was not until 1899 that the Syrians received separate classification among emigrants from the Turkish Empire.

Although this differentiation helped in the tabulation of their numbers, age, sex, and destination, the identity of the Syrians remained hidden since they were denied naturalization on racial grounds. They were deemed "non-white," and anti-Syrian resentment reached its peak in 1914-1915, the years following the highest immigration rates. That a mere 10,000 immigrants a year could inspire such paranoid reactions among Americans indicates the general anti-immigrant climate prevalent in the country at the time.

Whether or not the Syrians as a "race" were entitled to the privileges of American citizenship was a common question. Edward Rose wrote of them in 1914 that "Mediterranean people are morally below the races of Northern Europe. This is as certain as any social fact."[3] The Levantines, grouped with the Finnish people and others of supposedly Mongolian origins, had "polluted" Europe earlier during the Saracen invasions and it was feared that this new emigration from the Eastern shores of the Mediterranean would biologically and socially pollute the already established Northern European blood strains in the United States. The nativism prevailing in the 1920's applied to Eastern Europeans as well.

The problem of origin became centered on the Syrians' eligibility for naturalization. The question was first raised in St. Louis when the United States District Court held that they could not become naturalized because they were aliens who were not white. The circuit court of appeals in that district reversed that decision, and the same question was raised in the southern district of New York City where the circuit court of appeals again affirmed the decision to naturalize them. Legally and politically the question was important. Socially, the Syrian Christians—often blond and blue-eyed—were not particularly handicapped.

In addition, while the passports of the Syrians were issued by Turkey, the work "Turk" used by the American press and community to describe them was actually an ethnophaulism similar in intent to "Spic," "Mick," "Wop," et. cetera. In lower Manhatten and downtown Brooklyn, the Syrians were displacing the Irish and hostility between the two groups was frequently in evidence. In the words of the Industrial Commission Report on Immigration, "The Syrian in New York has housed himself in the tenements of the old First Ward from which he has displaced an undesirable Irish population, the remnant of which torments him."[4] When the tormenting was not physical, it took the form of verbal abuse in the epithet "Turk"—implying that they were not Christians but "adulterous non-believers." This was, to say the least, an insult to the Syrians, who felt it a curse to be classified as Turks. The Syrian Christians and Moslem Turks were enemies after all!

To make matters worse, the Syrians' first settlement in New York was near Battery Park bordering on the area of debarkation from Ellis Island. This proximity to the emerging Wall Street banking community helped focus attention on them and their way of life. Social service workers, newspaper reporters looking for stories, and the immigration officials at Ellis Island had a new and available population at hand to scrutinize, and they did so regularly and often negatively. Generally, the Syrians received serious indictments of their culture and life-style.

A passage taken from the autobiography of an immigrant Melkite Catholic priest summarizes the difficulties in ethnic identity and relations faced by the early Syrian settlers of Paterson, New Jersey, a suburb of New York city. As was the case in other locations, the section in which they began settling was known as the "Dublin District" because it was inhabited mostly by Irish families.

> When the Syrians came to live there, the rentals became higher. This caused hard feelings between the Irish and the Syrians, which developed into a feud between the two nationalities. The fight started in the saloon on Grand and Mill Streets, first with bitter arguments and harsh words, and then threatening fist fights. From the saloon, the fight came out to the streets. It was like two armies in opposition facing each other. The Irish, experienced in boxing, tried to knock down the Syrians; but Mr. George Bastory, whose hand palm was like a plate of steel, was knocking the Irish down one after the other before they could reach him. The police force was called to put an end to this fight. All they could do was to throw water on them to disperse them. These fights continued for three days in the evening. Finally, a committee of Syrians went to talk to Dean McNulty of St. John's explaining to him that they were Christians coming from the Holy Land, not Mohammedans or Turks, as the Irish used to call them. They were Catholics and they wanted to live in peace with everybody. Then the good Dean, at Sunday masses, urged the Irish to stop fighting the Syrians, who were like them, Catholics. He succeeded in stopping this fighting better than the police.[5]

This serious confusion in identity existed in all the ports of entry to the New World since all the immigration centers registered Syrians as "Turks," forcing them to go under the name "Turcos." This situation persisted for many decades, especially in Central and South America.

In the early 1900's legal emigration from the Middle East required a Turkish passport regardless of one's port of departure. Many different nationals consequently arrived in the United States as "passport Turks" even though they may have been Syrians, Palestinians, Jordanians, Egyptians, et cetera. The situation was further complicated by the fact that Lebanon had consistently been regarded as part of Syria. Thus, even after Lebanon passed under the French mandate and even after World War I, immigrants from this "new province" entered not as Lebanese but as "passport Syrians."

In spite of her pre-Arab, Phoenician origins, Lebanon was considered, both legally and politically, a province of Syria and it was not until General Allenby's Egyptian Expeditionary Force with Arab help drove out the Turks in 1917 that the Lebanese took seriously their desire to be a separate nation. On September 15, 1919, the French and English secretly signed the Sykes-Picot Treaty which gave the former control of what was then known as Syria including Palestine and Lebanon. It was not until 1920, when the Moslem Prince Faisal was proclaimed king of Syria, that Lebanon repudiated the government and declared itself independent.

Acquiescing to the demands of the Lebanese Maronites who were determined not to be engulfed by the Moslems, the French declared Lebanon a republic, but under a continuing mandate this amounted to little more than a title. However, with the collapse of the Vichy government during World War II, the last French troops were forced to withdraw after Lebanon successfully protested their presence to the new United Nations in 1946. By that time Lebanon had already successfully elected its first president according to a constitution drawn up under the direction of the high commissioner of the League of Nations.

As far as self-identity was concerned, however, the immigrants to America from this province considered themselves "Syrians" until the Great Depression of 1932. It was then that they began to realize the benefits of being known as progressive Lebanese Christians.

Our use of the term "Syrian," then, will include all turn-of-the-century immigrants from the modern nations of Jordan, Israel (Palestine), Lebanon and Syria who are either Melkites, Maronites, or Syrian-Orthodox Christians. Most scholars agree that this was the custom of the immigrants themselves.[6] Demographically, however, it is true that most Arabic-speaking Americans are descendants of modern Lebanon. Yet, the word Lebanese was never publicly used by any Arab-American publication until 1930. Hitti tells us that

> while at home they thought of themselves as Beiruties, Zahlawis, Dayranis, Hasrunis, Haqilanis, or as Maronites, Druses, Greek-Orthodox, Metawilah, in their lands of emigration they had to answer the question "What are you?" in broader terms. Even then some replied "Suri" (Syrian).[7]

It was only after the founding of the Al-Hoda Press by a Lebanese Maronite family that a campaign, often unsuccessful, was seriously undertaken to make the Syrians believe that they had Lebanese origins. Eventually, they succeeded, and some Syrian-Americans began identifying themselves as Lebanese some thirty years after their migration. As would be expected, this was especially true among those Syrians who did in fact come from villages now inside geographic Lebanon. But this was not always the case. Many Lebanese refused to identify themselves accordingly, preferring the term Syrian, and many "authentic" Syrians began calling themselves Lebanese.

Undoubtedly because of the progressiveness that Lebanon represents (it has a higher per capita income than most Arab nations as well as a 90 percent literacy rate as compared to about 25 percent for the rest of the Arab world), the present generation of Arabic-speaking Americans prefer to be identified as Lebanese and assume, partially out of ignorance, that this has always been their practice. A revealing summary of this development is recorded by *Al-Hoda* itself:

> When the U.S. entered the war, a controversy over Lebanese identity emerged following a decision to raise funds for the Red Cross. Politics were inserted into the humanitarian campaign by the proposal that Lebanon be excluded from the committee's title. It would be called "The Syrian Committee for Raising Funds for the American Red Cross." The

prominent industrialist Assad Abood protested, arguing that the Lebanese formed more than 85% of the entire Arab-speaking communities in the United States. But the Syrians and some Lebanese who did not recognize the independence of Lebanon insisted on identifying the committee as Syrian on the ground that the community was known in America as the Syrian community. Others argued against including Lebanon in the title in order to avoid a disruptive controversy.[8]

For our purposes, then, the immigrants from the Middle East at the turn of the century are ethnically "Syrian." The term primarily refers to Arabic-speaking Christians (Melkites, Maronites, Orthodox) from both Lebanon and Syria. We hesitate to use the term "Arab" to describe these people unless the intended meaning of the word "Arab" is made explicit. Generally speaking, this label has been used to categorize all the inhabitants of the Middle East—whoever they may be—whether they are Bedouins (desert wanderers) or settled city people. If "Arab" is made synonymous with the former, then the Syrian-Lebanese Christians are not Arabs. Nor are they "Arab" in nationality. Rather, they are "Arab" in culture, language, and custom. Many times, the word "Arab" is used to imply a follower of Mohammed. True, "Arab" came to mean "Moslem" in a society that seemed to always confuse or fuse religion and nationality. This application would naturally exclude all Arabic-speaking Christians.

Essentially the only factors common across the Arab world are language and culture, including food, music, and dance. But, according to the late President Nasser of Egypt, an Arab is "anyone whose mother tongue is Arabic." So, in compliance with this definition, all Syrian-Lebanese Christians are Arabs. Since Arab nationalism calls all Arabic-speaking people to celebrate their freedom and emancipation from foreign domination, the term no longer has only negative connotations attached to it. In this way and for these reasons, and because their countries of origin are identified with and participate in international Arab political organizations such as the Arab League, the Syrian-Lebanese American Christian population may be considered to be "Arab."[9]

How Many Christian Arab Immigrants?

Because of the identification problem previously discussed, the number of Syrians in the United States for any given decade is at best conjectural. Nevertheless, the Industrial Commission Reports, though prejudiced, suggest that "an aggregate of 1,000,000 Syrians have migrated."[10] If this were the case, there would be no Christians in the Holy Land today! Most likely, the commission wished to make fearsome the American Syrian's cultural background, social traits, and potential numerical strength and distribution in this country. Numerically, Syrians threatened no one. Racist fears, however, have little to do with reason and fact. Anxiety over the "growing Arab menace" undoubtedly added to Congress's desire to contain Syrian immigration to the United States.

Estimates of American Syrians have therefore varied from 25,000 by the Industrial Commission in 1901 to 60,000 by P. Roberts in 1910[11] and 400,000 by the *Literary Digest* in 1919.[12] The United States' thirteenth census (1910) reduces the figures of foreign stock speaking "Syrian" and Arabic to 46,727.[13] This confusion in data is further outlined in Habib Katibah's chapter on Syrian-Americans in Brown and Roucek's *One America.*[14] Says he,

> It is not easy to estimate the number of Syrians in the United States. The 1940 federal census gives the urban population of the Syrians (which includes the Palestinians and the Lebanese) as 136,849. Of these, approximately 50,000 are classed as foreign born, the rest as native born of foreign or mixed parentage. Adding to these numbers some 3,500 who are classed as rural farm population, and 11,000 rural nonfarm population, gives us a total of 151,300.[15]

This is about 50,000 less than the 1924 estimate given by Philip Hitti in *Syrians in America,*[16] and 100,000 less than that given by W. I. Cole in his brochure on the Syrians for the Massachusetts Department of Education in 1921.[17]

Mrs. Louise Houghton, who conducted the most extensive study of Syrians in the United States, says that between 1899 and 1907, 41,404 Syrians were admitted to the United States. "Although," she continues, "100,000 is the usual estimate, 70,000 is that of the best informed Syrian."[18] Yet, some Syrian authorities, Katibah tells us, "put the figures for the total number of Syrians in the United States as high as 500,000."[19] For 1946, this figure seems exaggerated by at least 250,000 people.

Official government reports can be summarized as follows:[20]

Source	Number
1) Reports of the Commissioner General on Syrian Immigration, 1899-1919	— 89,971 (Cf. Table II)
2) Fourteenth Census Report: 1920	— 104,139
3) International Migration Statistics 1899-1925 and Annual Reports of the Commissioner General, 1926–1933	— 106,391 (Cf. Table II)
4) Abstract of the Fifteenth Census of the United States, 1930	— 137,756 (Including American born)
5) Estimates of Morroe Berger in "America's Syrian Community,"[21] 1940	— 350,000
1958	— 450,000

Basing his estimates on the cumulative immigration by 1919, Hitti suggests that by 1924 if we take into account those Syrians entering the United States during the twenty years prior to 1899 as well as those who were born there, while making allowance for those who returned to Syria or died, there were 200,000 Syrians in the United States.[22]

While no data are available on the birthrates of Syrians in the United States, or on the percentage increase of the in-population per decade, it is still rather dubious that the community could have reproduced itself so rapidly in such a short span of time. Although Morroe Berger's estimates are probably exaggerated as well, his percentage increases between 1940 and 1958 seem reasonable, though the more accurate figure for 1958 would probably be nearer to 380,000. Recently, the Association of Arab-American University Graduates estimated the number of all Arabic-speaking people, including the old immigrants, the newly arrived Palestinians and Egyptians, the Christians and the Moslems, and their American-born children, to be 900,000.[23]

This much is certain: Syrians did not exceed one-hundredth of the total immigration to this country. Considering the relatively large numbers barred from entry because of trachoma, even this figure is questionable. Syrian Christians have always been and will always be a minority!

The widespread distribution of the Syrian population in the United States minimized their visibility. Every village of Mount Lebanon and Syria had one or more of its members as permanent emigrants living in North or South America. So too did Syrians settle everywhere within these continents. So extensive is their dispersal in the United States that the Reports of the Industrial Commission say that "no nook escapes him, and neither Canada, Latin America, the East Indies, or the Philippines is foreign to their enterprise."[24]

Dr. Adele Younis, a student of the Arab migrations to America, estimates the following distribution for the 3,698 Syrians who entered through the Port of New York in 1901:

> The six New England States with New York, New Jersey and Pennsylvania, attracted the largest number with about 42 percent preferring New York City. . . . Massachusetts ranked second in appeal, attracting 598 or 13 percent. There were token distributions elsewhere in New England. But following Massachusetts, Pennsylvania ranked third with 398 or under 10 percent going there. In all, 2,828 preferred the Northern states. This left the number of 873 to be distributed in the remaining four regions—South Atlantic, North Central, South Central, and the Western states. Ohio led the group with 205, Louisiana 96, Texas 88, Indiana 75, West Virginia 72, Illinois and Iowa each receiving 66, Maryland 41, Georgia 30, and only one indicating Kansas. Colorado and California in the West were favored; the first received 13; the latter 12.[25]

Since even the rural Syrians came from villages with close-knit social networks, the agricultural sections of the United States, particularly the mountain states, the eastern south-central states and the Pacific states have the smallest number of Syrians. The census of 1930 shows that of the estimated 57,227 foreign-born Syrians in the country, 90 percent were living in urban districts; 1.9 percent were in rural farm districts; and 8.1 percent were living in rural, nonfarm districts.[26]

Even though many had probably worked the land in the old country, the Syrians were not attracted to farming in the United States. This was probably due to the isolation and loneliness of American farm life, the great necessity for knowing English, the need for starting with a fund of money or land, the strange food and lack of church facilities, the competitiveness of the farm operation, and the less abundant economic remuneration of the American farm system. Because the familiar social life of the old country villages was absent from rural America, the immigrants settled in manufacturing centers where the probability of establishing some form of stable communal life was greater.

While industrial states have the largest number of Syrians, hardly a town with a population of 5,000 or over is without them. The Reports of the Immigration Commission for the years 1899-1910 show that the destinations named by the 56,909 Syrians admited included every state of the Union, without a single exception, as well as Alaska, Hawaii, and Puerto Rico.[27]

Syrian-American Communities–Where Are They?

By 1925 the distribution of the Syrians in the United States was fairly stabilized. Even when they clustered in smaller cities and towns they retained some homogeneity. Once an immigrant family settled, they invariably sent for their remaining kin and townsfolk, who upon arrival in America went to the town or city they had heard about in letters. Nevertheless, they essentially followed the patterns of other ethnic groups by settling and concentrating in urban areas. "Little Syrias" emerged in many an American city. Today, three-quarters of all American Christian Arabs live in the industrialized Northeast.

During the last decade of the nineteenth century a number of Syrian and Lebanese families settled in the Boston area, drawn by the promise of employment in that city's expanding garment industry and by the hope of engaging in trade in that already thriving commercial center. The first Syrian-Lebanese settlers in Lawrence, Massachusetts, seem also to have come during this period, attracted by employment possibilities in the many textile mills then dotting the city. As early as 1896, they secured the services of a Melkite Catholic priest who began organizing the Arab Christian community of the city.

Syrians from Aleppo and Damascus were drawn to Paterson, New Jersey, also to work in the textile mills. Around World War I, with the decline in the silk industry in Paterson, many of these Syrians or their children migrated again to Miami, Florida, which now houses a prosperous and growing Arab Christian community. The first immigrants from the Near East to settle in Utica, New York, were Maronites from Mount Lebanon. They were soon followed by a group of Syrians, mostly Melkites from Aleppo. By the beginning of the First World War, there were approximately seventy families of Syrian origin in Utica, forty of them operating grocery stores.

The Syrians had begun to settle in Birmingham, Alabama, in 1903 and as early as 1909 had compatriots in Los Angeles, California. The Melkites of Danbury, Connecticut, began to build a church in 1910, and the Chicago Melkite community did the same as early as 1905. Because of the language needs of the people, which required the services of an Arabic-speaking priest, both these congregations served the Orthodox and Maronites as well. The Maronites began a parish in St. Louis as early as 1898 and another parish was begun there in 1913 specifically for the people from Hadchite, a small mountain village near the Cedars.

With the rise of the automotive industry in Detroit, and its need for a great number of factory workers, many Syrian and Lebanese entered the area and by 1920 they were able to establish churches for the Melkites, Maronites, and Syrian Orthodox among them. The first Christian Arabs arrived in Rochester in 1899. By 1906, Christians from the town of Saghbeen and Kirbet Anafar, in the neighborhood of Zahle, Lebanon, began arriving in Akron, Ohio. A smaller group from Ain Bourie, near Baalbeck, began settling in the Milwaukee area around 1895. In 1901, the first Eastern Christian liturgy was offered in Cleveland for the growing community there. The number of Syrian immigrants to Central Falls, Rhode Island, increased so rapidly that by 1900 they began to construct a permanent church.

Even before 1890 Syrians began to settle in New York. Between 1890 and 1920 some 20,000 Near Easterners actually made this city their permanent home. Manhattan and Brooklyn eventually emerged as the largest Arab Christian communities in the country. Recently, however, Detroit, Michigan, has received a substantial influx of new immigrants, especially Chaldean-rite Christians from Iraq and Palestinians and Jordanians. The total Arabic-speaking community there might now number 70,000. A small but significant group of Coptic Christians from Egypt has recently settled in Jersey City, New Jersey, and has already established a church of their rite there as well as their own newspapers. Their specialty shops seem to be thriving among the native Americans, who have received them warmly.

Basically, the emergence of a strong ethnic identity and community was both delayed and facilitated by these churches, which became responsible for preserving the ethnic cultural heritage. Generally, where the Syrians failed to establish these churches, their maintenance of ethnic continuity was severely hampered. Their secular clubs and associations simply lacked the wherewithal to successfully guide them through the assimilation experience. When they were not attached to a community, especially one that was sustained by their churches, the Syrians simply disappeared as a cultural entity. In a sense, the Syrians in the American diaspora, separated from their ethnic community, became Americans of Syrian ancestry while their counterparts in the cities remained "Syrian-Americans," i.e., they had a cultural, communal, and institutional life with which they identified.

Except for those in principal cities, there are no other significant communities of Syrians. Unlike other ethnics, the Syrians were neither able, nor interested, in establishing community-wide associations based solely on ethnicity, in order to pass on the cultural heritage. Rather, they pinned their interests and hopes on the family and church. At first, the tendency natural to all immigrants to group themselves in colonies was not particularly prevalent among them. This may have been due to their small numbers and their limited social consciousness. Most likely it was a consequence of the way they traditionally defined and structured their communities. The *Literary Digest* wrote of the Syrians in 1919 that "they disincline to gather in colonies and do not usually assert themselves as Syrians . . . [yet] where there are colonies of Syrians it will be found that they hold together because of similarity of business interests."[28] And this meant, in effect, "family business."

Younis gives an account of the importance of such "business interests" and ties in the New York community:

> New York City remained the most important center of attraction, particularly because of its commercial advantages. Small factories had already been well established producing white goods in underwear and household items as well as combs, mirrors, pocketbooks, kimonos and related items. The interest in commerce was well reflected in their early

newspapers. The first page did not carry the most important political or social news of the day. Instead, large advertising space displayed either the pictures of the plants in operation or the articles produced for sale. The names appeared in bold type in English and Arabic to emphasize their importance. News of national or international value appeared on succeeding pages. Their wide diversity of activities included the founding of a Syrian bank in an imposing building of its own. The residential area of lower Manhattan extended to South Brooklyn. From this center the more prosperous families entered select communities. From the New York center, communities radiated into New Jersey and Connecticut.[29]

Syrian newspapers were established between 1898 and 1907 and kept the community informed of the happenings in the old country. They also circulated the social news of each community. It is interesting to note that the community had already started to utilize English in its public pronouncements. This undoubtedly helped the more "Americanized" of the group identify with the larger ethnic community. The newspapers also kept the mobile community informed of the latest business ventures of emerging Syrian entrepreneurs.

Indeed, the scattering of the community and the need for a common medium of communication can be partially explained by the Syrian's desire to succeed economically. He is a trader by disposition and he probably began to wander as he always had wandered. Being disinclined to compete with fellow Syrians for a limited market, he would rather trade with the "Americans" who were unfamiliar with his products and selling techniques. Even today, the relationship of the major Syrian enterprises is one of helpful cooperation rather than competition.

In spite of their dispersion, however, it was New York, the favored port of entry, which became both the mecca for emigrants to the United States and eventually their point of departure to other parts of the country. Washington Street, located in lower Manhattan, became the cultural base for Syrians throughout the United States and was responsible for the literary life of all American Syrian communities. In addition to a scholarly journal entitled *The Syrian World*, the creation of a viable Arabic press was a primary concern of the immigrants. According to Dr. Younis,

Of first importance was the Arabic press. Other newspapers and journals followed *Kowkab America*. Joseph Malouf, the dean of Arabic literature, issued *Al-Ayam* ("The Days"); Shibli N. Damus founded *Al-Islah* ("The Reform"); the Mokarzel brothers, Nahum and Salloum, established *Al-Hoda* ("The Guidance"); and Najeeb Diab published *Murrat-el-Gharb* ("The Mirror of the West"). In the early twentieth century Abdulmesiah A. Haddad brought out *As-Sayeh* ("The Traveler"). Elia D. Madey, an early editor of *Murrat-el-Gharb*, issued a separate literary publication, *As-Sameer* ("The Entertainer" or "Friend"), which was later published as a daily paper.[30]

These publications not only played an important role in tying scattered people together, but it was through them that the classical Arabic language was made colloquial and functional, and hence suitable to the needs of the immigrants. Once established, the technique was followed elsewhere, including the Middle East.

Washington Street and its environs was destined to become the principal Syrian colony in the country. Most of what the local and dispersed community needed to survive could be found within its confines. Since it was a voluntary community located in the midst of the expanding banking community, its existence was short-lived. At its height, the colony was contained in approximately seven city blocks, bounded on the south by Battery Place, on the west by West Street, on the east by Greenwich Street and Trinity Place, and on the north by Cedar Street.

At one time the neighborhood had been in the hands of the Dutch, who were eventually followed by the Irish and Italians. Syrians eventually dispersed these two ethnic groups. Symbolically, their homes were conveniently located near the piers—the center of trade for the city and country. As the immigrants stepped from the steamers into Castle Garden, they not only found available lodgings close by but trading establishments whose methods they would soon learn to duplicate.

The same occurred in other parts of the city and also throughout the country. Often the newcomers established their residences within the area in which they first arrived. The homes along Washington Street had grown dingy and dilapidated by the time the Syrians inherited them. But the Arab community, once in possession of this area, turned it into a thriving Oriental trading mart that made the neighborhood internationally famous.

Washington and Rector Streets represented great investments

in American and imported merchandise. It became the shopping center for those who sought the exotic East in the United States. Many merchants in the area not only shipped goods to other settlements but also engaged in a lively export trade to the West Indies and South America. Unfortunately, its days as a residence quarter were numbered, for the colony was being reduced yearly by the constant erection of office buildings and factories. The year 1930 found the community completely dispersed to Brooklyn and Long Island.

The only remaining evidence of the Syrians' presence in downtown Manhattan are the "Syrian churches," Saint George's (Melkite) and Saint Joseph's (Maronite). Several prosperous stores owned by Syrians can also be found (Awns, Jabbour's), but they cater now to a strictly Wall Street clientele. Their owners have long since moved to Brooklyn and the churches, because they are Catholic, have been taken over by the New York Archdiocese and now serve the Roman Catholics of the business district. Gone is the confinement of crowded quarters and the sporadic native American hostilities leveled against these "undesirable Turks."

Like the Jews, whose experiences they seem to have duplicated, the Syrians opened small businesses and succeeded, but unlike them, they were never socially or involuntarily confined to any particular occupation or neighborhood as the Jews were on the Lower East Side. Even in New York, Syrian families were scattered into three areas by the time Lucius H. Miller did his study of them in 1904.[31] The New York *Daily Tribune* (October 2, 1892) and the Brooklyn *Daily Eagle* (May 10, 1892) described the movements of the better class of Syrians into the newer suburbs. It was felt that the Brooklyn colony of Syrians was financially more solvent than most immigrant colonies in any part of the United States and was really a "residence district" for well-to-do Syrians.

Eventually, Brooklyn absorbed virtually all of New York's Syrians into very fashionable neighborhoods. By the 1930's they were heavily settled in the "Park Slope" section of the borough, which even today is one of the better residential areas in the city. At present, however, a substantial majority lives on or near Shore Road in Bay Ridge. A small and extremely wealthy group is scattered on New York's Fifth and Park Avenues and in Westchester

County and Manhasset, Long Island. According to Dr. Younis, many prominent merchants had begun moving to Fifth Avenue as early as 1900.

Saleem Mallouk, a man of learning and wealth before his emigration, became one of the influential importers on Fifth Avenue. A patron of literature, he generously supported the budding literary circle which reached its heights during the 1920's. The Bardawill family enjoyed affluence in trade and social life, as did the Jabbaras. The Kiamies practically monopolized the silk manufacturing industry. Wadie Beder extended the silk industry to Shanghai, China. Others had plants in the Philippines. Naimi Tadross was among the first of the prominent Persian rug importers, as were Albert Sleiman and the Atiyeh brothers. . . . Antone Tadross and George Ackary, friends since Tripoli days, joined their efforts to establish an impressive warehouse on lower Broadway. Their textile products helped to supply out-of-town Syrian business houses just getting started in many more remote parts of the United States. Dr. Amin Haddad and Dr. Risq. George Haddad had studied in American schools before their emigration. Both devoted their energies to giving medical care to their people in lower Manhattan and Brooklyn which was an extension of the Washington Street district. The R. G. Haddad Educational Foundation was established after Dr. Haddad's death in 1943 for the purpose of awarding scholarships to young men of Arabic origin. In its twenty-fifth year, friends of the Foundation are actively engaged in a drive to make the foundation self-sustaining.[32]

One thing is certain. Syrians generally do not reside or settle within cities or towns at random. Rather, they move as family units with special religious interests. Both forces keep them close to and dependent on one another. Today, for example, the younger generation of Brooklyn Syrians is following a predictable demographic pattern. Young Catholic couples who wish to escape the city are moving mostly to the Emerson Hill area of Staten Island while the young Orthodox are moving to Tenafly-Englewood, New Jersey, where they are beginning to establish a church. The effort should help to ensure the community's collective future.

CHAPTER V

The Syrians Succeed

ORIGINALLY, THE SYRIANS' ENTRANCE INTO AMERICAN LIFE DID not look very promising. Though this was true for most ethnic groups, unfavorable attitudes toward the Syrians were largely based on two or three unrepresentative encounters with the New York police. At the turn of the century several misunderstood and exaggerated newspaper accounts of the Manhattan colony's sporadic "factional wars" were reported in the major tabloids of the city. In 1902 and 1905 two situations in New York City reached the attention of police and the general public. The first involved a fracas that led to possible abusive treatment of five Syrians by the police. A difficulty at 71 Washington Street led one of the officers to wield his club indiscriminately, causing blood to flow and heads to be bandaged. One man described as a giant who could hold nine men on his shoulders was severely beaten and the case involved several appearances in court.

In the other instance, the *New York Times* reported on October 24, 1905, that "wild-eyed Syrians battled fiercely for a quarter of an hour in the lower Westside last night. The dim light from barroom and club windows showed the glint of steel in two hundred swarthy hands. Reserves from three police precincts were rushed to the battleground, but there was plenty of time for a fight before they got there," et cetera. A similar description was carried by the *New York Herald* on October 29, 1905: "Factional War is waged between Syrians in New York City. Cutting and shooting. Brother against Brother, villagers, and old time friends are parted. Oriental warfare is carried on with American modifications. Voices of women heard."[1]

It was a misleading account and the publicity resulting from it created a poor impression of Syrians in general. It was a repetition of the historic religious feuds and frays that characterized social life in their former homeland. Until they became "Syrians," the immigrants identified themselves as "Maronites," "Melkites," or "Syrian Orthodox," and proceeded to act accordingly, that is, in a competitive rather than a cooperative fashion. When one recalls that so many of the petty disputes in Syria were caused by religious antagonism, it is no surprise to find religious dissensions and rivalries at the bottom of their quarrels in America too. The difficulties of 1905, for example, revolved around disputes among members of the Syrian-Orthodox faith over the qualifications of their bishop.

The Stereotypes Continue

There were also disturbances between the Catholic Maronites and the Orthodox over control of the community's press. Since the emerging Arab-American press played an important role in imparting news about local communities or the homeland, it mattered to the readership whether or not the press depicted the "right community." Eventually, the *Al-Hoda* publishing house became the organ of the Maronites and the other Catholic Syrians; *Murrat-ul-Garb* spoke for the Orthodox. By the time the problem was resolved in 1906, one young man, the Maronite priest's brother, was killed as a result of street fighting and knife wielding.

Nor did the financial aptitude shown by the American Syrians protect them from hostile criticism. After noting that there was a substantial number of wealthy Syrians in the Washington Street colony of "peasant extractions, who have concentrated their energies upon the dollar rather than upon the better aspects of Americanism," the Industrial Commission Report on Immigration went on to say:

> It is these alleged proselytes (those who become temporary Protestants to get an education), who have contributed largely to bring into relief the instinctively servile character of the Syrian, his ingratitude and mendacity, his prostitution of all ideals to the huckster level. . . . The Syrian possesses an ingrained indolence better suited to Oriental bazaar methods than to American business life. . . .[2]

This criticism reflected the attitude of the period toward factory workers in general and toward Syrian women, who were often employed in family-controlled businesses. Given the nature of the rapid industrialization of the nation at the time of the emigration, it is no wonder that the bulk of the commission's criticism deals with the alleged Syrian "disdain" for industrial labor:

> His docility as a proletarian is offset from the managerial standpoint by his fatalism—if driven too hard he simply lies down. Less vigorous than the others . . . with whom he competes, he is much less fettered than they. Worked too hard or paid too little in the mill, he becomes a peddler; a member of no union.[3]

Rather than being the consequence of any inherent laziness as the report suggests, his "docility" is more properly due to the Syrian's traditional dislike of working for someone else as well as his historic attraction to commerce and trade. Being an employee was equated with financial exploitation and was seen as a handicap and hindrance to financial success.

The Syrian-Lebanese newcomers were a leaven from the Levant, and by nature, circumstance and inclination preferred trading to any other type of work. What better place than America, the home of hard work and free enterprise to ply their wares? Their mercantile mentality was more than an ethnic oddity. It was part of an emotional, psychological, social and historical inheritance. When we look at the Syrian peddler/trader we are looking at the key to the Syrian-Lebanese Americanization process.

It is no accident that America's foremost heart surgeon and America's tireless consumer advocate are sons of Lebanese immigrants who were themselves in trade. Shaker Morris DeBakey came to the United States in 1855 at the age of 15 and ran a drugstore where the celebrated heart surgeon Michael E. Debakey first dreamed of medicine. For Ralph Nader, the king of consumer crusading in America, it was a family restaurant in Winsted, Connecticut, where, like DeBakey, he imbibed the meaning of hard work and tireless effort.

Unfortunately, this expression of hard work through peddling actually tarnished the Syrian image. Native Americans looked down on peddling as an activity to be followed by the destitute rather than as a first step in the economic success of an immigrant group.

Similarly, the exigencies of the migratory experience as well as the early conditions of life here also facilitated the autonomy of the Syrian woman, which seemed to especially irk the prudish commission. Accordingly, Syrian economic enterprise is described as

> consisting of sending his wife and daughters, or the wives and daughters of his countrymen, out to peddle from door to door, the silks, rugs, bijouterie, and antiques in which he traffics . . . . The real offenders are merchants (so called) whose cupidity and indolence reinforced by exaggerated partiarchal authority, enables them to make use of the pleasing appearance, glib tongues and insinuating manner of their women. . . .[4]

As for women's work (notwithstanding the fact that peddling is an acceptable profession in Syria), a very small proportion of Syrian women were the actual breadwinners of the family —except as the associates of their husbands. Married Syrian women were not expected to contribute to the support of the family except through the care of the household, which was considered their share of the "partnership." The "better class" of Christian women in Syria or in America did no work other than housework. This was due not so much to a lack of financial ability or to the spirit of economy as to the persistence of the belief that a women's place is in the home where she is to do all the household work.

Moreover, Syrian entrepreneurs generally mistrusted partners and preferred to own and operate their own businesses. When they did organize partnerships, the partners were close relatives, including their wives, sisters, and mothers.

With the coming of the Depression, critics of the Syrians actually began to equate its causes with the presence of unassimilable immigrants. Yet Syrian immigrant labor (unlike that of other ethnic groups) did not swell the ranks of the unskilled to any great degree. One writer felt, however, that "the Syrians, Assyrians, and Armenians are regarded unfavorably in several quarters. Some employers do not engage Syrians because they're a lot of troublemakers, much too fond of the radical labor movement."[5]

This chronicler went on to contradict himself by next noting that the Syrians are "potentially dangerous rivals who use their employment to learn the business and set up competing concerns."[6]

Edward Corsi, who had served for a short time as United States Commissioner of Immigration and Naturalization in New York, criticized the Syrians for arriving at a time when the country was "deluged with numbers of fakirs belonging to a group called 'Maronites,' followers of Maron, a supposed saint who lived in the fifth century. These people spoke Arabic and came here from Lebanon and Syria."[7] He went on to say that the Syrians traveled the country in gangs trying to peddle their wares to unsuspecting Americans.

Depictions of the Syrians did not remain entirely negative, however. Eventually, more accurate descriptions of their life-styles and culture became available to the public. The most important tract in their favor was prepared by Professor William I. Cole of the applied sociology department of Wheaton College, Massachusettes. After tracing their origins and occupations in the old country, he emphasized the immigrants' cooperative loyalties to family and church, and their "love of domestic life [and] courtesy," as well as the proverbial Arabic hospitality. In her review of his study, Dr. Younis writes:

> In total, he defined their traits as strong in "self-respect" and "self-reliance." He felt that in Boston the Syrians had made rapid progress in assimilation. A score or more had received their learning at Harvard and Massachusetts Institute of Technology. For recent arrivals this progress appeared quite remarkable to Professor Cole. He asserted that their strong individualistic and capitalistic inclinations made them averse to ideas either socialistic or radical. In conclusion he stated: When, through the opportunities and influence of America, they shall have come fully to their own, we shall number among our "foreign-born neighbors" no better residents and citizens than this people from Syria.[8]

Complimentary reviews of the Syrians were not limited to Massachusetts. In Chicago, a survey of Syrians generally revealed that they had a higher proportion of professional and skilled workers and a lower proportion of laborers than other groups in the city. They also ranked high in the number of teachers, clergymen, and physicians available to them from their own community.[9]

Nevertheless, the Syrians were considered "illiterate" while in reality the Christians among them were some of the best-educated people in the Middle East. Prior to the arrival of the

American Protestant missionaries, the Turkish overlords established only occasional public schools, which were essentially anti-Christian. The Protestants supplied the Christians with Arabic texts by means of which they became informed of their own heritage. Many actually emigrated to the United States to complete their education! Although illiteracy may have been high among the early immigrants, by 1919 a population of 70,000 in the United States was supporting ten Arabic newspapers and magazines.

The statistics on illiteracy given by the Immigration Department before 1910 puts the rate at 56.42 percent and 43 percent illiterate for women and men respectively between the ages of fourteen and forty-five. Undoubtedly, the Eastern custom of neglecting the education of girls was a factor in the difference. Houghton notes that for Syrian parents to send a daughter to school away from home requires "courage, and resolution quite heroic on the part of both daughter and parents. A generation ago it was still more unusual. Therefore, the proportion of illiterate middle-aged women to the men in their generation is necessarily large."[10]

By 1930, however, the percentage of illiteracy of foreign-born Syrians in the United States was only 25.2 percent; 16 percent of the males over ten years of age were illiterate, and 37.4 percent of the females. Of those Syrians born in the United States the percentage of illiteracy was 0.7 of those over the age of ten.[11]

Philip Hitti noted that however poor the family may have been, the parents usually insisted on giving the child a primary education. But once grade school was finished, the student was considered "educated" with no further necessity for study.[12] There also seemed to be a tendency for Syrian families to imitate a custom of the old country by having their children put into educational boarding schools run by various religious denominations. In time, practically all the Syrian children of the Catholic faith (Maronites and Melkites) attended parochial schools while the Orthodox and Presbyterians had only the public system to depend on.

The Emergence of the Entrepreneurs

It would not be an understatement to say that the Syrians arrived here as "ready made Yankees." While they were poor, they were psychologically ready for the American middle class. Imbued with a desire to succeed and own property, a readiness to gain financial security and independence, they looked for and found opportunity in the free-enterprise climate of America. Indeed, one immigrant became nationally known in the 1930's as a Syrian Yankee after arriving as a poor orphan boy from the forsaken village of Ain Arab (Arab's Spring). Salom Rizk lectured throughout the United States for *Reader's Digest* and described his Americanization experience in a book aptly-titled *Syrian Yankee*. Rizk celebrated the opportunities offered by America and proclaimed the responsibility to do something for America in return. According to Lebanese-American journalist Edward Wakin, "he mixed the practical with a populist idealism tinged with sentimentality, the kind of mixture that appealed to Americans and also reflected the Lebanese-Syrian mentality."[13]

As with his compatriots, peddling was Rizk's first pursuit in America. He wrote of being on the road with a partner, Joe Solmon, selling rugs and tapestries packed into a Model-T Ford. On the very first day out, poetry and practicalities emerged—"my joy in being a citizen of this land was almost unbounded. . . . When I remarked to Joe about the richness of the countryside and the prosperous look of the farms, he said there was only one thing they needed to be complete: a lovely oriental tapestry on the living-room wall and an oriental rug on the floor."[14]

In many ways then the Syrians always seemed to be typically American: they were frugal, religious, non-criminal, industrious, mobile and dedicated. As Morroe Berger says:

> even while they were still in the lower income brackets and in working class occupations, the "Syrians" displayed the social characteristics of the middle classes in American urban centers. Studies of these Arab immigrants in Chicago, Pittsburgh and the South reveal a common pattern: low crime rates, better than average health, higher I.Q.'s, and more regular school attendance among the children, few intermarriages and divorces.[15]

These traits served them well and helped support their basic desire for a separate communal life. Their rapid accumulation of wealth was in large part due to their cultural values, social characteristics, and business acumen. Syrian values, it seems, never really had to be greatly modified during the process of assimilation. The immigrants' success began quite early so that by 1895 there were some importers of Syrian goods who were quite prosperous. In 1919, the community in New York was characterized as generally prosperous—not wealthy, but independent.[16]

According to Houghton (1911), the Syrians in the lake cities were "comparatively prosperous and generally respected. . . . The Cincinnati and Pittsburgh colonies were inferior economically to any of the lake cities yet the organized charities report 'no poor Syrians in Cincinnati.' "[17]

It was financial success motivated by their desire for freedom and financial independence that set the stage for their assimilation into the dominant society around them and which led to their overall monetary accomplishments no matter where they settled. Indeed profitable Syrian enterprise was not limited to the United States and in some respects was even more spectacular elsewhere. Philip Hitti mentions that "he who amassed the largest fortune in Australia was there two years before he realized that he was not in 'Al-Na-Yurk,' the shipping agent in Marseilles having put him on the wrong boat." "In Brazil," he further notes, "the trade of that country passes more and more into Syrian hands every year."[18] As Benedicto Chuaqui writes of the immigrants' Chilean experience, so was it in the United States:

> Those who came first were forced to carry on commerce at its most elementary level: selling trinkets in the streets. No one would believe that the enormous factories in operation today are the product of the very hands that humbly peddled baskets of baubles. It is not that several generations have come and gone; in many cases it is the same little man that emigrated in the early 1900's who now sits in the front office of a factory which supplies jobs for thousands of laborers and white collar workers.[19]

In the United States, the emergence from immigrant poverty began on the Lower West Side of Manhattan—the cradle from which practically all Syrian "colonies" in the country emerged. Even in its early days this community had much within it that was creditable to the people—a number of prosperous factories, several importing houses, a travel bureau, steamship agency, and several real estate brokers in addition to restaurants and other small industries which dotted Washington Street and its environs.

Among the other means of livelihood for the early Syrian settlers were the clothing and manufacturing industries, grocery businesses, industrial work, and exporting. Mines, packing firms, and the possibility for trade brought the Syrians as far west as Minnesota.

In and near New York, thirty-five kimono factories operated by their owners helped establish early financial independence. In Paterson, New Jersey, the Syrians literally took over the silk industry, establishing more than twenty-five silk factories by 1924. Considerable wealth was also accumulated through the manufacture of cigarettes, embroidery, suspenders, gloves, and shoes.

While some groceries were established by Syrians in the Northeast (including New York), it was more typical of their development in the Middle and Far West. In the interior of the country, if the Syrian was not a lace or dry-goods merchant, he was usually selling food or sweets. Detroit, at one time, housed some three-hundred Syrian groceries.

Writing in *One America,* Habib Katibah notes that Syrians were among the foremost fruit and vegetable shippers and commission merchants in the country.

> In some cities, as in Utica, New York; Charleston, West Virginia; and . . . in Detroit, they seem to dominate the business. A Syrian in Detroit publishes a trade magazine for the grocers of Michigan and neighboring states.[20]

Dr. Adele Younis tells a typical Syrian-American success story. According to her, the story of Betrus Saad is not uncommon:

> Saad left Biskinta, Syria, as a young man and arrived in New York in the blizzard of 1888. New York City was a world of snow. Merchants directed Saad and four companions to go up-country as "walking merchants." The journey lasted three years. The young men had set out to sell, see America, and learn English. At Utica, New York, they paused to trade and attend evening school. The name Cheyenne, Wyoming, exerted a certain charm on their imagination, and they moved on toward that northwest outpost. California then beckoned. The circle completed, they returned to New York City. After his excursion, Saad wished to share his good fortune and sent a $200 check to his brother in Syria. The day the money arrived, forty energetic Biskinta youth left Syria for New York City.[21]

The accomplishments of the late patriarch of the Coury (Khuri) family, who died in 1956 at the age of eighty-four, are recounted by Morroe Berger:

> He came to the United States in 1891 at 19 years of age, almost penniless. With a little borrowed money he bought a meagre stock of goods which he peddled across the country. He soon acquired a store, then branched out until he made several fortunes in various businesses. Retiring to Miami, he found it difficult to do nothing but relax; so he made another fortune through a chain of self-service laundries. His son, typically, has moved up the ladder of prestige but (and less typically) without sacrificing opportunities to acquire more wealth; he is a prominent investment broker in Miami.[22]

Although not so prosperous as this particular family, most Syrians are in the comfortable income brackets. More important, they can be found in virtually all professions and occupations. While the Syrians did not take to some types of factory work very easily, they still contributed to the industrialization of Lawrence, Worcester, and Fall River, Massachusetts, where many became quite prosperous. Their achievements in this regard are even more impressive in Latin America. Indeed, they are particularly responsible for the industrialization of São Paulo, Brazil, having established many of the textile, iron, and steelworks there.

In the United States, criticism of Syrians as workers came from the misconception that they would not do manual labor. In truth, they did not like working for someone else and they were usually busy elsewhere in types of work that made them independent employers. Where they did have to work "indoors," as it were, they would rarely go underground, but sought work in textile mills and factories. At one time, 60 percent of the Syrians living in Connecticut were employed in this industry. Generally speaking, however, they disliked factory work because of the low wages paid, the confining hours behind closed doors, and the driving taskmasters.

Peddling–The Vehicle of Success

Of all their economic endeavors, however, none compares with peddling in terms of its influence on the future direction of Syrian economic mobility. Many enterprising young men among the immigrants wished to relocate beyond crowded Manhattan. So they took to the road, traveling first to nearby communities and later across the country. Indeed, if it were not for the peddling "instinct" of the Syrians, it is conceivable that there would be no other Syrian communities in the United States today besides that of New York. The long working hours in factories and farms before World War I as well as the distance to commercial centers made the peddler a welcome visitor to most American homes. "He was a friend who brought needed goods as well as news from the world beyond. At night his reward could be a place to sleep and a warm meal."[23]

A Syrian peddler filled an important vacuum in the American economy, and his disposition to travel served him well. "The Syrian is a trader wherever and whenever he can be," according to Hitti, "a laborer only where he must be."[24] His familiarity with buying and selling was described by Edward Corsi in his book, *The Shadow of Liberty*:

> They began coming in small groups in the garb of mendicants. They wore red fezzez, short open jackets, short baggy blue trousers to the calves of the legs and ill-fitting shoes. As soon as they had passed the immigration authorities, they would at once go out into the street to ply their trade. At the end of the first day in America the whining Maronite would have added five dollars to his hoard, while the Irish or German immigrant would be bustling about trying to find work to enable him to earn a dollar.[25]

The trading instinct of the Syrians carried them over both North and South America as well as Africa and Southern Asia. They penetrated the headwaters of the Amazon and are found all over the west coast of Latin America. More than one national legislature and city ordinance has acknowledged the superior commercial ability of the Syrian by trying to exclude him altogether! The Syrians who followed this activity did not always return to New York. Rather, they began to attract friends and relatives in the remote cities and towns they concentrated on. "Here and there," writes Younis, "little Aleys, Aleppos, Sidons, Zahlehs and Beiruts emerged. Group living brought relief from loneliness, but a few daring souls struck out by themselves to settle on the prairie or in a remote town."[26]

She continues:

Philadelphia attracted traders from Jerusalem, Beirut and Damascus during the Centennial Exposition of 1876. Constantinople and several North African cities sent representative displays to the Exposition. This introduction of Near Eastern art works motivated expansion of trade in Oriental goods. In Philadelphia several wealthy families established themselves in desirable neighborhoods, avoiding colonial settlements.

The Columbian Exposition of 1892/93 similarly affected the Great Lakes region. Near Eastern presses publicized the event, bringing visitors and settlers into the region. Similarly, the St. Louis Exposition of 1904 led settlers into the Mississippi region. Many prominent Syrian families from Damascus, for example, remained in St. Louis.[27]

"Trade will lead a man far," is an old Arab proverb, as Younis reminds us. Many Syrians responded to the call and were successful.

Michael K. Joulan, who came in 1889 at the age of 23, discovered Pottsville, Pennsylvania. He was a scholarly man from a priestly Maronite family. One of Pottsville's special attractions was spring water, which reminded Joulan of his beloved home in Tula. Here he decided to stay; he married a Tula girl, and friends joined them. In 1900 Joe Cantees, a peddler, entered Williamson, West Virginia; he received a welcome from the town settlers who urged him to make his home among them. As the little community prospered, so did Cantees and his family and . . . friends.[28]

Those who could not immediately go into business for themselves sought employment in mills and factories. The textile industry in New England was at its zenith before 1925 and the assurance of immediate employment led the Syrians to such places as Fall River, New Bedford, and Lawrence, Massachusetts. Syrians from Aleppo were attracted to Pawtucket, Rhode Island, and many Syrians from Southern Lebanon went to Willimantic, Connecticut.

Wherever they went and whatever they did, however, their frugality and temperance enabled them to accumulate money rapidly. Once they did, they invested it either in business or in real estate, following the custom of the old country where nearly every man owned the house he lived in.

A review of the immigration reports of the years 1899 to 1907 would not have predicted the Syrians' rapid economic success. The statistics show that of 41,404 Syrian immigrants, 3,200, or a trifle less than 8 percent, were professional men, and 6,193, or a little less than 15 percent, were skilled laborers of various sorts; 14,320 (or 34.5 percent) were entered as having no occupation, and 20,564, or nearly 50 percent, as having "miscellaneous callings" such as clergymen, teachers, barbers, blacksmiths, carpenters, and clerks.[29] By 1911, however, Syrians had entered every branch of commerce from banking and importing expensive Oriental commodities to small trading and the furnishing of peddlers' supplies—a very lucrative business.

Peddling as a profession became even more prominent when some kindly souls, probably Jewish wholesale merchants, showed the Syrians how to successfully trade in the American style. In time, they learned how to keep the wolf from the door by peddling trinkets and household necessities to the outlying American public. Successful peddling became the base industry through which the community entered the American mainstream. They were so accomplished at it that an article in the *New York American* of 1927[30] suggested that a statue be erected to the enterprising commercial spirit of the Syrian as symbolized by the pioneer peddler. After vilifying them, the Industrial Commission itself pointed out that, because of peddling, the peasant or workmen class of Syrians made up only a small proportion of their population. "Their characteristics, in general, pursuers of trade. In New York a score of more of the Syrians are reputed to be worth between $10,000 and $40,000, representing the most enterprising of the Syrian population."[31]

For these immigrants, then, the immediate expression of their trading instinct was peddling. They could thus make up for lack of capital with energy, taking goods on consignment or rounding up enough money to buy inexpensive trinkets and dry goods. Going from door to door and town to town, they could be on their own and even get by with a very limited knowledge of English. All they had to do was show their goods and count the change. Consequently, peddling saved them from the long cramped hours of factories and sweatshops. They were people of the outdoors and resisted confinement. Merchandise in hand, they could see the country, practice their English and go as far as their energy, enterprise and determination would take them.

The study by Lucius Hopkins Miller in 1904 indicated that about one out of three New York Syrians were engaged in peddling, and industrious peddlers were earning $10 to $12 a week, a very respectable income considering the fact that they were unskilled, new in the country, and just learning the language. It was almost as much as the typical income of $665 reported in 1911 for men over 18 whose parents were born in the United States.

The money made by the young men who went on the road supported families, built businesses, and kept these immigrants financially self-sufficient. Sometimes they saved their money and went to school, as was the case of a peddler who saved $5,000 for his medical education and became famous as a doctor. He was Dr. Michael A. Shadid of Elk City, Oklahoma, an 1890 immigrant who eventually set up the first cooperative hospital in the United States to provide inexpensive medical care.[32]

Dr. Shadid was inspired to do something for America while peddling in the South and Southwest and his very explanation was in trader's terms: "When I was peddling jewelry from door to door those first years in America, I saw a lot of America. And the more I saw of it, the more I loved it. But some things disturbed me. Here and there were injustice, oppression and discrimination. . . . I owed a debt to America for the opportunities she had given me, and I felt I ought to repay it in some concrete way. This hospital is part of my payment. Let's say it's the down payment."[33] It was the same dedication to ideals and sense of gratitude that prompted entertainer Danny Thomas to build St. Jude's Hospital in Tennessee for children with leukemia.

Peddling included everyone from the lowest and cleverest vendor of collar buttons and laces to the highly respectable and straightforward sellers of Oriental goods. At first the Syrians sold only trinkets from the Holy Land as "religious articles," which Americans eagerly bought because of their "authenticity." Indeed, the fact that they themselves were from the Holy Land added immensely to their prestige and credibility. Most of them, however, eventually dealt mainly in lace and expensive Oriental goods not usually available elsewhere.

Among non-Syrian writers in the United States, there was a tendency to attribute peddling to reasons other than tradition. Undoubtedly, their being newly arrived, unfamiliar with English, and disdainful of inside work helped propel them into that profession. Yet the immigrants' familiarity with the dynamics of the Oriental marketplace cannot be underestimated. Though trading, another area they excelled in, is not the same as peddling, there is an affinity.

Familiarity with the one will add to success in the other, and through these mediums the Syrians boosted their position in all their worldwide settlements. Early Arab immigrants to Mexico, for example, though unable to speak Spanish fluently and with no capital to open shops, filled suitcases with ready-to-wear clothes and cloth and, as itinerant merchants, carried their goods from town to town. At one time they were familiar figures in Georgia, Alabama, Mississippi and Brazil. Once they had earned enough money, they opened shops that eventually evolved into large stores and/or factories. Their success in the southern United States is recounted by J. K. David: "They worked, opened stores, traded, and saved, until in the course of time, they became able to establish businesses, to acquire real estate, to erect buildings, to build homes, etc."[34]

The "peddling" we are describing here was of a different character than that of the Italians or Greeks. It usually consisted of carrying those items that were different or difficult to find to regular customers throughout the country. Peddlers at the door were nothing new on the American scene. The Irish sold farm produce while the Germans sold dry goods, clothing, and other manufactured goods. Although the selling of fruits and vegetables or flowers from pushcarts was not part of the Syrian peddling tradition, their activity was still not accepted by the American public as a respectable or honorable profession—especially when undertaken by women.

And Syrian women did peddle quite frequently—not because their husbands were idle, but because they wanted to accumulate enough capital to open a small store. Since the Syrian family tended to be a tight, self-contained, self-sufficient unit, the whole family was organized toward the achievement of wealth. One could speculate as to the origins of the emancipation of these Syrian Christian women. After all, the Syrian immigrants did discover new and diversified possibilities in this country that were not always available in the homeland. Willingness to work hard, an asset in America, led eventually not only to financial security but also to a better position in society.[35]

The trend in the working distribution among Syrian-born husbands and their wives suggested that by combining their efforts they could provide maximum comfort for the family and satisfy the emotional need involved in the acquisition of certain status symbols. In other words, to the Syrian husband in America, especially if he had recently migrated to this land, the woman proved what is stressed in a well-known Arabic saying: "A girl is good in the house and in the field."[36]

The wife, if and when she worked, was at once the partner and agent of her husband. Her help was important because she usually had access to more homes than her male counterpart. In the cities where factory workers put in a ten- or twelve-hour day, five and a half days a week, the woman peddler was welcomed in the evening and at other off hours. Those who followed a regular route and sold on the installment plan found ready responses among the industrial workers with limited budgets. Although she was violating popular American mores concerning the place of women, the female peddler maintained her pride.

> Several years ago, dining with a Syrian family in one of our large cities, I met among the guests a beautifully dressed woman who spoke English almost perfectly, having been educated in one of the best girl's schools of the American Mission in Syria. Her manners were exquisite in which fact there was nothing distinctive, but her name would have sufficed to show anyone familiar with her native land that her family was one of the best in Syria. She took leave of the company somewhat earlier than the other guests, giving as her reason that she was to start early next morning on a peddling tour. Two or three years later, meeting her again, she asked me why it was that American ladies took it for granted that women peddlers were of low class. Though she had been half a dozen years in this country, she simply could not understand it. "Why is it," she asked, "that American ladies don't know the difference between well-born and low-born people."[37]

Typical of the American views on the subject, the Boston Associated Charities reacted to peddling by offering its practitioners "charity" since they thought peddling could only be practiced by the destitute. The association tried to induce them to "give it up for some more self-respecting occupation."[38] Apparently, some Syrians accepted that interpretation of their profession and "improved" their status and social standing by turning to other work. According to Miller:

> [Peddling] was irregular, as was the financial return and the whole effect upon the social and moral nature is more or less injurious. . . . This fact, coupled with the contempt Americans have for this type of work, has been the cause of a great increase in factory workers among the more settled Syrian immigrants.[39]

Social Mobility

If peddling had any real deleterious effect it was probably in temporarily separating spouses as well as limiting the Syrian's community life. It has been suggested, however, that the Syrians separated themselves from one another, not to avoid their fellows socially, but to avoid the competition of compatriots in their adopted land. In reference to this "cooperative competitiveness," Hitti writes:

> Because of the nature of their work (trade), Syrians do not congregate in colonies. Whether peddlers or dealers in lace, kimonos and underwear, they must keep close to American home life. In Xenia, Ohio, I came across a Syrian family which has lived there for the last dozen years without attracting another Syrian. When asking someone in Lafayette, Indiana, who said he had been there by himself since 1890 and with his family since 1908 as to whether there were other Syrians in the town, the sharp reply came back. "No, Al-hamd-li'Allah" (Thank Goodness!).[40]

However, distance did not rule out the cooperative element between family members, village dwellers, or fellow ethnics in general. It has even been suggested that settlers in New York went so far as to establish business liaisons with Syrians as far away as Buenos Aires, Argentina.

Furthermore, the Syrians began to develop a remarkable capacity for administration as well as for factory work. This reflects a later stage of their history in America. While some Syrians always worked in industry, the appearance of the factory workers was, in their case, a one-generation occurrence, for neither their sons nor grandchildren would ever know this form of employment. If a Syrian father had been a petty merchant, laborer, or artisan, his son was to become a businessman or professional. Indeed, those who entered the textile plants in New England came to be considered pariahs among the Arabic-speaking people in other parts of the country where success in business and later in professional fields came more rapidly to them. Those who eventually succeeded in the textile areas did so because of thrift rather than high wages. Their investments in real estate also helped to boost their income.

While factory work represented, in some cases, an improvement over peddling, it also helped create an economically stratified Syrian community. The upwardly mobile children of the factory workers sought employment outside their fathers' occupations. Eventually, the children of these laborers, through years of hard work on the part of their parents, went on to become solidly middle class and integrated into the American mainstream. Of course, they are not nearly so wealthy as the entrepreneurs and their offspring. Yet, it was the children of these workers who were the most occupationally mobile, i.e., they have entered nearly all professions and some have become recognizable to the American public. In the New York community, however, many of the sons of the successful manufacturers and distributors, in spite of professional and college training, seem to have taken over their fathers' businesses.

The Syrian-Lebanese community is filled with Horatio Alger stories whose heroes are immigrants. They include nationally-known manufacturers like J. M. Haggar, Sr. who founded the Haggar Company of Dallas, Texas; the Farah Slack Company also of Texas; the Jerro Bros. Shoe Company of New York and the Saybury housecoats of New York established by Elias Sayour, an immigrant from Damascus.

A random sample of news reports in the July, 1972 issues of the *Lebanese-American Journal* gives an idea of the range of achievements that one generation of residence in this country has nurtured: William L. Kattak, candidate for surrogate judge in New Jersey. . . Miss Jemille A. Zaydon of Florida, an educator now working in the Scranton, Pa., area, named to *Who's Who of American Women*. . . . Broadway librettist Fred Saidly and his physician-chess master son play host to world chess champion Bobby Fischer. . . . Helen Thomas, United Press International Washington correspondent, once more in the news as the recipient of a phone call from Mrs. Martha Mitchell, wife of the former Attorney-General. . . . State Senator Mike McKool of Austin, Texas, completes a record-breaking 42 hour and 33 minute filibuster on behalf of appropriations for mental services. . . .

Rosalind Elias joins Metropolitan Opera Company. . . . Sister M. Michel Boulus elected member of the General Council of the Sisters of Mercy in Belmont, North Carolina. . . .the Michigan Federation of American Syrian-Lebanese Clubs, honors John Shaheen, a general foreman at the Fisher Body plant in Flint as its man of the year. . . . W. Nicholas Kerbawy, commissioner of the Michigan Sports Hall of Fame, as civic leader of the year. . . Probate Judge George N. Bashara, Jr. as attorney of the year. . . . Sister Agnes Mary Mansour, president of Detroit's Mercy College, as educator of the year. . . . Also a feature on 36-year old Eddie Khayat as coach of the Philadelphia Eagles and an announcement that Chicago Bears Coach Abe Gibron was going to address the annual convention of the Midwest Federation of American Syrian-Lebanese Clubs.

According to Wakin, these children and grandchildren of Levantine immigrants were bearing out the prediction of a noted Protestant missionary who reported in 1887 that the "character of these emigrants will compare most favorably with that of any nationality reaching American shores." His endorsement stressed: "They are not drunkards, they are not turbulent, they do not carry revolutionary theories or propensities. They come from very frugal homes where ties of parental affection and kinship are very strong; their ideas of marriage and of parental authority are Biblical and pure; they are all pious believers in God and providence. . . ."[41]

Popular stereotypes of the Syrian-American community would lead one to believe that there are no "poor Syrians" in the United States. But there are today and always have been some Syrian families who receive some form of aid from Syrian charitable associations. Most are middle class, however, if not in wealth or income then in life-style. Many of the old-timers, having propelled their offspring into the professions, are now relatively poor. Their pride keeps them off the public welfare system and their children and brothers and sisters help them out. The profits made in peddling or in business did not always last very long.

It was when the peddlers settled down (after they acquired some capital) that their wealth became more secure. In time, the evolution of the shopkeeper into the wholesaler took place. In the Middle and Far West, some of these "peddlers turned businessmen" opened up successful department stores. By 1904

Syrians throughout the country were engaged largely in the retailing of cheap dry goods and notions. This accounted for the presence in New York of several large wholesale dry goods houses which distributed products to Syrian retailers all over the world. With their connections and complete knowledge of the field, the Syrian wholesalers became supreme in the industry.

The business acumen of Syrians is described by interviewees of Houghton. "In business, they are considered 'very shrewd and clever.' A New York banker says they are 'smarter than Jews or even Americans, well understanding our banking and business laws.' The Syrian business man is 'self-denying, abstemious, very industrious, too busy for rivalry.' All seem to have a 'keen sense of business.' "[42]

Apparently, a contributing factor to their entrepreneurial success was the fear of "disgrace" and scandal pursuant upon failure. The "shame" would reflect on the whole family and would be borne by and in the community.

By the end of the Korean War, Syrian Americans had given up their "nomadic" life and moved into quite diversified occupations. They had entered completely the mainstream of American economic and social life and are today represented in practically every industry and profession. The immigrants' prosperity permitted their children to go into the sciences, professions, politics, and the arts, and they have distinguished themselves in each of these fields.

While various studies on the Syrian-Americans allude to their mobility, wealth, and occupational diversity, few offer any statistical data. A survey of the Maronite community of St. Louis concluded that they were upwardly mobile to an exceptional degree. "Fifty-six percent of the respondents were employed in professional, self-employed or clerical positions; whereas only twenty-eight percent of their (immigrant) fathers held similar positions. While only thirteen percent of the respondents were employed in skilled, semiskilled or unskilled capacities, forty-four percent of their fathers were so employed. A number of the fathers (five) functioned as independent merchants and peddlers."[43]

Data on the Christian "Lebanese" community of Los Angeles, California, reveals that there is a "preponderant number of individuals who work in, or own, market stores, cocktail lounges, restaurants, nightclubs and dry goods stores, retail and/or wholesale. Also the large number of professional persons listed is striking."[44]

In a 1969 sample of the Syrians of Springfield, Massachusetts, political scientist Naseer Aruri notes that

> a very distinctive characteristic of the community is the relatively high (55%) of self employed and owners or part-owners of a business. This represents a continuation of the pattern which characterized the immigrants who showed a strong inclination for business. Today, the grandchildren of the immigrants are moving rapidly into the professions and other enterprises requiring special skills such as manufacturing, insurance and real estate. . . .[45]

He continues,

> The occupational picture shows the majority of the gainfully employed in the community are self-employed. To work for somebody is neither desirable nor profitable; the occupational gulf between the generations is wide. It is reflected in the disparity between respondents and fathers in the professional and manual occupations. Continuity, however, is revealed in self-employment, a pattern which characterized the two generations.[46]

In his comparison of occupational and income statistics between immigrant parents and their children, Aruri writes that "the overwhelming majority of the college graduates whose income is over $25,000 are professionals."

> Together with the managers and owners of business establishments, most of whom are also college graduates, they constitute the highest income groups in our sample. Age does not seem to be a factor in the determination of income. Most of those who earn the highest incomes tend to be in their thirties and forties. As may be expected, the income picture demonstrates a wide gulf between the generations. While 40% of the parents earned less than $5,000, only 9% of their male children are receiving such income, and while only 20% of the parents earn over $10,000, some 48% of their children are earning incomes exceeding $10,000.[47]

An important factor in the upward mobility of the Syrians was the lack of deep, traditional, and long-time historical prejudices against them. Hardly an unfavorable stereotype of them existed except, perhaps, those that stemmed from the immediate response to "high" immigration levels, previously described, and their "questionable" business ethics. Beyond a limited number of stabbing and shooting frays, cases of smuggling and fraudulent bankruptcy, the only serious accusations brought against Syrians is that their standards of business probity and veracity were not up to the American mark.

This situation resulted from a conflict of business custom with ethics—not a lack of them! Syrians were unfamiliar with the non-negotiable one-price system. In the old country, the responsibility for customer satisfaction with price and quality lies with the buyer, not the seller. The duty and responsibility of the former is to create the business challenge which, if he fails, leaves the seller with the right to "wheel and deal" for what he can get. A passive, trusting purchaser is an enigma who actually insults his host by not challenging him! He, instead, deprives him of a skilled debate.

There are other explanations for the Syrians' general success in business besides the suggestion that they were dishonest merchants. First, many of them were familiar with urban life and associated occupations as well as with buying and selling in a money economy. "Moreover," as Berger notes, "those who did not come from cities came from villages . . . in which they performed certain business functions avoided by the Moslems."[48] Finally, the Syrians were accustomed to a frugal existence in the old country; they were, therefore, able and anxious to subsist on relatively little and to save much of what they earned. A tight family structure sustained them when they were impoverished.

These characteristics helped to differentiate the Syrians from other ethnics like the Irish and Italians who migrated before them. In the long run the Syrians passed imperceptibly into American economic life without having to overcome any strong objections to their presence or severe barriers of discrimination. Their numbers in any given location were infinitesimal compared to the other ethnics around them. While limiting their ability to organize, their small numbers helped reduce native hostility against them as members of a "competing" or threatening interest group. Had they been challenged, perhaps they would have had to develop more viable community institutions to defend themselves other than those known in the old country. Undoubtedly, their adjustment to American society would have been different had this been the case.

Unlike other immigrant groups who had to wait two or three generations to exert their independence from ghetto life and to satisfy their desire for mobility, it was the Syrian immigrants (first generation) who amassed the wealth that their sons used as a lever for bringing themselves into wider contacts with society.

This situation was unusual for neither the Latin American[49] nor the Canadian Arab Christian community, which is said to have "twenty or twenty-five 'millionaires' among the old Arab immigrants to Montreal."[50] Though the United States had its share of accomplished entrepreneurs, their success was more spectacular in those countries that were less industrialized. Syrian values and living habits suggest an entrepreneurial uniformity that might be operative among Arabic-speaking people no matter where they settle.

As a consequence of their overall economic success, the viability of Syrian ethnicity in the United States is less secure. Any ethnic group that has been as financially successful in so short a time must face conflicts and cleavages within its own ranks. Why and how do they continue as an ethnic community? Should they? What will be their family patterns? Can they sustain their churches? What will be their collective future?

The successful immersion of the Syrians in the American middle class and its life-style might be the very source of their dissolution as an ethnoreligious community. On occasion the older Syrian communities were able to muster support for causes and problems that were imminently present or recognizable. Today, the problems that previously justified the need for community "togetherness" no longer exist. It is possible that today, the "enemy" may overcome before it is even perceived as such.

CHAPTER VI

The Roots of Syrian Ethnicity

The Beginnings of a "Syrian-American" Consciousness

THE ELIMINATION OF THE NEED TO MAINTAIN AN ETHNIC GROUP consciousness is a recent phenomenon and became evident some seventy years after the original Syrian settlement here. At one time an ethnic identity was needed. After all, the first Syrian Christians to arrive here were labeled "Arabs" and "Turks" and treated as such by their hosts. Even when a proper label was arrived at, it was still one that was imposed on them from without. Consequently, its form and content were derived from the Syrians' symbiotic relationship with the outside world. The imposition of an ethnic identity such as "Syrian" was done without regard for their own historical sense of nationality. The institutions or cultural modes developed and used by the Syrian community were either created in America or modified from the past.

Also, acceptance of the designation "Syrian," both useful and not of their own making, did not mean that the early collective discrimination they experienced on the part of native Americans would cease even though the term "Syrian" was then considered socially more acceptable than "Turk" or "Arab." Rather, it forced them into cooperation and common recognition of who they were historically and nationally. Certainly, they did share some common ancestry, and discrimination helped them to recognize this. Thus, when the problem of being refused citizenship because of their "non-Caucasian origins" arose, they solved it collectively because they were being discriminated against as "Syrians," and not Melkites, Orthodox, or Aleppians, et cetera. With the racial question behind them, but still in their recollections, the Syrians were on the way to becoming another American ethnic group and their destiny was shaped by the interaction of their own culture with that of the dominant society. The "ethnic group" concept is an American creation and the Arabs became "Syrian-Americans" accordingly. Their final emergence into the plural ethnic network of the nation was predicated on their ability to successfully integrate several factors: their social and economic position, their values, religious heritage, and social organization. All these have influenced the opinion formed by them by their host culture. Today, their communities reflect the Syrians' desire to be accepted without being made culturally bankrupt. However, the conflict they experienced with the outside world forced them to adapt by altering the essence of their cultural heritage.

Village and Family Life and Group Consciousness

A people organized socially around their religion and village express most of their values in relation to family life. It is the family that passes on the socioreligious values of the culture to its offspring. Indeed, proper introduction and identification of a Middle Easterner does not end with the announcement of his name and profession. Rather, his family group must be ascertained as well as his village community. For the Levantine immigrant, the family was an extension of himself, and his religion an extension of his family. From this bedrock commitment to family came both identity and strength, loyalty and love, and on occasion feuds and fracases. For them, blood was not only thicker than water; it should never turn into water. The individual in isolation does not amount to much. He is complete as a social being only when related to his family and community. These are the primary units on whose foundation Middle Eastern culture has developed since biblical times.

The emphasis on the family was upon the blood tie not only within the conjugal unit but also within the large extended family, particularly on the fathers' side. The patriarchal system developed in all the communities of the East and prevails even at the present. This pervasive pattern resulted in a sharp division between the sexes. Yet, the Arab mother and particularly her brothers still exercised considerable influence over her children. The general pattern consisted of a joint family, a large family group made up of the parents and their children, the paternal grandparents, uncles and their families on both sides, unmarried paternal aunts, and the extended kinship group, which consisted of all those who claimed descent from the same paternal ancestor. The individual learned to identify himself with this family group from the moment of birth and his behavior was established accordingly.

So intensive was the predominance of kinship positions in patterning and regulating interpersonal affairs that intermarriage within the same lineage was often the preferred form. This was especially true of many American families of Syrian ancestry who did not have the range of eligible marriage mates available to them that they had had in the old country. The only alternative was marriage within the village community that drew its strength from the intensive association and social intercourse afforded people in such close proximity. So the village often became nothing more than the extension of the family.

Each Syrian village in the homeland defined clearly the boundaries of its territory with respect to other villages. The situation was encouraged by the unique topology of the area which made intervillage communication and cooperation almost impossible since the land was divided by mountain ranges and narrow elongated strips of usable land. Except for a few Roman military roads, the country was almost devoid of good roads until the French began building them in this century. The effect was to leave the population divided socially, politically, and economically. Syria never was a strong and distinct political unit; it was rather a group of locally ruled city-states.

Each town with its surrounding district constituted a small separate state in which the management of affairs was conducted by families of the nobility. This served to perpetuate the prejudices of the various segments of Syrian society. Moreover, each village defined clearly the boundaries of its psychosocial identification, that is, it defined everyone's "in" and "out" group. At the same time, within each village, subgroup identifications were clearly defined and shifts in these identifications were not encouraged. If they took place, they did so according to a regular pattern. For example, wives would take on the religion or rite of their husbands rather than maintain their own, and Moslems never became Christians although the reverse was possible.

This psychosocial situation prevailed in America. For example, the Catholic Syrian community of Paterson, New Jersey, is derived almost exclusively from Aleppo, Syria. It is tied socially to other "Aleppians" in Brooklyn, Miami, and Pawtucket, Rhode Island. For the Patersonians, Paterson has become their new "village," and they identify with it as a place of residence. The psychosocial community is biased in favor of Patersonians, but they maintain extended relations with other Catholic Aleppians in other cities, and it is to this group that their emotional feelings are tied.

Life in Syria's urban districts was not very different from that just described. Syrian towns were often divided into sections inhabited by particular religious and ethnic groups. There was little sense of real identification with the larger community. Individuals were identified by their "quarters," creating an aura of mistrust between the segments. With Westernization and urbanization, however, this custom began to recede, as did the absolute patriarchal structure of the family. This was especially true in Lebanon.

In light of this, it is no wonder that the Syrians in America and the Middle East have never gotten over their distrust of one another. This has handicapped studies of their cultural life here,[1] as well as their ability to develop viable political and social institutions outside the sphere of religion. It also deprived Syria of a common and national identity. The Reverend Abraham Rihbany, who wrote an autobiography of his journey to the United States, sums it up:

> Thus deprived of all the agencies which make for enlightened nationalism, she [Syria] could not follow one path. . . . There is no higher education to rid the mind of trivialities and superstitions; no industry to teach the value of time and create a longing for peace; no civic spirit to convert life's activities into ethical and social values.[2]

In the United States, the aspect of Syrian life that suffered most from this lack of broad social consciousness was the political, followed closely by the social. This is to be expected from a culture that never encouraged a "we the people" concept. Their individualism and social provincialism meant political impotence. Syrians have cut no figure in the political life of this nation because they could never unite to place a Syrian candidate in office. Nor could they place any confidence in the electoral system, never having been exposed to its processes in the old country.

Moreover, they never constituted a majority vote in any district. Any Syrian-American candidate who did succeed did so without the united support of the ethnic group. In 1910, the Syrians failed, for example, to elect a Syrian-American senator from Manhattan's fifth district and more recently failed in Bay Ridge, Brooklyn, where a "Lebanese" ran on the Democratic ticket in an area that has the largest density of Arabic-speaking people in the country. Syrians are predominantly Republican and would not or could not change party lines even to put one of "their own" in office.[3]

The other important force in Syrian social life that affected the emergence of a strong community in the United States was religion. A Syrian's religious identification is so intense that he is the proverbial "man without a country." His patriotism and group identification is based on love for family and religion. For all practical purposes his family and church take the place of the state for him. In both Syria and Lebanon, religion is the practical equivalent of nationality, with each religious community recognized in and within the structure of the state. All cooperation between individuals, therefore, is limited to their traditional groups—family, village, and religion. This attitude was carried to America in the earliest stages of the emigration and was an important factor not only in the structuring of the early Syrian-American communities but also in the present development (or lack of it) of Syrian ethnicity.

Syrian Values and Group Consciousness

Most Syrians believe in a God to whom they are subordinate in all their actions and who rewards or punishes them after death on the basis of their behavior in this life. Consequently, all their social relations reflect a religious attitude which demands adherence to a "proper" pattern to ensure respectability and acceptability. It is incumbent upon the Syrian to be moral, not so much because it is expedient, or fashionable, but because it is his religious duty.

A good "Arab" then, is a man of honor who is hospitable, dignified, and brave and who adheres to his group's expectations and norms. In a reflective statement on the Syrians' normative order, Cole writes:

> Pride and race, a high degree of native intelligence, an individualism which retards cooperative effort and often passes into factionalism,

shrewdness and cleverness in business, devotion to the institutions of this country, imaginativeness, religious loyalty, love of domestic life, courtesy, and hospitality, eagerness for education, fondness for music and poetry, temperance in the men and chastity in the women, self-respect and self-reliance . . . such are some of the more obvious traits of the Syrians.[4]

A Syrian's honor is closely regulated by his participation in a family system. It is the family that institutionalizes, structures, and transmits cultural values to the offspring. If a man acts dishonorably, he "blackens his family name"; if his family has been dishonored by the actions of either a member or an outsider, the individual is shamed until the guilty person is punished. Unfortunately, an individual's commitments and obligations rarely, if ever, extend further than to his own kinsmen.

It is this type of social consciousness that regulates all aspects of his life. Sexuality, sobriety, and morality all reflect the social control exercised by the family, which defines all public acts as social acts with social roots and consequences. To act indiscreetly in any area is to reflect upon the whole clan. In Syria, the existence of a communal life, centered on the prerogatives of the family which holds itself accountable for the individual acts of its members, was responsible for a high level of general "morality" among the people that continued even after they came to America.

This is why female chastity is treated as one of the higher virtues, making sexual offenses crimes against honor. According to the *Area Handbook of Syria*, a man of honor "sees that his daughters and other females of his lineage do not act wantonly toward men, and to a lesser extent, that his sons do not misbehave toward the daughters of other men. He joins together with the men of his kin group to punish offenders within the group and to seek redress against members of other kin groups who offend his own kinsmen."[5]

Accordingly, the saloon, an Anglo-Saxon institution, found no patrons among the immigrant Syrians or even among their offspring. Syrian socializing took place in the home of relatives and family friends. Bars were for lonely people and those who were socially isolated. Until recently, drinking as a social act was always confined to the home which gave it its meaning.

In the area of criminal deviance, Hitti tells us that "police blotters are virtually divest of Syrian names . . . there have never been any Syrians who stand out prominently as offenders of law, property or person."[6] Criminal notoriety is still not prevalent among them to any significant degree. Hitti goes on to mention that there are no known instances of Syrian prostitution in this country.

The same force kept the Syrian from ever applying for public charity even though there was occasional need for it. Social welfare was a family, not a public, affair. In a related vein, the Syrian abhorrence of debt is proverbial. An immigrant would go hungry and sleep on the floor to pay back borrowed money. Houghton tells us that as soon as it was paid back "they buy furniture and clothes and begin to live more like Americans."[7] This terminology—"be like the Americans"—is commonly used even today. The Syrians wanted "in," that is, they wanted to be like the Americans in all their ways, and very quickly imitated their life-style.

It was this limited sense of social responsibility that also shaped Syrian philanthropy. Not only would families not seek public assistance, but when it was offered, it would be accepted only if it came from a recognized group or church society and after anonymity was assured. Syrian philanthropy was limited to helping one's own kind—those within the same religious tradition (rite) and/or of the same home-town origin. Instead of helping one another on a pan-Arab or pan-Syrian basis, social welfare was limited to those with whom social interaction would be expected and encouraged.

An interesting account of this value at work is given by Morris Zelditch, who, after noting that a neighbor may occasionally assist another for a brief period, says:

> The only community activity among the Syrians in Pittsburgh which approaches a philanthropic action is the existence of a St. Vincent dePaul Society branch organization at the Church. This organization led by the Priest, gives out Christmas baskets to needy members of the congregation, sends an occasional load of coal, and contributes old clothes to needy members. These contributions, are, however, restricted to members of the Church. When the priest was approached by the writer with a view to expanding the church's philanthropic activities so they would take in any part of the Syrian community, [the priest] could not understand the viewpoint. Only his congregation counted.[8]

On the other hand millions of dollars have been given to the American Near East Welfare Association of the American Catholic Church for orphanages, schools, and hospitals in Syria and Lebanon over the years, while virtually no institutions have been built in the United States for the American Syrians and Lebanese. Catholic Syrian-Americans gained recognition and prestige from their Latin Catholic compatriots because of their generosity to this Church in general and to their fellow Catholics of the same rite in particular. In America, they had no intermediary organization to help them because they saw no need for one. Aid in this country was to be gotten from the family and then from the church, so a community-wide organization was not particularly necessary.

Interestingly, the amount of financial aid sent back to Syrian villages in the old country is rather exceptional in view of the small numbers of the immigrants and it attests to their rather rapid accumulation of wealth. Up to 1920, the individual contributions sent through the Near East Relief by Syrians amounted to $168,000. Up to the first of December, 1919, the Presbyterian Board of Foreign Missions had transmitted $2,250,360 to Syrian relatives and friends from Syrians in America. The Syrian Mount Lebanon Relief Committee raised in the same period some $165,815 in two and a half years from about 15,000 Syrian subscribers in America. How much more was sent through the papal legation at Washington and the Spanish embassy is hard to ascertain.[9]

According to a correspondent who accompanied a subcommittee of the United States Immigration Commission on its visits to Turkey in 1907, the Syrian immigrants "send more money per capita than the immigrants of any other nationality. Between Beirut and Damascus one sees more houses built with American money than one sees in a trip to South Italy five times as long."[10]

It is estimated that the village of Zahleh, which has a large representation in the United States, received an average of five hundred dollars a day. In 1885, Zahleh boasted only one stone building—the church; a quarter of a century later, it had almost nothing but stone buildings. Today, hardly a village or town of Lebanon does not exhibit a red-tile-roofed house built by money from abroad. According to Lebanese government statistics, in

1951–52, emigrants' remittances (from all countries) to charitable religious and educational institutions and to friends and relatives amounted to $18,000,000 and $22,000,000 respectively.

In the Syrian-American "value system," then, social *obligations* are exceptionally demanding and strong, while social *consciousness* is limited. With regard to his fellows (who are limited in definition) the Syrian doesn't say "mind your own business" since the weal and woe of one is the concern of all "his people." This characteristic and the high value set upon reputation kept the Syrian immigrant and his children safe in the midst of unfamiliar surroundings. Yet, it was this same provincial force that prevented the Syrians from giving really strong institutional form to their feelings for Arabic life and culture. For example, while claiming to want to see the "old ways"—language and culture, and so on—continued among their offspring in the United States, they never established programs and schools to facilitate this.

If they could have gotten together as "Arab" or "Syrian" Americans they might have been able to cooperate together on community-wide projects. Regardless of where they have settled, however, they have not deviated significantly from their old pattern. In general, their colonies are so divided by religious, political, regional, and family rivalries that it has not been possible to organize an association to represent the entire community. Pan-Syrian societies are a phenomenon of the present generation but arose only in those places least represented by traditional Syrian institutions like the church. This occurred especially in the South and Midwest. Even here the organizations established are primarily apolitical and merely social. Many attempts to organize other communities along anything but social lines have ended in failure.

By the late 1950's the Syrians were able to establish ethnic clubs that coexisted with their churches. Yet, they never succeeded in involving the total community in them or in effectively changing people's allegiances. Organizational planning that required everyone's participation was beyond the historical experience of the group. Leadership that did emerge came from traditional sources like the clergy, who then surrounded themselves with a few select or elite faithful. This may have stemmed from the Syrian's inherent distrust for organization and his preferring to let fate dictate the outcome of events. Ironically, it was this passivity and fatalism that helped the Christians survive in an overwhelmingly Moslem world. In America, this approach became self-destructive.

At the same time that today's Syrians are very verbal about their commitment to high communal ideals, they are incapable of institutionalizing their objectives in practical programs. Hence, they speak in platitudes (reflective of their language patterns and poetic leanings) and project master plans, but they fail on the empirical, practical level of implementation. Syrians tend to ignore the pleas to help integrate and stabilize their communities for collective security or ethnic survival. The needs of the family and the church come first.

This situation cannot be properly understood outside the framework of the most basic and influential forces that affect the Oriental mind; namely, the deep values supplied by the village-family-religion complex the Syrian immigrant identified with.

Social Relations in the Early Settlement

As previously discussed, it was the Washington Street community in lower Manhattan that ushered most of the Syrian immigrants into American economic life. And it was to the relatives and friends remaining there that many returned after making good somewhere in the interior of the country. In its day, Washington Street was called "little Syria" because it duplicated Syrian daily life with the utmost fidelity. But it was, after all, an American creation—born out of the struggle for survival of a displaced and confused people. Hitti has observed that it was old Syria in the New World, but much more perplexed. "It is far from being for the Syrians what little Sicily is for the Italians, the ghetto for the Russian Jews, and Chinatown for the Chinese."[11] Like other "nationalities" that arrived in the United States without strong national identities, Syrian life was constantly fractionalized by religion and region and this pattern, continued in America, marred the growth of a strong Syrian-American community in terms of emotion and identity.

The same applies to the Brooklyn community, which has always housed the most important, if not the largest, Arabic-speaking population in the country. Its preeminence lies not in its numerical strength nor in its deep feelings of loyalty and identity—which in fact it has always lacked. Rather, it is the result of its economic dynamism and its age—it is the oldest of the existing Syrian communities in the United States.

The ethnic flavor created and maintained by the Syrians on Brooklyn's Atlantic Avenue places then squarely in the consciousness of America's most ethnically minded metropolis. Arab ethnicity has not been reproduced as accurately anywhere else in the United States. Arab-American hearts turn to Brooklyn when they think of their past or of their culture, for it is there that Middle Eastern merchandise is stored and shipped throughout the continent. Syrian bread, Arabic music, home furnishings, clothing, and cuisine are all available on the two short blocks between Henry and Court Streets.

No other cities, not Miàmi, Boston, or Paterson—all of which house substantial Syrian communities—have been able to duplicate the prosperity or prestige of the Brooklyn "Arab quarter." Brooklyn, consequently, has come to be considered the economic and social "home base" for most American Syrians—especially since the Manhattan "ghetto" is now extinct.

For the Syrians though, Brooklyn, like Washington Street, could ultimately be only a place. It is neither home nor a ghetto in the true sense. It is neither an extension of oneself nor the center or source of one's strongest identity. It was always merely a geographic area in which economic and social intercourse was to take place. The population of Syria had been fragmented for so long that the Syrians naturally reproduced and maintained their old loyalties and divisions in this country. Syrians do not regard "place" as the root of their community identification. Rather, they prefer to utilize the primordial ties of blood and faith. This helps explain why they did not form the traditional, large, stable, and integrated settlements that characterized other American ethnic groups.

The lack of strong community integration is one of the most distinguishing characteristics of Syrians throughout the United States. Syrian communal life is not directly related in any way to size or density of population. Indeed, the number of Syrians in any given place was so insignificant that they could barely rely on population density as a basis for even communal sociability. In Manhattan, for example, they never exceeded more than 10,000 people at the height of their settlement. Even then, the Syrians were very selective in their social interaction. Even if their numbers were larger, they would not have been able to overcome the narrow definition of "acceptable society" (good family from the same town and religious tradition) they brought with them from the old country. The immigrant Syrians would never "mix" indiscriminately with one another purely on the basis of common national background or because they accidentally occupied the same neighborhood in America. Indeed, they never thought of ancestry in terms of country and only partially and rather ineffectively learned to do so upon settlement here.

With the third generation the unfulfilled need to maintain a strong ethnic community ceased. The Syrian immigrants themselves never thought it terribly important to create or be part of an institutionally complete "Syrian-American community." But to please inquisitive and prejudiced native Americans, who lumped them together as Arabs or Turks and who were always wondering who they really were, they became Syrian-Americans. Americans understood nationalities and not millets, and the Syrians learned to accommodate their hosts.

Because Syrian social relations are predicated on membership not in the same nation, but in the same home town (Aleppo, Beirut, Damascus, et cetera), religion (Moslem, Catholic, Eastern Orthodox), or rite (Catholic Melkites and Maronites, et cetera) the source of Syrian communal strength is sociopsychological and not derived from territorial closeness or national identity. For example, Melkite Catholics from Aleppo, Syria, perceive themselves as belonging to a community comprised primarily of other Melkites (wherever they may be) and then other Aleppian Syrians. The appellation "my people" for a Melkite would be applied to Melkites regardless of where they reside. To this day, Melkite Aleppians in Brooklyn mix more freely and intimately with the Aleppian Melkites of Paterson, New Jersey, than they do with their fellow ethnics in the same city.

This pattern continued in America and indicated a continuity with the past that acculturation did not wipe out. The Syrians' origins were also reflected in their emerging political, religious, and economic attitudes. Their overall social and moral values were those of American society in general and speeded up their economic integration and assimilation into American life to the point where ghetto existence became even less useful. In a sense, these traits, coupled with a certain degree of economic prosperity, served to undermine their older, more narrowly based loyalties. And, like other ethnic groups, the Syrians did not foresee that their desire for material success would be at the root of the disintegration of what little community life and common identity they did have.

The prosperous, college-educated, and English-speaking offspring of the immigrant factory owner, wholesaler, or peddler could not fully relate to a cultural past that was quickly becoming a memory. Ironically, by the time the American social order created and recognized them as "Syrians," and they came to accept this definition, they also discovered that they not only had "made it" economically and socially in the overall society, but that maintaining a Syrian identity would impede further mobility. It was their own cultural values—favoring acculturation—that lessened their ability to develop an integrated, ethnically-based communal life. The new identity—Syrian-American—became an irrelevant one for the English-speaking, Americanized, and assimilated third generation. No sooner had they overcome the handicap of defining everything in terms of family and religion, than they discovered that they were not especially poor or working class in orientation and that relationships based solely on ethnicity would no longer be particularly attractive or necessary.

After all, it was not really popular or functional to be a "Syrian" especially after one had begun to assimilate on his own. Also, the substance of Arabic culture had been altered beyond recognition. The differences between what was Arab and what was American had become quite hazy!

CHAPTER VII

The Search for an Identity

THE MOST SUCCESSFUL AMERICAN ETHNIC GROUP TO CREATE A functional identity was the American Irish. They did so by becoming Irish-Catholic-Democrats and they were reacted to as such by the rest of American society. The Syrians in America could not do the same; they could not even think along these lines. Ethnically, they could be either Syrians or Lebanese—indeed, many "Syrians" rediscovered their "Lebanese" origins sometime after World War II. Religiously, they were either Protestants, Eastern Orthodox, or Roman Catholics of either the Melkite, Maronite, Syriac, or Armenian rites. Politically, they were divided: the entrepreneurs among them generally becoming Republicans and the others Democrats.

Syrians or Lebanese?

As was previously noted, national consciousness was the least likely area in which the Syrian could find his identity or sense of belonging. Integration into a single religious group was also out of the question. Because of the Middle Eastern organizational mode that inextricably intertwined the family system with the religious (the latter supplying the sociopolitical reality and sense of nationhood), Syrian-Americans would not easily merge into a single, integrated "nationality" group. Even today, there are in the United States three structurally distinct yet interrelated Syrian populations—Melkites, Maronites, and Syrian-Orthodox—which, when taken together, make up the Syrian-Lebanese American community. These identities interfered with the development of "pan-Arabic" institutions and caused each sect to act as if it were a different "nationality group."

This reduced the functional importance of the extended community to a general and diffuse level. "Syrian" became a term that summarized a broad social whole. For example, as Treudley notes, "the phrase, 'Syrians of Boston,' labels the category which is to be dealt with but does not indicate the source of the sense of belongingness which makes an individual a member of the collectivity. Geography [Boston] supplies only the framework within which sociological analysis is applied."[1] Not having a recognizable secular identity directly affected their adjustment to American society.

Even when the Syrian immigrant did utilize a geographic referent it was only to the town or village of his origin. The effect of this on emerging national identities in America cannot be overestimated,[2] since ethnic identification has been commonly defined as a "person's use of racial, national or religious terms to identify himself, and thereby, to relate himself to others."[3] These broad national categories allegedly provide a universalistic framework for ordering social relationships.

Many immigrants were not responsive to such comprehensive categories. Nahirny and Fishman write:

> The very mode of orientation toward ethnicity largely barred most immigrant fathers from being sensitive to general ethnic categories. Being an outgrowth of past personal experience, the ethnic identification of the immigrant fathers constituted something deeply subjective and concrete; that is to say, it was hardly externalized or expressed in general symbolic terms. So much was this the case that many of them were simply ignorant of their national identity.[4]

Thus, when "national consciousness" emerged among the Syrians in the United States, it proved to be as dissociative as it was unifying. It was based on a misunderstanding of their own history and consequently it never served to unify them into one group. Just as they had begun to identify themselves as "American Syrian Catholics," or "Syrian-Orthodox Americans," the question of Lebanese nationalism arose and modified these alternatives. Many Syrian-Americans became (after Lebanon was granted full autonomy) adamant and vocal "Lebanese-Americans," and the process split the Arabic-speaking people in two. Younis summarizes:

To the Americans who had already accepted the term "Syrian" once divorced from the general name "Turk," the rise of the new Near Eastern nations caused confusion in the identities of those already here. Some groups began to call themselves "Lebanese"—since they were in the majority—while others retained the term "Syrian" whether originally so or not. But the two decades of the 1920's and 1930's still favored the name "Syrian." Not until after the Second World War, when the nations emerged in full sovereignty, did the two names become permanently separated.[5]

The forces that partially account for this split national identity are to be found in Lebanon's historical relationship to France. "The Lebanon" (in the old parlance) reacted strongly and singularly to Western cultural influences initiated by the French in dress, social mores, cultural outlooks and, most important, in government. Unlike Syria, which is prone to dictatorship, Lebanon has maintained a stable and flourishing democracy that has also become the leading Christian center for the entire Middle East. From the Arab perspective, these achievements do not outweigh the harm done to the Arab cultural inheritance which Lebanon is supposed to represent.

The importance of this situation cannot be overestimated. The balance of power in the Middle East among Moslems, Christians, and Israel is in a very precarious state and it is felt by some that any shift could mean the eventual disappearance of Christianity in some of its traditional centers. Lebanese-Americans are acutely aware of this and feel that "their" beloved homeland might very well be the last, best hope of Christianity in the East since it reflects the so-called progressive and valued things in Western life.

Syria, on the other hand, still retains its pro-Arab orientation, its interest in Russian-sponsored socialism as well as an image of desolateness, disorder, and backwardness. This may be the case, but when compared to Lebanon, Syria has maintained its cultural integrity, has recognized the French influence as essentially imperialistic, and has generally avoided the dilemma of "Levantism" that was previously described. In bastardizing themselves socially and culturally, the Lebanese have merely continued in secular terms the religious equivalent we described as "latinization."

The attitude toward Lebanon is revealed in a recent article by the Reverend Thomas J. McMahon, former secretary of Near

East welfare. The fact that these remarks came from a Latin Catholic working in the Middle East on terms detrimental to the Maronite Church did not interest the Catholic Lebanese. That a Western Catholic priest was speaking for them and on their behalf seemed to enthrall them enormously. He speaks of "Lebanon's Glory" saying: "Today the little republic of Lebanon, independent, represents spiritual freedom . . . and all these days the Lebanon has been not only a Catholic fortress, but has been a haven and refuge for persecuted Christians, Catholic and non-Catholic."[6]

After the bombing of Beirut airport by the Israelis in 1969, the editors of the largest Arabic newspaper in the United States wrote:

> The ire of the Lebanese, whose sole desire is the independence of Lebanon, that it may continue to function as the basis for hope and peace in that area and the center of the world's hub, was aroused by this attack on their beloved country. This peaceful country . . . which has always been a refuge for the oppressed and stricken, harboring them with full protection, from the Armenians to the Jews, to the Palestinians. Lebanon has been the shining beacon of freedom for all people, of varying faiths and races, with the greatest tolerance of perhaps any other country.[7]

Before this national pride and interest in Lebanon could be cultivated, America's Syrian community had to redefine itself in terms of the legitimate grievances of its Lebanese members. In the mid-1940's, Syrian community organizations were often forced to change their names from "American Syrian" clubs to "Lebanese-Syrian-American" clubs. Syrian priests were surprised to find themselves with "Lebanese" congregations and "Syrian food" became "Lebanese" food.

If the new Lebanese-Americans thought they could unite all Arab-Americans in a common identity and heritage, they were mistaken—for the identity acted like another provincialism and consisted of a truncated cultural reality. Actually, it further divided the Arabic-speaking community. The Lebanese were sensitive to being identified as Syrians, and the latter could not tolerate the new superior attitude of the mountain folk who were, historically and traditionally, farmers and uncultivated Syrians. All other Arab-Americans, especially the Moslems, refused to associate with the Lebanese because of the latter's tendency to disassociate themselves from Arab sociopolitical thought.

As Morroe Berger notes,

> Religious affiliation usually determines the "Syrians' " attitude toward the West. The Maronites from Lebanon, who have for centuries looked to France as their protector and many of whom were educated in French schools, have been least affected by the growth of Arab nationalism in the Middle East and the anti-Western outlook of some Arab spokesmen. In 1956, two . . . newspapers attacked the Eastern States Federation of Syrian-Lebanese American clubs for devoting too much attention to Pan Arab matters instead of confining itself to Lebanese affairs; the leaders of the Federation were accused of slighting the distinction between Lebanon (whose population is roughly half-Christian and half-Moslem) and other Arabic-speaking states (whose Christian element is much smaller).[8]

Just as third-generation American Syrians began to band together in clubs that theoretically transcended religious and village differences, the Lebanese nationality controversy emerged and forced them to deal again with the question of a national identity. Of this transfer of identity, *Al-Hoda* writes:

> The campaign for absorption of Lebanon into Syria was particularly active West of New York and particularly aimed at the younger generation which was more vulnerable. Among the members of the new generation, ties with the old country were not as strong and most of them were not familiar with the ins and outs of the Lebanese situation. A disturbing sign was the progress made even among the older generation; many were identifying with Syria. A number of associations and clubs with a majority of Lebanese members were identifying themselves with Syria rather than with Lebanon. The new associations also called themselves Syrians.[9]

In time, resistance to *Al-Hoda*'s attempt to create a Lebanese consciousness receded and the Lebanese-American community was born. Even many Syrian Melkites and Orthodox are beginning to show a preference for this new identity. When this writer visited Rochester, New York, several years ago and was a guest at "St. Nicholas *Syrian* Catholic Church" (sign posted in front), circulars advertising the availability of "Lebanese food" and "Lebanese bread" at the parish bazaar appeared throughout the city. In no other city, save perhaps Cleveland, has he ever observed this custom regardless of the proportion of Lebanese therein. In Brooklyn and Boston, for example, which have large numbers of "Lebanese-Americans," Arabic food is still called "Syrian food." Arabic-speaking Americans seemingly will identify with either category (Syrian or Lebanese) as circumstances dictate.

Given their ambivalent attitude toward national identities and their lack of familiarity with national terms, even identification as Lebanese might be temporary. Writing of the Syrians of Brazil, whose experience in this regard greatly parallels that of the Syrians in the United States, a *Newsweek* correspondent recently noted:

> Perhaps the most revealing index of the rise of the Lebanese in Brazilian society . . . lies in the different names that have been applied to them over the years. At first, they were known by the slightly derogatory term, "Turks." That was replaced later by the somewhat more prestigious "Syrians," which, in turn, gave way to the current—and still more respectful—"Lebanese." Now, however, even that degree of esteem is being escalated. "In university circles," reports a scholar of Lebanese ancestry, "we are now called Phoenicians."[10]

Whatever the case may be, this lack of a common awareness of origins, coupled with the confusion in identity upon arrival in America, caused the Syrians to continue the patterns of the old country which meant primarily relating only to those who could be considered an extension of the family. In a perceptive realization of this, Treudley again notes:

> All members of the collectivity have, to be sure, come themselves or are descendents from immigrants who came from Syria, Lebanon or Palestine. Only Christians, however, are considered to be "our kind of people." Moslems and Jews are, with few exceptions, excluded from the in-group. Furthermore, membership is felt to rest not so much on the country of origin as on the biological position of the individual. The collectivity is less a nationality group to the ordinary person than a union of extended kinships.[11]

The Maronites in America

Subscribing to the philosophy that "our Lebanese community is supported by our culture and religion . . . both of them reflecting our soul and spirit,"[12] the Maronite Church in the United States has become the primary bearer and preserver of an unauthentic form of "Arabic culture," as interpreted by Lebanon, rather than a Catholic Eastern rite that is universal in appeal and composition and that could be open to all non-Arab ethnics.

Lebanon is probably the least likely place in the Middle East where Arabic culture is being preserved. Most Lebanese speak French as a second language, and consider it a sign of respectability to be as "Franji" as possible. Perhaps the most obvious "Westernization" in their culture is in music. Oriental rhythms and instruments have given way to Western sounds, as evidenced by the most popular record album produced there in recent years. "Evening in Beirut" is complete with Western instrumentation and retains its Arabic flavor only in the language used.

More important, however, is the effect of this on the religious life of the Lebanese in America. The French influence, the historical tie to Lebanon, their attachment to the Roman See, and their tenacity of faith have all combined to place the American Maronites in the mainstream of American Catholic life while seemingly allowing them to maintain their ethnic and cultural identity in the eyes of undiscriminating outside observers. Not unlike the American Irish, who have made Catholic and Irish synonymous, the Maronites did very much the same thing. They became the "Irish of the East," since for them being Lebanese and Maronite Catholic was the same.

In the United States, religious latinization became synonymous in the Lebanese mind with Americanization, and vice versa. Their wholesale adoption of "Latinisms" or Latin Catholic religious practices not only indicated the Maronites' attachment to the Roman See and their idealization of Western culture, but it also impinged on their identity as a distinct Catholic group. Though this gave them security as a legitimate Catholic religious and ethnic group, it generated hostility from their Melkite and Syrian-Orthodox brothers who were trying to adapt to Western political and social institutions without having to adopt Western religious forms as well.

What the Byzantine Catholics (Melkites) and Syrian Orthodox have always acknowledged, in principle at least, is the separation of culture from rite allowing one to vary independently of the other. For the Melkites, the Byzantine rite is universal and can be (and is today) used by many national groups and native cultures. For the Maronites, rite and culture have become one and the same. The result is that being a good Maronite means being devoted to Lebanese culture and society and vice versa.

Professor Naseer Aruri's study of the Springfield Lebanese community gives evidence of this. The Maronite Church there not only provided facilities for worship but it also perpetuated Lebanese self-consciousness. The Reverend Michael Saab, who came to this country from Lebanon as a young man, encouraged his Maronite parishioners to retain their Lebanese traditions. He preached the desirability of loyalty to the United States and integration with American society without losing sight of the Lebanese heritage that was theirs. The following statement made during his investiture as pastor is typical of the feelings and orientation of the American Lebanese:

> The most important part of my work was to help my people remain ever closer to God and to realize that they could live as full a life in this country . . . as in Lebanon. . . . I did not want them to forget their Lebanese heritage because this is a wonderful thing.[12]

In America, this has created several problems for the Lebanese. If ethnic religions are doomed to failure, then the Maronite rite, as it is presently consituted, possesses within itself the seeds of its own demise. Second, the Maronites' pro-Roman orientation has made their claim of "distinctiveness" somewhat dubious. For all practical purposes, the only difference remaining between the Maronites and the Latin-rite Catholics is the commitment of the former to maintaining Lebanese culture.

Given the experiences of other ethnic groups, it would seem that only isolation of the Maronites from other, more assimilated American Catholics would enable them to keep their form of Lebanese culture-religion alive. On the other hand, it is possible that they will be able to continue as an ethnic-national group since their cultural symbols have been totally confused with their religious faith. Since their ethnic heritage is now disguised as a religious tradition and since Americans tend to prefer religious pluralism and toleration to ethnic divisiveness, they may have developed a satisfactory mode of relating to American society.

The Preference for American (Latin) Catholicism

In spite of their verbalizations to the contrary, however, the Catholic Syrians and Lebanese have not been able to stem the transfer of allegiance to the Roman rite which has taken place among the community's young. The American-born Syrians and Lebanese are not institutionally bound like their fathers. They participate in American society. Desiring acceptance, the Syrians have pushed their children through the Catholic school system and these children have responded by both negating their ethnic past and prefering the services of the Latin Catholic Church.

This situation has affected the community dramatically. The Catholic Syrians and Lebanese considered their acceptance by the Catholic schools a point of pride. It made them feel that their Latin Catholic neighbors (the Irish in particular) understood and accepted them. But it also meant that the Catholic Syrians would be drawn into the network of Roman Catholic institutions and away from those of their own community. Their interests would become those of Roman Catholicism and they would no longer be able to recognize their Orthodox compatriots as fellow ethnics. The Orthodox children would be in public schools and make their social adjustment outside a Catholic framework. Religion would not or could not serve to unify their community as it did for so many other ethnic groups.

Socialized effectively by their Irish-Latin Catholic mentors, the Syrians who were Melkites and Maronites became essentially American Catholics—which meant Latin-rite (Western) Catholics. The Orthodox Syrians began to join together with Greeks, Russians, Slovaks, et cetera, of the same faith to lay the groundwork for an emerging de-ethnicized American Eastern Orthodox Church. The Presbyterian Syrians merely let their ethnicity die by becoming absorbed into American Protestantism.

Ironically, many of the earliest migrants were the products of the Protestant Mission Schools, especially those of Lebanon, which were established at the turn of the century. The Protestants represented a new tradition that could not be easily incorporated into the traditional social order of the area, which historically evolved around the rights and privileges of Muslims and Eastern Christians. The Protestants also represented Western values and life-styles and hence caused the most disruption. Only a substantial migration would ensure their safety.

The French, being Catholic, were somewhat better received in Lebanon. Indeed, their effect on the East was of a completely different order. While the Protestants Westernized, i.e., transmitted Western values, attitudes, thought patterns, and customs, the French "latinized." Their primary influence was to make Roman or Latin Catholics out of the native Melkites and Maronites. Westernization would still result but it would be a secondary effect of becoming Latin. The French attempts were not always direct or systematic. Rather, the Eastern Catholics were won over because they generally envied the prosperity and generosity of the Western, Latin Catholics. They began to lose sight of their own traditions and it soon became more desirable to be a Latin Catholic than to remain in the Melkite or Maronite rite.

It was the relative insignificance and poverty of some of these Eastern churches and the obscurity of the individuals and traditions composing them that made the Western Church more attractive. Consequently, many "Easterners" sought direct affiliation with the Latin Church at the expense of their own rite. They did so because of their desire for the material goods associated with Western Catholicism rather than as a result of any theological or aesthetic appreciation of it. Donald Atwater, who wrote the first English history of the Syrian Eastern Churches, writes:

> The Latin rite stands for European (and Christian) civilization and influence; for its attractive ideas of progress, for prestige, education, commerce, pseudo-Parisian clothes, for being "in" with the Franks; Eastern rites are looked down on as being for mere peasants, too often, nay ordinarily, Latins accept rather than oppose such wrong views.[13]

The Latin Catholic Church has traditionally used the rewards of material and intellectual progress as the "bait" with which to retain its present Arab membership and convert the Eastern Catholics and Orthodox of other nationalities. As the recently appointed Archbishop of Galilee noted:

> In order to keep these Orientals in the Latin Church . . . it was necessary to create in them a superiority complex. This complex is maintained by an exaggerated display of wealth and power. . . . The orientals who remained faithful to their Church of the East find themselves humiliated and looked down upon by the others, their brothers.[14]

Traditionally, the use of religion as a form of personal and family mobility has been very strong in the East. Becoming a priest in the Eastern Church elevated the candidate to a position of status, honor, and respect. For many it was the least expensive means of receiving an education and becoming socially mobile at the same time. The establishment of schools by the Latin patriarchate of Jerusalem, however, altered the situation. More education was made available to the general population and the attraction of the Latin rite and its traditions was also enhanced. As the archbishop further notes:

> This morning . . . the father of a family came to see me and said in all tranquility: "If you don't tell the Director of our college seminary in Nazareth to admit my children for nothing, I will become Latin!"

The Archbishop continues:

> Is it normal that a superior of a school should answer me, a Bishop responsible for his flock, when I posed the question: "Do you encourage, dear Sister, the Greek-Catholic [Melkite] children to go to prayers in their Church?" . . . "Your excellency, here we are missionaries of the Latin Patriarchate. The children have to become Latin; otherwise open up a school yourself for them."[15]

While the Westerners, in particular the French, were mainly responsible for the preservation of the Eastern Churches from the onslaughts of the Turks and Moslems, their presence in the East resulted in a certain ambivalence: on the one hand, the Syrian Christians saw the Latins as "saviors" in times of persecution, and on the other, it was the Latin Westerners who administered and introduced the policies that made the Eastern traditions and customs appear inferior.

The Latin rite for the Syrians reflected the West and the material benefits that Western civilization brought. Thus, those adhering to the authentic and majority traditions of the East received satisfaction in knowing that they were following the indigenous customs, but it was little compensation for being poor and essentially nonprogressive. In the minds of the Syrians, then, to be "Western" meant to be Latin, and vice versa.

If this awareness was such in Syria, it became even more pronounced upon the immigrants' arrival in the United States. The Syrians' Eastern Catholicism would not find the same "recognition" it had in the old country. Indeed, if anything, their traditions represented a totally new and foreign type of Catholicism that American Catholics apparently would not or could not understand and that was matched by the Syrians' noncomprehension of America's religious traditions. Thus, the predilection to imitate the West, or at least the Western Christians, crystallized in America, where they became totally overwhelmed by the power and prestige of their fellow Catholics. In America, the Eastern Catholic immigrants had two options open to them: they could stay backward Arabs—at least in the popular mind—or they could become another Catholic ethnic group, leaving behind the Syrian Orthodox to represent the East. They chose the latter, and formalized their commitment to American society by attending and supporting the educational institutions of the Latin Catholic Church.

The Syrian Catholic reaction to American society was expressed in two nearly opposite ways. The Maronites actually joined their religious pursuits or interests with their social and cultural activities to form a Lebanese Catholic ethnic group, while the Melkite Syrians seemed to separate religion and culture. American Melkites originally did not demand respect for themselves as a separate and valid Catholic tradition. That they eventually did so was a result of their ethic which demands that Byzantine Christians not only adapt to new surroundings and cultures, but inform these cultures as well.

Melkites in America would attempt to survive because their rite has, in theological terms, something special to offer American society. They assume that their rite is unique and different enough to attract Americans of all persuasions who are in search of spiritual succor. The Maronites, on the other hand, still feel that the soul of their tradition—which is also unique when presented in a pure state—lies in its Arabic origins and not in the beauty or religious essence of the rite itself.

Regardless of this divergence, however, both groups acted somewhat uniformly until the present decade. As we shall demonstrate, Melkites and Maronites have both latinized in the past and have consequently come together to form an ethnic group with their old religious traditions supporting and containing them. The Eastern Orthodox Syrians also had to accommodate themselves to the changing interests and needs of their "Americanizing" constituency until that time when a unified (together with Greeks and Russians, et cetera) American Orthodox

Church restressing faith emerged. Catholics and Orthodox were thus brought together over the ethnocultural issue and the perplexing question of how to acculturate without being assimilated into oblivion. And so, the desire for ethnicity flourished for a time.

Unfortunately, this solution did not last very long or sustain them as a community much beyond the Korean War. Ethnicity in the late 1950's and early 1960's was a thing of the past—existing mainly in the minds and memories of the people. New leadership to meet new challenges was needed and the Syrians had no one to call upon except a clergy that frequently included crass and uninformed opportunists who came to America to send money back to their status-conscious relatives.

No leaders seemed ever to have emerged who could educate the Syrians in their own socioreligious history. They were simply ignorant about their religious past. The second generation could not learn what no one was willing or able to teach them. The typical immigrant Syrian Catholic and his children know little or nothing about their rite or faith. The third generation does, however! Texts have now been written in English about the Christian East which all Americans can refer to. This information is for everyone and the Syrians generally learn about their past from non-Arab teachers in formalized institutional settings open to non-Syrians.

The Syrians are not unlettered. They are writers and poets and classical storytellers. Unfortunately, they applied their native intelligence to cultural and economic pursuits rather than to the education of their own countrymen in America. Other than the writings of Kalil Gibran, most Arabic-American literature is kept within the ethnic community and is not intended for or available to the general American audience. It has even been suggested that the independence and nationalist movements of Syria and Lebanon were considerably indebted to the activities and writings of Syrian nationalists in America. All this took place while they were becoming Americanized, yet they could do nothing for themselves in America as an integrated ethnic community.

Dr. Adele Younis tells us that "they were eager to please their non-Arabic neighbors by means of the press or personal contacts. They wished to convey to the American populace their philosophy and ancestral history."[16] Unfortunately, their desire to please meant that they would negate their own heritage —especially their religious origins. They gave America a bastardized version of their Arab past. This, plus their inability to effectively resolve their vertical religious cleavages, left them completely prey to the forces of Americanization. These Middle Easterners became Americans before they had a chance to become unified American "Syrians." Those of them who were Catholic became like the Irish before they learned about and transmitted their own heritage to their own children.

Rather than attempting to survive by relying on the merits of their religious heritage as a distinctive and legitimate form of Catholic worship, spirituality, and theology, they presented it only in the context of "Arabic culture." Indeed, the Maronites drew their strength from their culture rather than from the potential theological and liturgical uniqueness of their rite itself. Not realizing that the educated, acculturated, and American-born Maronite would eventually reject his church as he found his ethnic identity and culture dysfunctional or shallow or irrelevant, they insisted on maintaining the old ethnic traditions as distinctive religious supports.

Moreover, rather than adding to Catholic pluralism in the United States, the Maronites would become unnecessary as they became no different in genuine religious practice from Latin-rite Catholics. Maronites, and to a degree Melkites, have deprived themselves of a raison d'être.

CHAPTER VIII

America and the Syrian Easterners

IN THE PROCESS OF ADJUSTING TO AMERICAN SOCIETY, THE SYRIANS had to learn to deal more effectively with one another across religious lines. At the same time, each separate religious group within the collectivity responded somewhat differently to America's environment and culture.

The Confrontation

The Protestant Syrians, for example, were not only educated and better prepared for their encounter with America, but experienced little overt hostility from the Protestant community in general. The early Protestant emigrants were somewhat more mobile than the other Syrians because of their affiliation with Presbyterianism, a dominant American religious community. The Syrian Orthodox were completely unfamiliar with the host society and had to contend with both an emerging American Catholicism and an established Protestantism. Because of their historic dislike of the former, they often opted for closer cooperation with the latter, even though this greatly increased the chances of apostasy from the Eastern tradition that they and the Catholics shared.

Fr. Alan Maloof cites a typical Orthodox response to Protestantism:

> . . . many Orthodox became Protestants—going to the nearest church no matter what sect it might be. (They carefully avoided going to the nearest Catholic Church.) I, personally, know Orthodox families who send their children to Protestant Sunday schools in the neighborhood and often a Protestant has stood sponsor at an Orthodox baptism.[1]

Often, when they could not build their own churches, the Orthodox would use the halls and basements of the Protestant churches (especially those of the Episcopalians, who somehow were perceived as the Western equivalent to Eastern Orthodoxy). The losses of the Orthodox to Protestantism are difficult to estimate accurately. As reported to this writer by Fr. Gregory Aboud, Dean of Saint Nicholas Syrian Orthodox Cathedral, Brooklyn, there are only 60,000 Orthodox Syrians registered in their archdiocese out of an estimated 110,000 official Orthodox in their geographic region.[2]

When the Syrian Orthodox Church lost members, it was usually because of the general shortage of priests and facilities. The religious needs of a rather dispersed population had to be fulfilled outside the faith. There was also the problem of being a totally new and misunderstood Christian tradition in America. Eventually, the Orthodox established a strong hierarchy and church administration in the United States and apostasy from the faith was reversed. Presently, they are discussing with other Eastern Orthodox groups the forming of an indigenous English-speaking American Eastern Orthodox Church which will become America's fourth great religion with some 6,000,000 members.

The Syrian Catholic confrontation with America's religious traditions differed from that of the Orthodox and seemed to mirror the Irish-Catholic encounter with American Protestantism more than anything else. The Catholic Syrians, to be sure, were rarely, if ever, in contact with American culture or society except as it was mediated by the Irish, who submerged and transformed their own ethnicity into a religion.

Since group boundaries for the Syrians were really church boundaries, they had to enter American life through the Irish church. Until the present decade, Syrian Catholics still refered to the Irish church as the "American" church, and the Irish priest as the "American" priest. Their own church, clergy (even when American born), and hierarchy (as well as those of all non-Irish Catholics) are defined in ethnic terms.

Because of the language differences, of course, American Catholicism's conception of all non-Irish Americans as "ethnics" was not totally erroneous. As Chyz and Read have noted:

> In all facets of American life, the nationality groups which came from English speaking countries became the majority groups in the United States. They impressed their language and institutions on the new conti-

nent. The result has been a tendency to think of the agencies created by English speaking groups as "American," and of similar developments on the part of other nationality groups as "foreign."[3]

Moreover, as Raymond Breton says, "some of the most crucial factors bearing on absorption of immigrants would be in the social organization of the communities which the immigrant contacts in the receiving country."[4] Since the only parallel institution belonging to the Syrians which was different from the publicly sanctioned ways of the larger population was their church, and since "religious institutions have the greatest effect in keeping the immigrants' personal associations within the boundaries of the ethnic community,"[5] it would be in this area that they would most deeply experience the tensions of assimilation.

Canonically, since the Irish churches were Latin and hence "American," the Syrian reaction to them was not very different than that of other less "American" oriented Catholic ethnic groups. But while the Syrian confrontation with the Irish was like that of the Poles, Italians, and Germans, it differed considerably in that the Syrians were involved with more than just ethnic conflict: it was rather a confrontation between two religious disciplines, two ecclesiologies, and two religious-cultural traditions that never fully understood one another.

As already noted, the Syrians were immigrants who utilized identities that were outside Western concepts such as nation and state. The situation was further complicated by the historical relationship of the Eastern and Western churches in the Levant and the position of the Irish Catholics in American life at the time of the Syrians' arrival.

Traditionally, Eastern and Western Christians viewed each other with suspicion and each century that passed left its influence on their future relationships. Their accommodation became much more difficult in America, where ethnicity became intertwined with religion and "patriotism"; where competion set group against group; and where the assimilation process left the emigrants' culture and personality in a marginal state. For the Catholic Syrians the situation was further complicated by the great power of the Latin Church in the United States.

In the Middle East the Eastern-rite Catholic lived within a microcosm of the "universal church" which he understood and participated in regularly; that is, all the rites and disciplines of the entire church were in constant contact and equilibrium with one another. Lack of familiarity with another tradition was impossible for them, since the Catholics in Syria were constantly made aware of the liturgical variations in the life of the church around them.

Although there was substantial appreciation, on the part of the Catholics living in Syria of their own rites, they still found Western liturgical observances highly attractive. As was previously mentioned, this was more a result of the material and social appeal of Latin Christianity than of its religious or otherworldly significance.

To be modern, affluent, and American meant being Latin in the Syrian immigrants' mind. Unfortunately, of course, because of the narrow ethnocentric perspective of the American Irish Catholics, the Syrian Catholic religious traditions remained an enigma to them. This produced a similar reaction on the part of the Syrians, who then had difficulty understanding and accepting the American Latin Catholic disposition.

The situation, then, involved contradictory motivations on the part of the Syrians: a desire for all of the benefits and status of American Catholicism coupled with a mistrust and rejection of it.

American Catholicism

The forming spirit behind American Catholicism came from the Irish, who not only dominated the hierarchy but also reshaped the Church in a "Hibernian" mode not dissimilar to its counterpart in Europe. As such, the Catholic Church that the non-Irish Catholic immigrants found in the United States was, as Oscar Handlin put it, "as different from what was familiar to the newcomers as the chapels of the Episcopalians or Methodists."[6] It was English-speaking, puritanical, democratic, popular, activistic, and nationalistic. Irish, Catholic, and American became almost identical in the Irish-American mind.

According to Glazer and Moynihan, the Church that grew here was, from the very beginning, different from the historical Roman Catholic Church not only in theology, with its distinctive Jansenist tendencies, but also in culture:

> It was a Church with a decided aversion to the modern liberal state. It was a church that was decidedly separatist in its attitude toward the

non-Catholic community, which for a long time was the ascendent community. It was a church with almost no intellectual tradition. "Irish Catholicism . . . had developed many of the characteristics of English sectarianisms: defensive, insular, parochial, puritanical."[7]

Irish dominance did not immediately destroy the racial and cultural heterogeneity the other Catholic nationals insisted on maintaining. But since they controlled the hierarchy, they still defined Catholic ethnic pluralism as harmful to the unity and future of a growing "American" Church. In order to avoid schisms, though, the Irish had to allow the establishment of judicial "national parishes" that would serve the needs of the non-English-speaking immigrants. Naturally, they confused the Syrian Eastern Catholic Churches with these national parishes. But the Syrian churches had differences of rite as well as language!

In these cases, the ritual of church services, the meaning of the sacred symbols and the traditional religious exercises, the church architecture and decoration all added to the maintenance of the ethnic group. Through this method, the Church was able to hold together in one body diverse ethnic religious elements—each with its own idiosyncratic customs.

This approach of the church hierarchy was no problem for Western European Catholics who shared the same ecclesiology and liturgical history. Their religious symbols, as well as the language of their liturgy, were uniform (Latin) and recognizable. It was around these common symbols that an integrated American Catholic institutional life emerged. As Handlin notes:

> It was still possible to share the Mass! Ultimately Catholics like Lutherans and Jews achieved a workable compromise which gave communicants of every group the opportunity for identification they desired. Church-goers thus had a choice of affiliations and the churches ineluctably adapted themselves to their communicants' freedom to belong or not to belong.[8]

Eastern Catholic Reactions

Because the Syrians were adherents of Eastern rather than Latin Catholic rites, however, they were socially and religiously marginal in terms of ritual, language, and symbols to the developing American Catholic Church. In the first place, their churches and parishes were inclusive to a degree unmatched by other

Catholic groups. According to Neusee, there is substantial evidence available indicating that the "forms and symbols" of religious worship (ritual including music and song) were more completely integrated with the ethnic cultures of the Uniates (even linguistically) than they are for Catholics of the Roman rite, thus making for increased difficulties in assimilation.[9]

Second, as Eastern Catholics, they differed in their interpretation of Christian cosmology and morality. Third, their symbols and liturgical systems were different from those commonly used and understood in the West, and the structure of their parishes and dioceses varied accordingly. Finally, there were also differences in religious discipline—for example, a married clergy was accepted and commonplace among all the Eastern Christians including the Catholics.

More important, and in spite of the fact that the keystone in both churches is the office of the priest, the exact proportion of power and control between clergy and laity differs greatly between the Eastern and Western Churches:

> Whereas the Roman Church is integrated both symbolically and formally, with its priestly hierarchy providing the sinews of the extended church system, the Eastern Church system, while an integrated entity symbolically, is in organization atomistic. This deviation between symbolic and formal organization expresses itself in a division of functions within a church structure. While the Eastern priest is the guardian of the symbols and the ritualistic mediator for the community, the community itself is in control of the non-sacred aspects of the Church structure.[10]

The Eastern priest, then, is a member of the community—often elected or at least requested by them. He is deeply responsible for and to his flock and is a reflection of them as well as an extension of their family. The Roman priest, on the other hand, is somewhat removed from his congregation, not necessarily responsible to them, and obligated to the decisions of his bishop. His role as manager of the organization often overshadows his role as a member of the Christian community.

The Latins often overlooked the fact that priest and communicant in the Eastern Church were very much the same "person," so most of the conflicts between Latins and Easterners were usually group conflicts. These often resulted in whole communities of

Eastern faithful following their priest in submission to the Latins or, when they refused to be controlled by them, into Orthodoxy. The situation was further complicated by the particular problems facing the emerging American Catholic Church, which felt it to be in the best interests of an "American" Church to render these "strange" Catholics or Uniates peripheral to Catholic life. They would thus be reduced to another Catholic ethnic group that would be like all the others from Western Europe. In time, then, they too would be Americanized or "latinized," and hence assimilated.

For the Latins, the Syrians as Melkites and Maronites were merely another ethnic group that disrupted and discredited a church that was trying so desperately to be American and unified. Thus, the desire of the Syrians for legitimate ecclesiastical independence became confused in the minds of the Latins with "Cahenslyism"; the government of their churches with "Trusteeism"; and their married clergy with Protestantism. More important, they feared that the Easterners would disrupt the "universality" of the Church, which was narrowly defined at that time as uniformity and conformity.

Ultimately, the deciding factors in determining how the Easterners would deal with the Latin hierarchy came from their unique history, the frequency and nature of contact with the Latins in the old country, the number of priests available to them of their own rite in the new country, and, most important, their awareness, interest, and devotion to the prerogatives of their own rite. Thus, while all Eastern groups shared the same "conflict in symbols," ecclesiology, and discipline with the Latin Church in America, each of them reacted somewhat differently.

The Eastern-rite Catholic groups from Eastern Europe (Ukrainians, Russian-rite Catholics, Carpatho-Ruthenians), for example, often reacted violently to Latin attempts to change their ritual practices and Eastern patrimony. They often prefered to give up their "Catholicity" and become Eastern Orthodox than to submit to the wishes of the American Latin Catholic hierarchy. In all cases, these final shifts in allegiance were the consequence of serious misunderstandings with the Latins as to what being a real Catholic consisted of. Latin Catholics were conditioned to think that all Catholics followed the same rituals, prayed in Latin, had no married clergy, and were under the thumbs of their bishops.

But the Eastern rite groups from the Slavic countries chose to force the issue of demanded latinization with Rome—especially the issue of required clerical celibacy. Indeed, over 225,000 faithful of the Ruthenian rite left the Catholic Church rather than give up their married clergy. Only about one-third of the Carpatho-Ruthenians remain today under the jurisdiction of Catholic bishops. One-third have passed over to the Latin rite, and another third into Eastern Orthodoxy. Had they remained Catholic, there would be a million of them today in the United States. The same is true of the Ukrainians of North America, of which one-third abandoned the faith.

The Syrians, on the other hand, remained completely loyal Catholics of their respective rites. They had long been accustomed to accommodating themselves to the Latin personality and ideologically always believed that it was ultimately more important to be a Roman Catholic, i.e., in union with Rome, than a self-righteous schismatic Eastern Orthodox not in communion with the "other half" of the Christian Church. Rather than inform the American Catholic public of their legitimate differences, however, the Syrian Catholics allowed themselves to become a latinized Catholic ethnic group rather than make American Catholicism pluralistic in terms of rite, language, and liturgy.

The Melkite-Maronite Response

Obviously, the reaction of the Catholic Syrians to the American Irish church was quite different from that of the other non-Latin-rite groups. Had they been more militant at an earlier period, it is conceivable that they would have achieved independence from Latin domination somewhat earlier. The Melkites and Maronites, whose original accommodation was of a less than forceful nature, are only now being allowed to coalesce into nationally unified diocesan bodies. In 1966 Apostolic Exarchates were established for them by the Oriental Congregation in Rome. That they should have been able to appoint their own bishops earlier did not interest the Latin-controlled Congregation. While limited in scope and power (they are attached to Roman dioceses and not to their respective patriarchates), they are the first attempt at canonical and jurisdictional autonomy for them in this country. It may be assumed that if they stay faithful to Rome, the Oriental Congregation will then trust them enough to allow them to reenter full hierarchical communion with their own patriarchates.

Previously, the response of the Syrian Melkites and Maronites reflected both their estimate of the Latins and their desire to enter fully into American life, which for them was equated with entrance into American Catholicism. In a revealing interview with a student of Eastern Christian affairs in the United States, the following comparison between the "Slavic" and Arab Catholics was made:

> Unlike the Arab Maronites and Melkites, "assimilation" had taken on different forms for the "Slavs." In general, except for the initial contact as immigrants with the Latins there has been little desire for social assimilation among the Ukrainians. The early pioneer-priests "latinized" extensively—but Latinization among the "Slavs" worked in reverse to that of the Arabs. Our priests (Ukrainian and Ruthenian) Latinized for their own acceptance; the people never accepted it fully as they never admired the Latins—for both historical and cultural reasons. The Arab people, on the other hand, had more contact with the Latins, the people demanded Latinization for acceptance.[11]

The Syrians, then, sensing the demands of their new environment, desired to fit in as much as possible. Their ultimate objective was entrance into the prestructured sequence of American status positions exemplified and fulfilled by the Latins. Consequently, they proceeded to modify their rite and the symbols of their "corporate identity" in order to be more American. In so doing, however, they effectively destroyed the basis for a separate and meaningful religious (hence communal) life by making their arguments for boundary maintenance impractical if not completely implausible.

As a result the Syrians could either belong to an inauthentic or latinized Eastern Church, or simply become Latin-rite Catholics by supporting these churches and incorporating themselves informally into their social and religious life. Those Syrians, as we shall demonstrate, who stayed Melkites and Maronites did so more for the ethnic security and identity that these rites offered than for their spiritual nourishment. By pursuing the first alternative, the Syrians gained access to the channels of social acceptability and upward mobility while retaining their communal identity. This resolved the primary "culture conflict" they met with in

America, which arose out of their inherent deviancy, i.e., nonconformity to the expected religious practices of the American Catholic Church.

Whether they intended it or not, the weakening of their authentic distinctiveness cost the Syrian Eastern Catholics over half their faithful to the Latin rite anyway. While the official estimates of the Melkite and Maronite Exarchates place their numbers at 50,000 and 150,000 respectively,[12] there are fewer than 20,000 Melkites *registered* in the 25 Melkite "parishes" of the United States. A greater number, estimated at 30,000, are only nominally Melkite, practically Latin. The Maronites, on the other hand, who have over 40 parishes, claim to have 100,000 "active" Maronites and estimate their loss to other rites at 50,000. Moreover, an intensive study of the Brooklyn Melkite community, completed in 1964 by this writer, reveals that 46 percent of the second generation of canonical Melkites actually identified with the Latin rite, with the proportion increasing to 55 percent by the third generation.[13]

Adoption of and adaptation to the Latin rite was a consequence of several complicating factors. To begin with, the shortage of priests and the lack of a diocesan organization left the Syrians without a competent and centralized authority. So both rites were dependent on the Latin-rite hierarchies—a factor that tended to dilute the rite even in areas where parishes were established, but especially where people had to depend on the Latins for services like funerals, weddings, and so forth.

Also, the tendency of the Arabic-speaking emigrants to scatter all over the United States made it impossible to form either aggregate communities out of which parishes could grow or a sizable and stable ethnic community. In addition, the lack of Melkite and Maronite parochial schools made spiritual formation in their Eastern tradition practically impossible; and finally, the traditional Syrian disposition for fast adjustment to American culture especially necessitated the modification of their rites to "American usage."

The motivation for latinization for the Maronites differed a bit from that of the Melkites. For the Maronites, it will be recalled, latinization was the continuation of an ancient process they defined as proof of one's "Catholicity," while latinization for the Melkites stemmed from their deep-seated inferiority complex developed from years of subjugation to Roman authorities in the Holy Land and elsewhere.

The Melkites' feelings were a consequence of Rome's (1) forbidding Middle Eastern converts to Catholicism to join an Eastern rite; (2) offering the cardinalate to patriarchs who were already higher in rank than a Western cardinal; (3) outlawing the married clergy of the Easterners in the United States without their approval or consent; (4) formulating an Eastern Canon Law that was nothing more than a translation of its Latin-rite counterpart; and (5) interfering in the appointment of bishops and the election of patriarchs.

The Church of the West has consistently used the promise of material and intellectual progress to convert Catholics and Orthodox of other traditions. And so Melkites and Maronites came to view latinization in the United States as Americanization. Nor was their perception mistaken—at least as far as Will Herberg's thesis that to be an American means to be either a Protestant, Catholic (Latin), or Jew is true.[14] Speaking of this equation in the minds of the Syrians, Reverend Alan Maloof, the first American born Melkite to be ordained in this country, writes:

> They wanted to be more "American" in all aspects of the word. Americanization remolded home, family, work and recreation. Some unfortunately, overzealous in their good intentions, confused the word "Americanization" with "Latinization." The general idea seemed to be, "We are in America now, therefore, our churches and customs should be the same as those of the other American Catholics (Latins); so that we may all be alike; we should not confuse people."[15]

This orientation in their religious life reflected quite accurately their attitude and approach to American society in general. It complemented their tendency to seek rather than avoid some form of effective integration with American society—especially in religion, which was at the root of their integration conflict. Moreover, their Catholicism was taken seriously, as was indicated by their virtual lack of schism. They wanted to be Catholic Americans no matter what the cost to their communal life.

Their reaction also reflected their historical attempts at adapting to a new culture rapidly without being absorbed completely into it. So far they have successfully warded off total absorption. Philip K. Hitti states that "no other immigrant group to the

United States so swiftly felt the American spirit yet retained the spirit and culture of the old country as the Syrians."[16] He claims that this has been their particular genius throughout the centuries:

> Maintaining old home ties did not spell laxity in accepting obligations and responsibilities toward the land of adoption. With no strong nationalistic feeling of the modern variety, the emigrants had no insurmountable difficulty in acquiring the feeling of "at homeness" wherever they went. Their versatility and adaptability helped them to become "all things to all men." In Egypt, they became Egyptians, in France, Frenchmen, in America, Americans—all before they had even become Lebanese.[17]

More important, however, was the nature of their confrontation with the Latin Catholics, which resulted in the Syrians' submission to them and the subsequent dilution of their original religious identity pattern. While conflict can serve to establish full ego identity and autonomy, help differentiate the personality from the outside world, and strengthen the internal cohesion of a group while centralizing its political structure, it did no such things for the Syrians. Coming from a powerless and subdued socioreligious tradition, lacking any substantial and appreciative awareness of their past, and being unable to organize into a workable and acceptable identity, they were literally religiously overwhelmed by the Latins.

Not unexpectedly, therefore, the Syrians tried to create in the United States a new identity: one based on "ethnicity" rather than rite or religion. A unique ethnic heritage and past would at least be understood by the American public. Interestingly enough, their new identity also brought the Catholic Syrians into closer contact with the Orthodox Syrians who likewise had not yet fully separated their faith from dependence on ethnicity. An important factor influencing this development was the unwillingness of American Catholicism to accept an autonomous Eastern Catholicism (Melkite, Maronite, or otherwise) as a valid and legitimate part of itself.

Had the Latins been more accommodating, the Syrian Catholics would have undergone a different assimilation experience. Not only would their interior life not have been altered but their relationship to each other and their own religious-cultural traditions would have been different. Since American Catholic society was more willing to recognize a culturally pluralistic social pattern based on ethnicity—since it was temporary—than one based on religion, the Syrians began latinizing themselves religiously and Syrianizing themselves ethnically and socially. In time they effectively learned to synthesize both—though not permanently.

CHAPTER IX

The Americanization of the "Syrian Churches"

WHEREVER ARABIC-SPEAKING CHRISTIAN PEOPLE SETTLED IN sufficient numbers they established their particular religions and rites. But to avoid rejection by their English-speaking children, they substantially altered those aspects of their traditions that were incongruous with their new environment. By so doing, they also avoided the possible communal dissolution that would have resulted from conflict both within their community and between themselves and their American hosts. They could have been completely absorbed into the dominant American churches, but generally they chose to preserve those aspects of their own ethnic traditions that would let them carry on some form of social life together.

Churches Are Established

The church's importance in the old country made religion the primary and most significant institution established by the immigrants in America. As a means of comfort in the anonymity of their new urban environment, the church continued its traditional role of providing support for the insecure immigrant. However, the immigrant church was an instrument, not only of preservation, but of adaptation as well. Inevitably the change in environment meant that the churches would be transformed even while they were still being transplanted. The immigrants, of course, generally intended otherwise. As Handlin notes, "The immigrants in departing had no desire to abandon their religion; and most of them struggled earnestly to reconstruct the familiar ways of worship in the New World."[1]

The pressures to adapt to American culture persisted and forced the immigrant Syrians to develop a hybrid culture, that is, one that contained some of the institutions and customs of the old country and added some of the practices of the dominant society as well as some new forms that were distinctive adjustments to the new environment. Even the area of religion with its traditional, stable, and unalterable symbols was forced to change. This was especially the situation with the Syrians, who not only altered the essential meaning rite had for them, but also modified their religious organization, symbol usage, language, and leadership patterns in order to gain recognition and acceptance. While latinization, whether or not disguised as Americanization, was theologically anathema to the Melkites, it did help this integration-oriented ethnic group accommodate itself to a hostile environment.

The Syrians established their churches only after considerable difficulty and disappointment. Generally speaking, when the Syrian people in a given area reached a sizable proportion of the population they would try to retain the services of a priest of their faith and preferably of their rite. Because of language needs (to confess in Arabic), Maronites, Melkites, and Syrian Orthodox would often accept any Arabic priest. When the community and priest were heavily Catholic and if the cleric was willing to stay, the faithful would petition the local Latin Catholic ordinary for his acceptance. If the cleric's papers were in order, the petition generally was accepted. Services would first be held in the halls and basements of the Latin parishes until funds, permission, and property could be obtained. This often took years. The first Syrian family to reach Paterson, New Jersey, in 1899 had to wait until 1922 before a church was built.

The same procedure was followed by the Syrian Orthodox, who used the facilities of the Episcopalians. When their own hierarchy was established, it remained under the jurisdiction of the Russian Orthodox because this was the first Orthodox group to settle in the Western hemisphere. This brought them unintentionally into closer cooperation with other Orthodox groups at the same time that it limited their interaction with other Syrians. The Catholic Syrians, of course, always remained under the jurisdiction and authority of the Latins, who rarely, if ever, understood or sought to understand the mentality, customs, and traditions of their

Eastern subjects, who were consistently treated as foreigners and "fake" Catholics.

This situation caused acute problems in the area of clerical and lay education. Proper Eastern theological formation became virtually impossible in the United States for many years. All aspirants to the priesthood were forced to go to the Orient to study—and this was a sufficient deterrent for many, especially the American born and English speaking. Latin seminaries would not teach Eastern theology because they were suspicious of it. This situation undoubtedly contributed to the total lack of "Syrian" vocations in the Melkite rite until 1951. One could conclude that both the priestly and religious vocations before this time were ushered into the services of the Latin rite even though Church law insists that all Catholics must stay faithful to their rites, which descend from father to children. You are, in Catholicism, the rite of your father. Because the Latins wanted to romanize the Syrians, they actually violated their own statutes and permitted the changing of rite. Indeed, it is quite conceivable that today there are more American-born Syrian Catholics serving in the Latin rite than American Melkites or Maronites serving in their own.

The lack of an official Melkite jurisdiction in the United States for so many years and the attitude of the Latins resulted in a loss of two-hundred women from Melkite religious orders to the Latin and probably the loss of twice as many Maronites. Fr. Maloof cites one example: "I know of a case where three Melkite girls changed their rite in order to enter Latin religious orders. They could have been used to help their own rite. . . . However, neither their pastor nor the Latin bishop interested themselves in encouraging these girls to stay in their own rite."[2]

Of course, when Melkite clerical training did take place in America, it was often training in Latin theology with the retention only of Byzantine symbolization. The studies of a seminarian were usually arranged by his Latin ordinary at the diocesan major seminary. No provision for Oriental studies would be allowed him, and he would be obliged to study French, German, and Latin instead of Arabic and Greek—the social and religious languages of his congregation. His courses would lack the Oriental point of view necessary for a seminarian of an Eastern rite.

Finally, the willingness of the Latins to accept the Melkite and

Maronite students into the Latin rite eventually deprived these rites of their best students of American affairs. These conditions undoubtly intensified the latinization process for these rites and further weakened the content of Arabic culture in America.

Traditionally, the use of religion as a form of personal and family mobility has been strong in the East. Becoming a priest meant attaining a position of status, honor, and respect. More importantly, the priest invariably inherited the role of mediator with the broader community, and it became his particular responsibility to introduce the Eastern Church to the Latin hierarchy and faithful. He also mediated American society for the Syrian laymen. Indeed, he has always been the traditional spokesman for the community. This explains why a substantial portion of Syrian leaders in America are clerics and possibly why the Syrian-Lebanese layman is politically unaggressive. For these reasons we can also attribute the deterioration of Eastern Christian spirituality in this country to the Syrian priests.

Undoubtedly, many of these non-English-speaking immigrant clergy were opportunists whose original attraction to the priesthood and then to America was the access to wealth that their position afforded them. While all have attempted to serve the religious needs of their people in the United States, many have amassed private fortunes while striving actively to be accepted into the company of the Latins—both socially and religiously. This is a reenactment in the American milieu of their deep-seated inferiority complex. For the most part, many Eastern Catholic priests in America do not understand their own customs and traditions and fear fighting for them.

It can be argued, though, that latinization is merely the religious equivalent of the community's general desire for Americanization and that the clergy were merely responding to the overall pressures generated by an assimilating ethnic group. Had the clergy acted otherwise, the Syrian community would have been split asunder and the very institution they had burdened with supporting and sustaining the community would have been set adrift.

Generally speaking, the laity were uneducated and ill-informed of the prerogatives of their rite. Yet those of them who had attained a modicum of economic success did in fact become the trustees of the churches which the clergy learned to control with them. Given the traditional role of the laity in the affairs of the Eastern Church, it is conceivable that they did in fact willingly accept if not initiate the latinizing changes which their pastors, in most cases, seemed not to object to very vociferously.

Indeed, it was the desire to be "Americanized" together with the influence, prestige, and power of the priest that caused them to modify their structures and practices to conform to some of the more broadly shared cultural patterns of American religion and the normative expectations that most Americans had of Catholics in general. They became punctual and introduced the sermon as well as other practical American practices like the collection plate. Essentially, they shortened, "dignified," and refined the services.[3]

The Syrian elite had power and status because of the relatively high positions they held in the business world. Because of their financial independence they exerted a certain amount of influence in the overall life of the community. They maintained their position by maintaining close personal relationships with their group as well as devoting time to furthering its interests—as they defined them. Determination of the local Syrian elite was facilitated by the small size of their communities and the accruing to so many of the status of "knighthood"—an honor bestowed upon them by Rome.

Unfortunately, no one perceived it as problematic that so many leaders in the religious institutions of the community had attained their position, not because of demonstrated leadership, knowledge, religiosity, or religious administrative ability, but because of economic achievement and generosity toward the Latin hierarchs—the very group that looked down on them but that knew how to use them when their monies were needed. The members of a Syrian community were affected in at least two ways when the Latin diocese recognized an important Catholic philanthropist among them. First, they received a certain amount of recognition from American Catholic "society" at the same time they were supplied with recognizable and obviously acceptable leaders; and second, the "Catholicity" of the whole Melkite and Maronite community was thus reinforced.

This last factor was especially important for the Melkites, since they always carried with them the knowledge that they were closer in religious tradition to the Orthodox than to the Roman Catholics. It also explains the different motivations of the Melkites and the Maronites for latinizing. While the Maronites always imitated the Latins because of the prestige that being like Westerners gave them, the Syrian Melkites did so because their rite was so distinctive that they were assumed to be non-Christian if not Moslem! When it was proven that they were Christian, they were thought to be Eastern Orthodox, not Uniates. Desiring not to be recognized as Orthodox, they changed their rites and traditions to "American" (Latin) usage, and propelled their lay elite into the ranks of Catholic society.

Essentially, however, the Syrian select were strictly local celebrities. They had neither broad recognition nor the prestige that other individuals have by belonging to several high-status groups and categories simultaneously. The Syrian elite was created in America under American conditions, but its members never fully succeeded in emancipating themselves from the cultural limitations they brought with them. Consequently, none of them had a claim to total ethnic group support, because an institutionally integrated and homogeneous Syrian community had, by and large, no basis in reality. If one were a member of an "elite" it was primarily a Melkite, Maronite, or Orthodox elite; so leadership in the church became synonymous with community leadership. These church leaders had a reputation among the other groups but had no cross-institutional power or status.

It took three generations before a true ethnic elite could emerge among the Syrian-Lebanese. Today, the designation of its members is based on the criterion of general achievement outside the religious sphere. Ironically (or naturally), most of the new high-status individuals have received public recognition for services performed in and for the nonethnic community. Thus, famous Syrians are exalted by the ethnic community, even though they have a minimal tie to it and have risen to fame independently of it.

This situation reflects a fundamental weakness of the Syrian-Americans. They simply never learned how to cooperate fully with one another for the general good of the whole community. According to Hitti, the Syrian is simply unaccustomed to submitting to either the will of the majority or to an abstract principle.[4]

> This inability of the Syrian to accept the will of the majority without struggle and to sacrifice his own attitudes to the community welfare has been fostered and maintained by centuries of living in a city-state form of

community life which has been in existence in Syria since pre-historic times. This, together with religious sub-divisions and loyalties built around these, makes it difficult for the Syrians as a group to unite on any action.[5]

Eastern Catholic "Americanization"

If the influence of the Syrian Catholic elite was to bring them and the groups they represented into the consciousness of American Catholicism, it also helped to alter their rites to make them more acceptable to the society at large. Being in a somewhat marginal situation themselves, the Syrian select invariably were more aware of what was considered proper behavior in other American Catholic churches. Together with the clergy they transformed their rite beyond recognition. Rather than de-Arabize it, however, they choose to latinize it—for the probable reason that it was quite acceptable to have a "Syrian Church,"—at least from the point of view of Latin Catholicism. The Syrians thus chose to keep their churches to themselves, i.e., serving the ethnic group. A latinized Melkite church using Arabic and serving the Arab community was more to their liking than preserving their rite in its purity and opening it up to the American public.

This transformation of the Syrian Catholic churches into something less than recognizable appeared in various degrees and forms throughout the country and consisted of a modification of both their structures and practices. But, as H. Richard Niebuhr has pointed out, the problems of adaptation of the immigrant churches were further aggravated by the activism, voluntarism, and evangelical emphasis characteristic of the American religious scene in general.[6]

Originally, this created serious problems for the Irish Catholics, whose Church and traditions seemed, at first, particularly foreign and unadaptable to American life. The internal struggle between the Roman cultural tradition of their Church and its need for adaptability to Americanisms seemed, until very recently, to end in victory for the strict "Romanists." Ironically, the Eastern Catholic churches were structurally and organizationally more similar to American culture configurations than the Latin Church, but, being the later arrivals, they were powerless to transform or inform the established church of this. Moreover, they were more interested in maintaining the ethnic character of their churches than in adding to the religious plurality of their new homeland. Yet, it has become increasingly obvious that one need not be a Syrian to be a Melkite. In the words of the highest authority in the Melkite Church:

> . . . the style of Christian living which we call Eastern is as much American as any other. This is not a foreign way of life implanted here in an American milieu; this is as much American, as any other mode of Christian life and there are some who say that it is more in tune with American institutions than other forms of Christian living. Despite misconceptions to the contrary, our Melkite Greek Catholic rite is supranational and in no sense restricted to people of a particular ethnic background. It cannot be stressed too strongly that our Melkite way of Christian living is open to all people of all nationalities and ethnic origins.[7]

Generally ignorant of this possibility, the Syrians transformed themselves to conform to some of the more broadly shared socioreligious patterns of American religion by latinizing their rite on the levels of both symbol and ritual and, more important, that of attitude toward the nature of the Christian Church.

On the symbolic-ritual level, the purity of the Byzantine rite was lost through a process of hybridization. At one time, Archdale King could write of the Melkites that their rite "is substantially pure, and they are justifiably jealous for the correct observance of the Byzantine liturgy."[8] In America, however, they began to genuflect, began blessing themselves as Latins, insisted that Confirmation and Eucharist be given separately from Baptism, tolerated statues in their churches, more often than not built their churches without the "Ikonastasis" and domed altars, put Latin vestments on their priests, introduced Latin devotional practices, and so on. Most significantly, some parishes introduced the Latin communion host, which was given to kneeling communicants who responded with "Amen" to the priest's intonation of the Latin "Corpus Christi."

Religious symbols function as techniques or instruments for relating to some deity in a manner perceived as relevant by the communicant. They do not exist in a void, but reflect an inner attitude and disposition. Without them the interior life would have no means of expression and development. In terms of rite, symbols become the external and recognizable expression of the rite's deeper spirituality and theology. Thus, any changes in the external components necessarily induce changes on the deeper attitudinal level. Because they lacked a school system, an informed clergy, and an appreciation of their own importance, these Easterners chose to change the interior life of their rite to conform to their symbolization rather than to keep both intact and together in a more selective adaptation to their new environment.

Because they had no reasonable alternative, Melkites and Maronites internalized, in a psychodynamic sense, the logic, mentality, theology, and outlook of the Roman rite. For all practical purposes, the immigrant clergy and the immigrant generation are the only true religious Easterners in the United States. The other generations face a complex dilemma: if a parish is Byzantine in symbolization, it is Byzantine only in symbolization and probably has a laity that is Latin in attitude and mentality; if the parish is latinized in symbolization then it is probably latinized throughout. Realistically speaking, there is no Eastern Church in either case. In both instances, the "forms" of a different religious institution (Latin) were adopted by the group without the adoption of either its total purpose or total meaning. The Eastern laity was confronted with a religious and symbolic façade, a truncated spirituality, and an incoherent ritual system that was probably dysfunctional and confusing to the development of an integrated religious life.

Isolated from their Byzantine origins and traditions and only marginally accepted and mostly misunderstood by Latin Catholicism, the Syrian Easterners could not maintain that distinctiveness which could have enhanced their attractiveness to both the Eastern and Western faithful in America. For this reason, most Melkite students have condemned the latinization of the Eastern rites. Yet, it does seem that this latinization (Americanization) was a necessary factor for both making the Melkites comprehensible to the Latins and keeping the community intact.

In the first place, in their minds, to be a Roman Catholic in America was ultimately more important than the prerogatives of any single rite or tradition within that faith. To remain Catholic was the primary goal of the Syrian Catholics (even at the expense of their own traditions), and their latinization was merely an attempt to force other Catholics to recognize the validity of their Catholicism. Since symbols are incidentals and not essential to a faith, the Syrians altered them without intending to change the inner nature of the rite or its relationship to the other Syrian religious traditions present within the emerging community.

Second, the Syrian Catholics wanted to become latinized. In perceiving the social and religious milieu around them, they became acutely aware that their liturgical traditions were a source of apprehension among the Latins. The symbols that "proved" their Catholicism in the old country were the very ones that brought their faith into question in the new one. The easiest solution to the dilemma was to alter them.

Moreover, the alteration could be considered the natural consequence of emigration to the United States, as every ethnic group had to reorder aspects of its heritage to survive. Indeed, the emigration itself was tantamount to change, since the traditions of the past could never be fully reproduced out of their original cultural context. Some researchers have indicated that without some changes the adjustment process would have become so difficult that total withdrawal from the group might have increased.

In one sense, the Melkites' accommodation to American Catholicism lessened the possibility and speed of group dissolution. In another, it accelerated it by neutralizing the importance of religious differences between themselves and other Syrian religious groups. They could now mix socially with all other Syrians who were also interested in creating and sustaining a way of life that was socially inclusive yet culturally nondistinctive from the point of view of American society. They would become a tolerable American ethnic group that could be recognized by the rest of society.

In retrospect, it seems that this first attempt at Americanization not only helped Melkites and Maronites become more Americanized in the eyes of American Catholic society but also helped them keep their community together by warding off those difficulties that could have emerged from a too-rapid secular assimilation without a parallel adjustment in the religious sphere. They could now create a way of life based on selected Arabic cultural traits, termed "American Syrianisms," supported by all their religious traditions. Because they were a nationality group that wanted to acculturate, their own native religious traditions became maintainers and supporters of a new and developing

"Arab-culture religion." Their operative faith became Arab-American culture. Indeed, what sociologists often described as characteristic of the national or macrosocial level occurred on the microsocial level within the Syrian-American community.

Henceforth, Syrian-Americans would not be defined by rite or religious nation. Rather, they would be "Syrian Catholics" and their churches could now be "Syrian churches," in much the same fashion that the Italians had "Italian churches." They would become a "nationality" in the traditional or popular sense of the word and their churches would become the strongest institutional support of this new identity.

This transformation of the churches of the Syrians, then, was more than "latinization"—it was the beginning of the replacement of an old form of identification by a new, more "American" concept. It was for these Easterners an important event in the process of becoming part of a culturally pluralistic society.

Ironically, this accommodation may have come too late to stem the growing tide of disinterest in ethnic affairs characteristic of so many Americans of Syrian ancestry. After all is said and done, the processes referred to here did not in fact include a majority of the American-born Syrians. Rather, those Syrians who were active in the religious life of the community were the same ones enjoying or participating in its sociocultural life. This is the group that latinized the churches. We can refer to these people as Syrian-Americans because they do in fact identify with the community and organize much of their lives within its boundaries. Thousands of others, who prefer to be more fully American, never bothered with the life of the ethnic community. Institutionally speaking, they participate in and identify with a nonethnic social reality.

CHAPTER X

Syrian-American Religion

ALTHOUGH ETHNICITY IS AN ACCEPTABLE AND UNIQUELY American concept, it is generally viewed as a temporary or "marking time" phenomenon. The creation and maintenance of a Syrian ethnic life-style by the Melkite and Maronite immigrants was fraught with disadvantages since the "melting pot" character of American society was basically opposed to permanent ethnic differentiation. Because of the nature of group life in American society, the Syrians could not rest with the new working ethnic identity they had just created. Indeed, other ethnic groups had already merged into one of the three major religious systems that now characterize the social structure of the United States.[1] Moreover, the Syrian Catholics could not continue with their traditional Eastern religious identities within a Roman Catholic tradition that was decidedly and intentionally monolithic because this would antagonize the very host community that had to assimilate them.

The Syrian Catholics also had to resolve their relationship to the Syrian Orthodox, who were also experiencing the pangs of assimilation. Unaccepted by other American religions and intensely aware of their apostolic and historic origins, the Syrian Orthodox were not about to disappear or become just another American religious sect. They also had a constituency that was heavily Arab in culture, thought, and style. Orthodox Syrians were also interested in preserving a sense of community, fostering inmarriage, and celebrating their heritage while acculturating without disappearing as a distinctive social entity. Catholic and Orthodox Syrians were thus brought together over the ethnic-cultural issue and the problems of continuity in a foreign and ethnically indifferent social world. Syrian Catholics, of course, had different problems and institutions to contend with than the

Orthodox, but all were attempting to survive in a nation in which the myth of tolerance and encouragement of diversity was heavily propagated.

What they came to do, therefore, was to confuse or fuse their national cultural traits with their religious heritage. Almost by accident, they discovered that Americans were diversified not so much by ethnicity as by religion. They thus transformed their churches by making them important mechanisms for the preservation of their ethnicity, which now could operate under the guise of religious distinctiveness—the preferred form of American diversity. Marshall Sklare, a noted American scholar studying the same phenomenon among Jews, feels that this is an exceptional and necessary event in the battle for ethnic continuity. He writes:

> The church was one of the few institutions of the original culture capable of re-establishment in the new land. Also, since the ethnic church is the counterpart of non-ethnic institutions of the same order, it would automatically receive identical formal recognition, although of course its status position may not be on the same level. Furthermore, while ethnic separatism is not very highly valued in our culture, religious distinctiveness is allowable—even esteemed in a way because it is "American."[2]

These types of churches would now have two functions. Like all religious organizations, they sought to provide a way of facing the problem of ultimate and unavoidable frustration, of "evil," and the generalized problem of meaning in some supernatural way. They would also have the additional task of preserving a particular subculture or ethnic group.

Ethnicity passing as religion seems to have more survival potential than pure social ethnicity, which simply attempts to keep a sociocultural community together for historical-emotional reasons. The Syrian Catholics, who actively strove to be American yet socially separate from the overall society, chose to become a nationality group rather than to make American Catholicism religiously pluralistic. The Syrian Orthodox, likewise not wishing to lose their members to other faiths, had to accommodate themselves to the changing social interests and needs of their faithful until that time when a unified, American Church stressing faith emerged. Both religious groups had an interest in preserving ethnicity.

Indeed, their accommodation meant that their interests and

energies would be spent on the continuation of their cultural inheritance rather than on their religious traditions per se. Ironically, all this would happen in a nation that was beginning to succeed in creating a pluralistic society based more on religion than nationality. Even though they had no historical precedents for cooperating with one another, Syrian Catholics and Orthodox began incorporating a common ethnic heritage into their religious life-styles.

Nevertheless, the emergence of a Syrian-American community based on ethnicity was haphazard, decidedly nonuniform, sporadic, and in most places never reached completion or achieved institutional integration. The Syrians never overcame their religious biases completely. The extension of social intercourse with those of the same family and rite to social intercourse with those of the same religion and then with those of the same national background was incomplete. It never reached fruition in an overall commitment to Arab culture and its people. Religion became the extent of their nationality or ethnic identification. According to Treudley, "only Christians . . . are considered to be 'our kind of people.' "[3] Moslems, Arabic-speaking Jews, Palestinians, and Arabs in general are excluded from the in-group.

Oscar Handlin suggests, however, that a basic unifying factor available to the Syrians was language, despite the presence of strong divisive religious differences. He mentions that "Syrian societies" came to include, not simply those born in Syria, but all Arabic-speaking people.[4] American ethnic groups had long been labeled in terms of the language they used, especially when they had arrived in the country with no known national identity. Strangely enough, however, if language was going to serve as a basis for unity, then the Syrians should have been called "Arabs," not "Syrians." As Hitti notes, "There is no such thing as the 'Syrian language' of which we often hear in this country."[5] But Syrian Christians are not Arabs and rebel at being so classified since Arab really means Moslem and hence oppressor in their eyes. Rather than be identified as Arabs they became "Syrians who spoke Syrian" even though the language was really Arabic.

In the final analysis, it was the conditions of settlement that determined what type of group life the Syrians would lead in America. Arriving without any secular ideology for maintaining a separate political or social life and without an extensive knowledge of Arabic culture, they became sensitive to the multi-ethnic society they found. They recognized and respected the reality of American cultural pluralism even though this would be only a passing phenomenon. In spite of, or because of, the fact that their culture, which had provided them with both emotional and aesthetic satisfaction, had been wrenched away from its traditional milieu, they developed a myth of common origin that supplied them with a basis for a common order of living.

What they succeeded in doing was to re-create a common cultural tradition that would respect the religious prerogatives of those who would participate in it at the same time that it answered the social needs of a changing community. Culture is a basis for ethnicity insofar as it makes available a common value system and allows expectations for interpersonal behavior to be fulfilled.

Undoubtedly, it was the factor of common cultural heritage that allowed the Syrians to come together at least socially across religious lines. The fact that they did also illustrates the assertion that people who share a common culture do not have to have a common political government to form a socially integrated community.[6] At least their culture made the Syrians more similar to one another than dissimilar, and this made a fellow Syrian more agreeable than a total stranger. This did not mean, however, that they would now be able to consistently act uniformly or to create a community-wide institutional life.

Moreover, the degree to which consciousness of kind develops among people varies consistently with the treatment they encounter from outside. Maronites and Melkites and to a certain extent the Syrian Orthodox were thus brought into closer cooperation with one another as they confronted the established Americans. For example, whether these Easterners liked it or not, Americans thought them to be Turks, or non-whites, and it was desirable for them to unite to dispel these myths. Furthermore, the problems of daily existence, of death, sickness, and community organization and disorganization produced an inevitable dependency that supplied them with a motive to expand their commitments to those outside their own families.

In time, therefore, they would establish associations after their towns or origins (The Damascus Club, The Aleppian Fraternity, The Becharre Welfare Society), or their own religious traditions

(St. Vincent DePaul Society). They often used either Syrian or Lebanese national names when this was to their advantage. By so doing they could have a show of strength in the event of a major crisis like that of naturalization. They could also better keep up their ties with their scattered fellow nationals. Yet, it is the distinctive qualities of Syrian consciousness, that is, the extension of primary group contacts to only family members and/or village members within the same religious tradition, that explains the particular form of Syrian ethnicity in the United States.

In spite of their usefulness, the associations of the Syrian-American people were all apolitical. They seemed to be formed for only one purpose—the perpetuation of Arab-American culture. They were not educational, politically dynamic, controversial, nor really pertinent to the everyday survival of the community. Since the Syrian-Americans had never resolved their dislike and fear of "outsiders," a strong motivating force in forming broader Syrian-American organizations was their need and desire to increase the pool of eligible marriageables. According to Treudley

> To most of the group, Syrianisms take precedence over religious faith at the one point where they are most sharply in conflict, the marriage of a daughter since wives are expected to follow the religion of their husbands. Some parents choose to mate their daughters within their own faith, even if it means going outside the collectivity, but they seem to be exceptions to the general rule. Most parents prefer to have their children leave the church rather than cross nationality lines.[7]

Without a doubt, the question of "out-marriage" has been the deepest fear of Syrian parents since their emigration to America. Hitti's statement to this effect, while somewhat subdued, reveals their attitude accurately.

> . . . Aside from a few business partnerships and marriages between Syrians and Greeks and Armenians, the Syrians have no special relationship with any other racial group. They prefer to intermarry among themselves and those of them who are not fortunate enough to find brides here have to go to Syria for them.[8]

The common complaint aired by Syrian parents when marriage to a non-Arab is proposed is that "we don't know their family."

Knowing the family is the primary means available to them for locating the individual and dealing with him properly. Treudley even goes as far as saying that membership in the collectivity does not rest so much on the country of origin as it does on the biological position of the individual. "The collectivity is less a nationality group to the ordinary person than a union of extended kinships."[9]

While all immigrants have disliked out-marrying, the Syrians make no small case about their disdain for it. Their attitude toward out-marrying has been summarized by one researcher:

> In one of the larger cities, the purpose of a certain "Syrian-Lebanese club," as claimed by many people (even of the second generation) is to "let the Syrian and Lebanese young people meet each other in order to marry from their own nationality." In another large city, the spontaneous reaction of some members of the "Ladies' Sodality" concerning a group of non-Melkite female college students volunteering to form a choir for the Melkite Church was: "It is no good. These young girls will make acquaintance with our boys and steal them from us."[10]

Undoubtedly, the distinctive qualities of family life in the United States also helped make the need for anchorage to a larger group particularly acute. As Handlin suggests, American families and adjusting immigrant families were often physically and socially isolated from each other. The latter, thrown back on their own resources, suffered uncertainty as to the roles of their members. This frequently produced severe internal tensions. "Such conditions increased the desire for identification with a group that would provide the family with roots in the past, locate it in the larger society, and supply it both with a pattern of approved standards of behavior and with the moral sanctions to aid in maintaining internal discipline."[11]

And so, as we have indicated, a Syrian ethnic group-consciousness emerged with its cultural traditions, its broad links to the past, and its pride in its Christian origins. But this ethnic consciousness was not alone sufficient to maintain the community nor could it have continued to provide Syrian families with the broad philosophical perspectives, cultural integrity, and institutional completeness they so sorely needed.

Their lack of a common secular history and their confusion over their identity made it impossible for them to successfully sustain their ethnic community. Indeed, Naseer Aruri states quite categorically that "Arabic-speaking Americans" are "incapable of creating group-wide institutions to work for common ends."[12] Similarly, Morroe Berger writes that "family ties have been strong enough to preclude active interest in the wider community. . . . It is as though the Syrians' capacity for relating themselves to others . . . was exhausted by the family and the group from the same village in the old country."[13] Even though the Syrian people in the United States have modified their cultural inheritance somewhat, they have really never fully disengaged themselves from that strong consciousness of small-town identity which previously characterized their life abroad.

But when they did accept and utilize their national identity, they were able to constitute themselves something of a community within the larger urban centers where they settled.

> The social-psychological boundaries of this subcommunity are clear and definite, although they do not follow the lines of an ecological pattern. One clear manifestation of this is the Church. . . . Through its rituals, festivals, priest and social activities, the Church is a clear expression of community consciousness and identity.[14]

It was a community characterized by social intercourse and the free flow of news from family to family. There is literally a grapevine of information which transcends the previous structures of the community. This is sustained by the extended kinship system, which also acts as a liaison between the individual and the community. In commenting on the effects of a shared culture in a structurally splintered ethnic group, priest-sociologist Constantine Volaitis succinctly summarizes the situation:

> The Syrian community still maintains a strong extended kinship system even though marked by separation into Orthodox, Catholic and Protestant divisions. The important factor is identification with the Syrian community as a whole and especially with the larger family group from which one descends. Many Syrian parishes are practically a kinship system in themselves with almost everyone related in one way or another.[15]

Involvement with the family is really involvement in microcosm with the total ethnic community. Even if a particular individual renounces his ethnic affiliation, he still participates in ethnicity when the clan gathers to celebrate some collective event.

Since families tend to be religiously homogeneous, and since families maintain ties to one of the three religious traditions of the community, to be identified as "Syrian-American" would have to mean being identified with one of its religious institutions —that is, being Syrian Orthodox, Maronite, or Melkite Catholic. Conversely, association with one of these churches means being engulfed in a network of "processed" Arabic culture.

The primary interest and function of the churches became preserving ethnicity and attracting the American-born Syrians simply because they were all *wlad Arab* (children of the Arab East) and not because they had a religious obligation to serve a distinct community of believers. As we see it, it is difficult to speak of Syrian-Americans as ethnics without assuming that they are in fact actively involved in the life of their churches, since these are the main institutions founded by the immigrants and maintained today. Syrian-Americans not affiliated with any Syrian institutions are really Americans of Syrian ancestry.

In the words of Elaine Hagopian, the Syrians concentrated "on building their churches which became the focal points for most of their social, cultural, religious, and interpersonal activities."[16] The churches, consequently, became "ghetto-oriented," with membership in them presupposing some desire for identification with "Arabic-speaking people" or culture. This happened as they latinized for religious acceptance.

As such, the churches of the Syrians—romanized, Americanized and bastardized—emerged as additional pillars of Syrian ethnicity. It may have seemed contradictory for these churches, which had divested themselves of their Eastern symbols, ritual, attitude, and theology, to become powerful forces in the development of an ethnic consciousness. But it was through their activity in the nonreligious areas of social life that direction and control were rendered to the ethnic interests of the Syrians and hence to their self-perception as a culturally distinct American group.

The Syrians' ethnicity made them "hyphenated" Americans, but they solved this dilemma by making their churches especially ethnic and retaining their separateness and distinctiveness in a disguised and more acceptable form. Thus, the emerging Syrian ethnic group was based not only on its familial structure but also on its churches, which, while providing a scheme of salvation for their members, also had to preserve the culture of the group itself. The churches became the central institution which held the greatest promise of keeping some form of ethnic consciousness alive and transmittable.

Furthermore, since each religious group shared in a common Arabic culture pattern, it was possible to use culture as the basis for developing a recognizable unity across religious preferences.

Religiously there may be Christian, Moslem or Jewish centers, but should they gather at social functions the customs and foods prevailed in Arabic preference for their basic culture. They then became indiscernible as Arabic speaking people who hold one common bond: their language, food and social amenities.[17]

Because they had an orientation toward American society that was positive if not imitative, the American "Syrianisms" they sought to maintain in America were highly selective and specific. Furthermore, the Syrians never fully duplicated a complete Arabic life here because they were never fully convinced of its utility outside the social sphere. They had no ideological commitment to the politics of the Near East or to its total way of life. Chronicler Louise Houghton notes that even in 1911 there were a number of opinions prevalent in the Syrian community concerning the usefulness of Arabic culture and colony life, but "the dominant view," she wrote, "is that colony life is a mistake. The new immigrant should live among Americans, and though it would be very hard in the beginning, it would be much better in the end. In colony life, he cannot grasp American ideals."[18]

Even attempts at maintaining the Arabic language were not seriously undertaken because it was too "difficult" and there was no value in its continued use. Spoken Arabic also varies by district and many dialects are spoken. Speaking Arabic was a mark of foreignness and, therefore, of inferior origin. Indeed, such an attitude was publicly promulgated by the Arabic newspaper *Al-Wafa*, and reflected the confidence the Syrians had in their plans to be Americans while maintaining their own communal life.

Al-Wafa eagerly encouraged the Americanization of its readers. Instead of the self-conscious talk about retaining the mother tongue, *Al-Wafa* said simply: "Study English because it will help you earn money." It suggested that the Syrians use the United States as a college and take advantage of the great opportunity that was theirs. No immigrant should presume to improve the "magnificent constitution." The Syrian who did things the American way would get ahead much faster than the one who tried to retain the old customs.[19]

Yet, other issues of the same paper did carry articles supporting the general idea of separate Syrian schools and churches. This ambivalence mirrored that of the community, which was trying to be American yet ethnic at the same time. Such a situation helps explain the decline of the strong literary tradition in the American Arabic press. In South America, by contrast, where Syrians confronted a culture they held to be inferior to their own, and an economy and political system no more enlightened than the one they had fled, Arabic language, literature, and culture flourished. Undoubtedly, an intervening variable here would be the early ties North America established in the Middle East which made Syrians more aware and envious of the North American way of life.

Furthermore, the Arabic-speaking immigrants themselves were able to bring only an abbreviated culture with them. They were basically illiterate and acquainted only with those family and village customs of members low in the social structure.

Syrianisms had a simple meaning: food habits, crafts, music and dancing, the rites of hospitality, authoritarian family patterns, the closeness and warmth of family ties, a religious ritual with many common features, whether the church was Maronite, Melchite or Eastern Orthodox.[20]

A common though superficial style permeated the group's living and patterned all its expressive activities in the United States. It determined, for example, what foods were bought at what seasons of the year and in what quantities, as well as how they were to be cooked and eaten. It gave a touch of exotic color to conversation, provided idiomatic terms for the phrasing of friendships, and added a characteristic informality even to the most formal meetings. For most members of the ethnic group, Syrianisms consist only of these attributes and little more.

The Ethnic Commitment

The broadening of Syrian consciousness, as shallow as it was, could have taken place only at the expense of the old and narrower identity with church, rite, and home town. As it was, it produced a basic alteration of the value system of the Syrians. The people who previously would not allow strong social ties to develop outside their own family now actively participate in public affairs where their children can meet any variety of "Syrian." This represents a major change from the action patterns and identities of the past. The attitude that "any Syrian is better than no Syrian" is now commonplace.

The Melkite Catholic Church of Brooklyn, for example, inaugurated its Catholic Youth Organization in the fall of 1965 only to find that nearly 50 percent of its registered members were non-Melkite Syrians of either the Syriac, Armenian, Latin, or Maronite rites. Strictly speaking, the church in question was responsible for and to Byzantine Melkites only. Yet it has increasingly relied on non-Melkites for support and there are now over 150 non-Melkite families registered with the parish.

These families are Eastern rite in origin but lack a church and clergy of their own. Catholic canon law recommends that such families choose the rite most similar to their own for identification purposes. Nevertheless, attachment to another Eastern Church is not pursued out of a desire to stay Eastern Catholic but stems for many out of a fear of disappearing or being absorbed by American society. The fear is that of loss of ethnic heritage—especially through intermarriage. Many families thus associate with an Eastern-rite church simply because they want their children to meet other Syrians.

The subordination of Eastern-rite religious identity (Melkite or Maronite) or religion (Catholic or Orthodox) to ethnic identity (Syrian or Lebanese) received additional impetus in the summer of 1969 when the various and traditionally divided elements of the Arabic-speaking community of Paterson, New Jersey, collectively sponsored an Arabic picnic (*mahrajan*) which drew nearly 3,500 people from all over the Northeast. Previously, each church in the city had sponsored its own summer affair so that three or four such events took place annually. For the first time in the fifty-year history of the community all three religious groups (Melkite, Syrian Orthodox, Armenian-rite Catholic) sponsored a single event. (Interestingly, the *mahrajan* was held at a Jewish-American day camp during the time the Syrians were raising funds for Arab refugees in the Middle East.)

Not unexpectedly, there is some ambivalence toward this type of socializing. So each of the principal Syrian religious organizations (Melkite, Maronite, and Syrian Orthodox) also sponsors its own weekend-long convention in rotating cities throughout the country. On any Fourth of July weekend, there are more than 10,000 Syrian-Americans collectively participating in one or another of these conventions. While they are in-group oriented and intended to serve the needs of the sponsoring organization, a recent effort to separate the dates of the conventions so they won't conflict has been highly supported. In 1968, the largest contingent of representatives at the Maronite convention in Hartford, Connecticut, were the Melkites of Brooklyn and Paterson. At the Melkite convention in New York in 1965, the Syrian Orthodox were disproportionately represented on the high side as were the Maronites. At the 1969 Orthodox convention in New York, Melkites and Maronites traveled from all over New England to the Waldorf-Astoria rather than travel to the Midwest for their own conventions.

The motivating force here was undoubtedly attachment not to rite but to nationality and culture. That Maronite and Melkite Catholics should accept each other's participation in their own conventions and those of the non-Catholic Orthodox is a rather important and striking indication of the direction the collectivity has taken concerning its ethnic identity.

It was the similarity in content at each convention that brought the Syrian-Lebanese together across religious lines. All "Syrian conventions," as they are popularly called, share in the same basic symbolism regardless of their particular intent:

> The collectivity is most responsive to the intermingling of American and Syrian symbolism. . . . American culture provides the formal ends for such an organization and techniques for their achievement, while Syrian culture adds the colorful dances and pageantry that make for vivid enjoyment.[21]

Because all three national religious organizations present the same Arabic-American sociocultural program in addition to their own religious specialties, it really makes no difference to the Syrians which convention they attend since the primary objective will be met at any one of them, namely, to meet and socialize with other Americans of Syrian ancestry. For the Syrian-Americans, then, church and rite became part and parcel of the immigrant Arab heritage. They not only became intertwined with the culture of the ethnic group but became secondary in importance to it. Indeed, in religious terms, there is a definite decline in the attachment of people to their rite for purely religious reasons. Most American Melkites, for example, not only fulfill their Sunday obligations in Latin churches but rarely if ever use the Melkite churches for religious services other than baptism, marriage, and burial—all three required to be done in their own church by canon law.

The social affairs of any Syrian parish are more highly organized, more appreciated, and better attended than any specifically religious event except those held on the high holidays like Easter and Christmas. Churches that are crowded to capacity for Arabic social affairs are less than half-filled on Sundays. Since the immigrant Syrians were a collectivity intent on self-preservation, it became quite reasonable for their churches to support their social needs. Religiously, the churches were part of the ethnic heritage but not viable religious institutions in their own right. Moreover, the content of Eastern spirituality in the United States has been sufficiently minimized by the churches' failure to establish formal channels of religious transmission, like seminaries and Sunday schools, and the inability of clerics to maintain the purity of their religious traditions.

Being acculturated, the Syrians were not interested in maintaining Arabic culture per se, but they were interested in a separate social life—the specific content of which was never really enumerated. Thus, their churches tried to contain primary group ties within the collectivity while letting only secondary relations develop with the outside world. Consequently, those who became leaders of the ethnic group were, for all practical purposes, leaders in the church. Some students of assimilation believe that when this is so, rejection of one will automatically lead to rejection of the other. This is probably true.

With regard to the Syrians, however, rejection or lack of identification with their churches stemmed from other sources. To begin with, Syrian religiosity, as measured by church attendence, has never really declined in America. Indeed, as in the old country, almost all Syrian-Americans attend some church (Eastern or Western) on Sundays and holy days.[22] However, although religiosity didn't decline, it did change its orientation. Like other

American ethnic groups, the Syrians became more religious as they became more acculturated. But the Catholic Syrians generally transferred their allegiance from the Melkite and Maronite rites to the Latin or "American" rite in greatly increasing numbers. To the broader society, they wished to be known as American Catholics.

A survey of the disposition of second- and third-generation Melkite Syrians reveals that 46 percent of the second generation and 55 percent of the third actually identify with the Latin rite when asked what rite or church they consider themselves members of.[23] It seems that in their private lives they would be Syrian-Americans with access to their own churches when they needed or wanted them. Interestingly, they almost always refer to the Melkite Church in their daily parlance as the "Syrian Church," and as they became more American and/or mobile they became less Melkite identified.

The survey also reveals a more selective attachment by Melkites to their rite, since over half the respondents prefer to regularly use the facilities of the Latin church. We can conclude from this that identification as Melkite does not necessarily have to entail attendance at a Melkite church or consideration of this church as one's own. We are implying that identification with the Melkite rite may have nothing to do with reasons of history or faith but is a response to ethnicity.

For a substantial majority of both generations of Melkites who consider themselves Latin-rite Catholics, the Melkite Church is essentially a "Syrian Church." Those who vary from this opinion could be those educated parishioners who are attached to the rite for purely religious reasons. Our data probably mean that Syrians tend to accept "ethnic pluralism" as the basis for American life. Whether they are Latin identified or not, they support the notion of "pluralistic" Catholicism. But they do so from the perspective of "national churches" that serve ethnic communities rather than from an understanding of Catholicism's traditional pluralism of rite.

Originally, the Syrians' awareness of Catholic multiplicity came from their exposure to Eastern Christian plurality. However, this gave way to an acceptance of ethnic pluralism as legitimate and basically American. Essentially, the Syrians have come to believe that it is the right and duty of churches to support and serve the ethnic-social needs of their people. They are reasserting the right of churches and communities to be ethnic and yet American. But they are also saying that it may not always be the individual's desire to be ethnically identified.

The Latin-identified in our study are *not* saying they are identified with the Latin or American Church because the Melkite Church is too Arabic. On the contrary, they are probably so identified because it better suits their needs as a mobile, middle-class ethnic group.

Conversely, we can expect the Melkite-identified in our study to have a stronger attachment to their "latinized" Church because this Church is committed to maintaining an Arabic cultural tradition. The Church for them is a "Syrian Church." Yet it is an American Church as well, because it is now a "national church," and Catholicism has long since recognized their validity. The Latin identified would also see the Melkite Church not only as Syrian but also as a church with the duty to be ethnic so that it may better serve its clientele.

The Present Situation

As specialist in the field of American religion, Will Herberg has written "those who rejected their ethnic identification or felt uncomfortable in it transformed this rejection to the Church and religion of their immigrant parents."[24] He apparently feels that the second generation's eagerness to be American led to their wholesale rejection of ethnicity and the churches that are a part of it.

Although we subscribe generally to his thesis and although this occurrence is reflected somewhat in the following passage by an American-born Melkite pastor, our experience with American Syrians shows a minimum of culture conflict as the basis for ethnic "rejection," as little as there was of it among the Syrians.

> For too long our people have been treating St. Nicholas Church like a poor relative whom we don't want to turn out into the cold but whom we'd just as soon have nothing to do with. We have unconsciously been treating St. Nicholas not just as a foreigner but even as an alien who can never become a citizen. Some of us honestly admit we look down on St. Nicholas simply because we lack the charity and the courage to treat it like anything more than a Syrian-Lebanese institution which we use like

a temporary toy or pacifier instead of a necessary and important organization. . . . St. Nicholas is as Catholic as any other parish in the Diocese and even a little more so than the others. It not only shares in the social and sanctifying oneness of all of Catholicism but it makes a strong contribution and exerts a dynamic influence on its life. Recognize this and be proud of its lofty commitments and its many legitimate Catholic potentials. Its members are American citizens, who whether they love their national cultures or not, are still Americans whose prime function as Christians is to worship God in a special way and have a very important contribution to make to American Christianity.[25]

These remarks reflect the cleric's belief in the possibility and need for freeing the rite from dependence on ethnicity if it is to stem rejection by the assimilating second and third generations. Theologically, this would also be more in line with the nature and disposition of the Eastern Church. For Melkites like this cleric, the Eastern Catholic rites can and should survive by adapting to the culture they are living in and by serving the needs of all people who find these religious perspectives relevant.

Since the Syrian Catholics have not succeeded in creating a strong ideology for social inclusiveness and because they can't see their rites surviving independently of an Arab community (which, it must be assumed, is surviving), they may very well be fostering wholesale absorption into American society through the medium of American Catholicism.

Although the Syrians, at first, generally avoided full entry into the institutional life of American Catholicism, their children's continuous confrontation with it and their change of identity altered the situation drastically. Until recently, the Syrians never really sought identification with or found meaningful roles within the institutions of American Catholicism. Indeed, their intermingling with the "Latins" stopped at the church door. If and when they adopted the external forms of the Latin rite, they never fully succeeded in adopting its deeper content. The Syrian Melkites themselves, for example, were just interested in being passively accepted—even if this occurred at the expense of their own religious traditions and distinctiveness.

To use Witterman's concept, they were "structurally marginal,"[26] i.e., they were ecclesiastically separate (at least theoretically) and unique, yet made part of the Roman diocese. But later, tolerated by the Roman Catholics, yet never fully understood, accepted, or encouraged, they became liturgical hybrids with a negative self-evaluation. They actually internalized the symbols, goals, and style of the dominant, nonmarginal Latin Catholics. Melkites and Maronites became for all practical purposes "Latins" in both spiritual and theological affairs. When they came under the jurisdiction of American Latin priests, it became even more difficult for them not to internalize Latin values and lose control of their own collective destiny. Religion, again, was splitting the Syrian-American community.

The Syrian children's attachment to the Catholic faith became cemented by their strong tie to the Latin Catholic parochial school system and the parish that sponsored it, even though such ties could not help but weaken their understanding of and attachment to their own rites and culture. For the Syrians, attendance at a parochial school meant acceptance of their Eastern Catholicism by the Romans. The schools, however, looked at them as "ethnic Catholics" who needed to be Americanized. They were not perceived as Eastern Catholics who should be encouraged to maintain their traditions. Parents were not able or in a position to ask the schools to teach the Syrian students about their religious rites, and consequently knowledge of them declined even further.

Syrian Eastern-rite Catholics were fearful that the schools they helped build would be closed to them if they insisted upon religious training in their rite for their children. Some parents even insisted upon baptism in the Latin rite to ensure their children's entrance into the parochial school. Moreover, the school created even stronger ties between parents and the local sponsoring parish church, and as it became more of a burden to support two churches (Melkite and Latin), many parents opted for support of the Latin parish since their children were in its school system.

It is our impression, however, that many Syrian Catholic parents still supported their Eastern Churches, and while their children were becoming latinized they themselves steered clear of intensive affiliation with the organizations, clubs, et cetera, of the Latin parishes. They could do this because they really expected their children to be "Syrians" first rather than Melkites or Maronites. Thus, their churches would hold on to the ethnic content making them a Syrian American social club and they could be Catholics "like everyone else." The church was to exist for the people's use when they wanted to be identified by nationality, and the churches were to maintain the illusion that a real Arabic culture was indeed alive and available. It was only among a small minority that the religious traditions were appreciated for their own relevance and usefulness.

The result of this is that today, however unintentionally, Syrian Catholics have become active in the institutional and social life of the various Latin parishes they live in. They are now ushers, altar boys, choir singers, bingo and bazaar workers, chaperones, priests, and nuns in greater numbers than in their own Eastern-rite parishes. The following revealing account was reported by a young Melkite woman. It indicates the present content of Arab ethnicity and the relationship between Syrian Eastern-rite Catholics and American Catholicism:

> After "our" successful bazaar at St. Anselm's (Latin) there was a party for the staff workers. There were so many Syrians there that I thought I was at a "Hafli" (Syrian party). In fact, we told the band to play "Hava Nagila" (Jewish) and and we got up and did the Debke (folk dance) for everyone.[27]

At least in this parish, then, Syrian Catholics prefer to be recognized as another ethnic group. They are becoming assimilated because they have given up their own religious "particularisms" in favor of those of the dominant religious group. They became "Syrian, Latin Catholics." Predictably enough, neither the Latins nor the Easterners fully recognize the consequences of such behavior for these Eastern Christians. Canonically, Syrian Catholics will always be Easterners and will be treated as such when they can be recognized. Their official association with Latin Catholicism can only be peripheral or marginal. When they have something to offer the Latins like time, money, skills, and so on, they are welcomed, but when they need the services of the Latins to help them maintain their Eastern religious ritual then they suddenly become "Melkites" or "Maronites" who must look after their own.

This was emphasized quite strongly in the late 1960's when the Brooklyn Melkites attempted to build a youth center for their children in Bay Ridge, where most Syrians live. According to the Melkite pastor in Brooklyn,

We were repeatedly told by the Latin diocese that we cannot build a church in Bay Ridge even though we only requested a youth center and chapel there. This is in spite of the fact that most of our congregation is located there and our own Melkite bishop told us to go ahead. In their last letter to me, the Latins told me that I can go ahead with it, but said that if I did, they would like a list of all our students in Catholic schools so that they could "tax" us for using "their facilities." It seems when we build convents for them, donate money to their building funds we are accepted, but when we need something as basic as this, we are Melkites who are at their benevolent mercy. They act as if Catholic schools were only for Latins and that we are non-Catholic. What would happen to me if I decided to build? How many parents would support me under these conditions, two or three percent?[28]

With some variation the above situation has been repeated in nearly all Eastern-rite communities in the United States. Those who stay identified with their ethnic churches are older, more resigned, and essentially unaware of their prerogatives as Eastern Catholics. On the other hand, others stay identified with their Eastern churches when they deliberately desire an "ethnic" or ghetto existence or when they seek an identity in ethnic terms.

Syrians stay identified with their Eastern-rite churches when their tie to ethnicity is greater than their tie to Latin Catholicism, and when they must because Latin Catholicism cannot serve them ritually at the time of birth, marriage, or death. The churches then sponsor ethnic programs suited to those who are in fact actively affiliated with the parishes. And they come to reinforce their ethnic identity because the people attached to the churches are those who are ethnically inclined to begin with.

CHAPTER XI

Hazardous Survival: Syrian-American Ethnicity

THE NEW ETHNIC IDENTITY CREATED BY THESE DISPLACED Middle Easterners helped them maintain their independence from the rest of american society. However, it also introduced problems. While their ethnicity is delaying complete assimilation, it is also facilitating it by making a separate communal life impractical and functionless by reducing its ethnic content to a nondistinctive level. American Catholicism may now absorb them in the same way that it integrated its Irish, German, Polish, and Italian elements. Seemingly, Catholic nationality groups either become absorbed into the larger Catholic whole or remain isolated from the mainstream of American life. The Syrians were active integrationists as long as assimilation did not mean the complete destruction of their community.

It is this attempt at maintaining a separate social life that reveals the underlying Syrian attitude toward the nature of American society in general. The Syrian has come to appreciate, recommend, and insist upon "cultural pluralism" as the most acceptable way of expressing his attachment both to America and to his own small community. For him, the social reality of America is multiplicity in ethnicity just as much as in religion. And the Syrians managed to fuse both so successfully that the presence of one was intimately bound up with the presence of the other. For them, one is being fully American precisely when he is being an ethnic and/or religious.

Ethnicity and Acculturation

The development of ethnic self-consciousness among the Syrians was a reaction to social, economic, political, and religious factors. Always fearing rejection as non-Americans (or non-whites or hostile aliens), the Syrians necessarily became deeply attached to American political ideals though not active in political life. As in Syria, they merely wanted to be a tolerated and unharrassed minority. Thus, practically all articles written about them in the United States cite their devotion and patriotism to their adopted nation. As law-abiding Americans, however, who identified primarily with the United States, they became only peripherally interested in the politics and culture of the Arab world.

Assimilation, then and the potential rejection of ethnic identity among the American-born Syrians reflected the somewhat paradoxical position and attitude of the group itself toward both assimilation and American society. Whatever ethnic rejection was taking place was not overly visible because there was nothing particularly foreign or distinctive to reject. Their basic orientation and attitude toward American society and its values probably served as a link with the culture at the same time that it allowed for a transformation of their own cultural traditions into something less Arab and more recognizably American.

Indeed, as has been previously indicated modification of Syrian values was not urgently necessary. They arrived as ready-made Yankees! Thus, a comparison of these and other already mentioned "Syrian values" with those American value configurations suggested by Robin Williams and John Gillen[1] (like achievement drives) reveals a marked similarity. Moreover, Syrian social organization shows that behavioral similarity to Americans can prevail along with ethnic group structural pluralism, that is, Syrians participate in American economic, educational, and political systems at the same time that they pursue their other cultural and social objectives.

It is for this reason that the wholesale rejection of ethnic identity usually characteristic of assimilating second-generation Americans did not generally take place and when it did occur it did so in a selective way and was not induced by culture inadequacy or characterized by extreme culture rejection. Consequently, no great return to Syrian folkways or mores on the part of the subsequent generation of Syrians has taken place. The cultural deposit (including the religious tradition) has been altered so much that there is nothing distinctive or dysfunctional to reject or to return to. Syrian-Americans thus lack a rationale for staying ethnically inclusive.

To be sure, individual Syrians relate and have related differently to their ethnic group during the past half century. In addition to those who have renounced their ethnic heritage, Habib Katibah classifies Syrian-Americans into three groups:

> There is the clannish group, impervious to forces of integration; there is the cosmopolitan group, too easily and often superficially integrated; and there is the more enlightened heritage conscious and American conscious group. This last group, intensely aware of its ancient heritage and the problems of adoption to American life . . . has made the most distinct contributions to 1) an enlarged concept of American life, and 2) the future destiny of America.[2]

Katibah not only indicates the Syrian's attitude toward acculturation without assimilation but reveals the availability of dual life-styles or group memberships for them. The Syrians' philosophy can perhaps be construed as follows: "All Americans belong to some group whether chosen or not. We, therefore, offer our children the possibility of a group life based on values and a life-style distinctly in line with American life yet still ethnically and socially inclusive." In the private sector, they could now engage in a social life based on American Syrianisms.

Ethnic identification would provide the Syrians with a frame of reference that would locate and identify them and order their social relationships. As Andrew Greely says,

> Is everyone an ethnic? Do we all belong to some larger collectivity that stands between the family and society and is somehow based on common origins? . . . My own inclination is to say that most all of us need some collectivity with which to identify ourselves and that many, if not most of us, are still inclined to fall back on the primordial bonds of blood and land.[3]

This would be especially so if the cultural traits involved in the ethnic activities were predominantly those from which the individual could secure a variety of gratifications, especially in the area of friendship and socializing, which was precisely the case with the Syrians.

The ethnic collectivity known as the "Syrian-American community," then, exists as an alternate course of identification for the American born. To choose it rather than some other is more or less to align oneself with a network of cultural traditions that are essentially American yet borne by Syrians. It is a voluntary form of association that does not greatly conflict, in style, with American cultural values or traditions. Indeed, it becomes an acceptable form of identity in a society that prides itself on its tolerance and pluralism. As sociologist Amitai Etzoni says,

> American society is not a "society" . . . and is not a universal melting pot, into which all ethnic groups "blend" sooner or later, by accepting the dominant culture of the one "real" American tradition. It is as has often been pointed out a pluralistic society with many subcultures and subgroups. All integrated groups accept some values, the universal values of American society, but at the same time hold their own particularistic tradition and values; they also maintain their segregating norms in many spheres in which the American society is open to alternative values and norms of behavior.[4]

The Syrian community exists as such because people wish it to exist and it persists insofar as people wish to identify with it. For this reason it has been able to maintain itself in varied forms over the past half century. As Morroe Berger notes, "All studies of Syrian life in the United States emphasize the community's cohesion, its powerful loyalties to place and family, the high degree of control the group exercises over the individual and the extraordinary concern of each member for all the others."[5] Yet the cultural opportunities it offers its adherents are those which are essentially American in addition to those modified Arabic customs which revolve around food, music, and folk dancing. This emphasis on sociability did not mean that the community was organizationally and structurally integrated across religious lines. To the casual observer, the Syrians appear to belong to a tight-knit community simply because people are now superficially mixing with each other across religious lines, i.e., they attend the same dances together.

Moreover, there are many indications that the Syrians have become acculturated in both their social and political behavior. According to Naseer Aruri, the Lebanese (Syrian) community of Springfield, Massachusetts, "does not deviate sharply from the population at large in such social characteristics as birthrate, income, education, occupation and urbanization, and in such political behavior as the attachment to a particular political party or certain ideological outlook. . . ."[5] These characteristics as well as the adjustments and changes introduced into their institutional and social life have helped the Syrians to minimize wholesale ethnic rejection by succeeding generations.

The dislocation of cultural components that usually occurs during assimilation and that leads to ethnic group rejection and dissolution was minimized among the Syrian-Americans for several reasons. First, the fact that the immigrants themselves spoke English, were financially successful, and did not attempt to completely retard acculturation lessened the probability that their offspring would either feel less American or develop disjunctive personalities. Assimilation in economic terms was simply a one-generation phenomenon for most Syrians, i.e., it was the immigrant generation that more or less accumulated the wealth that was sustained by their children and used to bring them into ever-wider contact with American society. It can be argued that latinization, the unique process of religious accommodation to American society the Syrians underwent, was merely the religious equivalent of a rapid integration into the culture and life-style of the American middle class.

Similarly, Marcus Hansen suggests that, in general, successive generations no longer feel the urgent need to reject their ethnicity once their speech becomes the same as other Americans' and when their wealth is similar to that of their fellow citizens.[7] By analogy, it would seem that children born of parents with these characteristics would feel more secure in their ethnic identification than those who are not, and hence they would not utilize the mechanisms of rejection as a means of affirming some other identity.

Second, rather than being an interference, the extended family system of the Syrians probably was helpful in supplying them with ideals, goals, motivations, and business connections. Furthermore, unlike those of other immigrant groups, the Syrian family system was "accommodatingly" patriarchal. This not only kept the family intact during the assimilation process but directed its general development as well. Note that studies of Italian-Americans relate the role of family dissolution to the decline of patriarchal authority during Americanization.[8] On the other hand, the Syrians seemed not to have great difficulty transfering authority to their wives and then children as they matured.

The early Syrian immigrants encountered the hard economic conditions of the Great Depression, but their experience with subsistence-level living in Syria helped them to survive and prosper again. They found that economic opportunities existed for those who were willing to invest their energies and time in enterprises that could not directly be adversely affected by the economic cycle. "Grocery stores, restaurants, . . . itinerant peddling," writes Elkholy, "helped the Arab-American family to exceed the average income of all American families in this period."[9]

Undoubtedly, an important determinant in the upward mobility of the Syrian family was the position of women in its structure and their relationship to the outside world. In a study of the Syrians of Chicago, author Safia Haddad notes that the economic goals of the family had been stressed from the very start. Consequently, the entire family was organized toward that end.

> . . . While the Syrian man peddled notions, curios, and underwear, his wife often baked and sold bread or made kimonos and aprons at home. His children were often sent out to sell papers or peddle other items at a very early age. . . . Thus, economic self-sufficiency being a primary objective of the Syrian family in the homeland, labor was divided between the sexes and even children did their share.[10]

It is Haddad's thesis that the success of the family in economic terms cannot be understood without reference to the woman's position in the family, i.e., her early emancipation from dependence on her spouse. In many respects American women are only now catching up with them. Once in this country, the Syrian woman used and adapted all her traditional skills. Consequently, her spatial world changed considerably. Most important, she was learning English at the same time and as well as her husband. Many Syrian businesses were jointly owned and operated by husband and wife.[11] Since the Syrian man was dependent on his wife as a moneymaking agent for the family, the woman's position was made ambivalent within the home and considerably more secure in the overall community.

Given the Syrians' history and fear of outsiders, it is not surprising that their women made their families into productive economic units. Unfortunately, however, the women's entrance into the middle class on their own right made retention of ethnicity somewhat problematic for them. In most societies, it is the woman's role to socialize children into the expected cultural mode. An English-speaking, business-oriented, Syrian-American mother could hardly be expected to be the agent for ethnocultural transmission. Yet, in a culture where home life was highly stressed, where visiting and entertaining at home constituted the major form of relaxation, and where food symbolized friendliness and hospitality, the fact that women worked did not relieve them of the responsibility of taking care of the household. Only now the responsibility for cultural continuity would have to be shared with the institutions of the community if it was to be successful.

Women thus took on the additional tasks of being achievers and business agents in the outside world. Perhaps it was this equality between the spouses as well as the freedom of movement and association that has helped keep the Syrian family relatively intact and stable. On the other hand, this type of accommodation must also have informed them of options in careers, life-styles, and values outside the family. Ethnic enclosure made less sense with each passing decade. A mother's ability and confidence in ethnic continuity must be weakened in a situation where most of her daily contacts are in nonethnic settings. Not surprisingly, "twenty percent of the second generation," studied by Elkholy "and seventy-one percent of the third neither understand nor read Arabic."[12]

Social Life in the Community

As we have said, the Syrians have been so successful in Americanizing that they have become more or less nondistinctive and their success may actually help dissolve their community. If anything, it certainly has weakened their hopes for social inclusiveness. Nevertheless, if the Syrian-American community was to continue, it had to develop loyalty and the desire for preservation among its members. It had to stress certain actions as required in the interest of the collectivity, disapprove of others as incompatible with its integrity, and organize a system of sanctions to enforce the desired behavior. The Syrians accomplished this by maintaining the extended family as the primary form of interactive behavior. When Syrian families gather together in their homes, it is a celebration on a small scale of other realities as well, that is it is also a gathering of Melkites or Maronites, Aleppians or people of Damascus. The whole community is reproduced in miniature.

Indeed, the Syrian-Lebanese community as a whole became marked by absorption into American values and social structures, while it retained other identities as the basis for relating members of the community to each other.[13] The family remained the bearer as well as the preserver of ethnicity, rite, and religion, and yet it existed somewhat independently of them. The social life of the community was family oriented—the family was expected to participate in it as a unit.

The Syrians have also established a network of formal agencies for the preservation and broadcasting of information important to the collectivity. They began early to organize for the satisfaction of social needs and to solve collective problems. As they did so, they kept pace with the changing character of the ethnic community itself. As they advanced in wealth and social status they proceeded to change the character and nature of their organizations so as not to offend their members or make them incompatible with their new interests. They developed two organizations of national appeal which aided them in giving expression to American ideals and at the same time permitted them to maintain a somewhat separate social life.

The National ALSAC organization (previously called American Lebanese-Syrian Associated Club and now called Aiding Leukemia Stricken American Children) is almost entirely administered by American Syrian-Lebanese and maintains an Arabic character. As a nonprofit charitable organization devoted to raising funds for Saint Jude's Hospital, it has become the center of Syrian and Lebanese philanthropy in this country. While open to all and serving all races and creeds, the social life of the organization is basically Arabic.

ALSAC represents an exceptional display of group solidarity for a worthy cause that is not purely ethnic in purpose. Entertainer Danny Thomas had promised to build a hospital if he became a success. Fulfilling his obligation, he built Saint Jude's Hospital in Memphis, Tennessee, where leukemia research is conducted and children treated. Indeed, he has an enormous capacity for rallying the Syrian-Lebanese behind his annual campaign to raise funds for the hospital. The social activities at the organization's conventions are always held in Arabic, and for all practical purposes it serves to unify the Syrian-Lebanese in this country.

Naseer Aruri suggests that all this is possible because ALSAC represents fund raising on behalf of noncontroversial projects and because it has a social dimension to it:

> Fund-raising for the St. Jude Hospital for leukemia victims is also a source of pride to the community because of the hospital's association with the nationally famous comedian Danny Thomas and because of its humanitarian motives. Again, this project is safe, noncontroversial, prestigious, and above all, it was initiated outside the community. But projects which require primary responsibility of the community itself for the welfare of its members are seldom undertaken by its institutions. Nor do these institutions attempt to articulate the interest of the community, even when such articulation is an essential ingredient of the political system. Undoubtedly this political passiveness is due to certain characteristics which govern the social and political behavior of the people.[14]

The Risq. Haddad Foundation, on the other hand, is a nonprofit organization designed to administer scholarship funds for needy Syrian-Lebanese Americans. It differs from the ALSAC organization in terms of the high prestige of its community members and the medium in which it presents itself. The ties to Arabic culture are at an absolute minimum and consist merely of the fact that its members are of Arabic-speaking origin. All its public functions are non-Arabic in appeal and content. The foundation serves an important function for those Americans of Syrian-Lebanese ancestry who feel obliged to maintain some tie with their ethnic past. To succeed, the foundation's board of directors had to consist of members from all segments of the collectivity. There are Syrians, Lebanese, Aleppians, Beirutis, Damascenes, Melkites, Maronites, and Orthodox on the board who raise funds from their respective constituencies.

If social class differences are more decisive than differences in ethnicity in determining who people socialize with, the existence of the Haddad Foundation offers the Syrians an alternative to seeking social companionship commensurable with their status outside the ethnic group. Rather than leaving the ethnic group when a higher social stratum is achieved, the Syrians can now fill their social predilections within the Americanized social life offered them by the foundation.

On the negative side the foundation actually takes promising young Syrian-Americans and prepares them for a better life outside the community. Nor does the foundation ask for any return on the part of the recipient. One would expect that since the money for the scholarships is raised from within the community that the community would have the right to expect some services in return for its generosity. The foundation has actually given scholarships to children of mixed ethnic background who have absolutely no tie to any Arab institution in the United States and are only marginally tied to the Syrian-Lebanese American community.

Both associations suffer from the inability to completely transcend the old identities and loyalties. Indeed, they have failed to articulate their interests in the manner of most ethnic groups. No Syrian social federations have developed into a strong national organization like the NAACP or the American Jewish Committee. "Unlike the Italians," writes Aruri, "who organized a protest movement against television programs which portrayed Italians as gangsters, the Syrian-Lebanese as a group remained indifferent to the general bias of the American press against the Arabs."[15] As Treudley notes:

> The Syrian tends to reject universalistic criteria in assessing other persons, as too impersonal and abstract. He can grasp people only as they are related to himself and since his ancestors have always thought in kinship terms, he continues to think in such terms over here.[16]

Consequently, no single organization can speak for the community or represent it to the outside world. In the New York area during the 1970's many city-wide ethnic festivals were held without the participation of the Syrians. They were not prepared to participate. There was no single group to be approached for inclusion in these events. In September of 1973, for example, the Armenian community of New York sponsored an ethnic day at its Cathedral Church featuring Middle Eastern culture, cuisine, and entertainment. Although they have common ties with the Armenians, the Syrians of New York made no contribution to the event.

Because they neither fully duplicated the institutions of the broader society nor succeeded in creating adequate retention techniques for maintaining their modified culture in and through the institutions they had, the Syrians have not been able to continue their structural and cultural separation. Socially, they created an unobjectionable and alternative social life but they have not been able to create a strong ideology for keeping membership inclusive, nor have they been able to adequately create an institutional system that would better serve them in this regard. Lack of schools, historical societies, pure ethnic culture and differentiation, lack of a segregated and nonmobile population have made it all but impossible for them and their institutions to survive.

With reference to these factors, Elaine Hagopian gives the following perceptive summary of the Boston Syrian-Lebanese community which can, by analogy, be extended to nearly all others:

> . . . the Arab-American community is relatively prosperous, providing more education for its young, stressing mobility in middle class America, still arguing within its churches, still identifying themselves as separate Syrians and Lebanese, and yet they have a growing awareness of their common identity, the need for a set of ethnic institutions that are cultural and educational, a greater willingness to identify with their total Arab heritage, and they have a few groups attempting to assist in this transformation. It is true . . . that those few individuals and families who were aware in the earlier periods of their Arab heritage and the need to develop a common set of institutions for the community are still the main people involved today. A broader base of organization and membership would have to be developed in order to effect the transformation. As a part of securing this process, male leadership would have to develop that could relate Arab ethnicity to the national American scene as well as educating members of the community to the role of their ethnicity within America and for America by bringing balance into the present Middle East crisis.[17]

There seems to be abundant historical evidence that such intragroup cooperation is beyond their interests and ability. Cooperation is often stressed in their rhetoric but rarely is achieved. Working toward objective goals would mean more than a superficial comingling at social affairs. According to Hitti, this inability represents a historic flaw in the Arab social character. He writes:

> Of all the immigrant races, the Syrians seem to be the most jealous of those of their number who aspire to leadership and are consequently most leaderless. Intensely individualistic with a history and geography that militates against cooperative effort the modern Syrian has come to look upon organization with suspicion and contempt.[18]

If this was the curse of the immigrant generation, it has affected the American born by depriving them of issues and precedents around which they can mobilize. Nor are their motivation, experiences, and concern less poignant than those of their forefathers. Not only are these generational differences due to divergent political and social styles and modes of thought which greatly influence the character and content of public issues, but since the Syrians wanted to be Americanized their children can't help but query the usefulness of being Syrian-American. In the long run, it is easier and more useful merely to be Americans of Syrian ancestry.

More important, the primary focus and preoccupation of the Syrian collectivity is becoming nothing more than maintaining the community through the discouragement of out-marriage. The chief function of the Syrian community is not only acting as a buffer against anomie, but also acting as a "marriage-market" for eligible young Syrians. This required a redefinition of marriage eligibility such that partners no longer had to come from the same town, rite, or even religious grouping. As long as they are Syrians—that's all that matters.

To that end the *mahrajan* or "outdoor picnic" was born in August 31, 1930, in Bridgeport, Connecticut, and was soon imitated by other Arabic communities throughout the nation. The purpose of the festival was expressed in the following words:

> Our coming together in such a gathering is because we are influenced by the same traditions governing our former social conditions. We are, in the United States, a distinct group who owe their adopted country the contributions of the best that is in them towards its cultural and democratic progress. And we are proud to claim one of the most precious heritages that have fallen to the lot of any small nation in history. By coming together as an ethnological unit we propose to keep alive those distinct features of our racial heritage for permanent contributions to our land of adoption.[19]

As an attempt at expressing and reaffirming the collective sentiments of the Arabic-speaking communities in the United States and encouraging in-marriage, the *mahrajan* was unsurpassed. Many small and isolated communities sponsored the event each summer in a rotating fashion which drew thousands of people from across the nation. At first, it was used primarily for in-group socializing and fund raising. In time, however, the composition and direction of the *mahrajan* began to reflect the disposition and condition of the public it was intended to serve. By 1960, the largest *mahrajan* in New England became settled in Danbury, Connecticut, and was sponsored by the combined churches and Syrian-Lebanese clubs of the city. Drawing more than 5,000 people every Labor Day weekend, the *mahrajan* represents most clearly the melting of religious distinctions in favor of a common and broader ethnic identity.

The avowed purpose of the event is to keep Oriental cultural traditions alive among the young and, by so doing, to achieve success in keeping them attached to their churches, which in turn means attachment to their ethnic past. The emphasis is on culture—food, music, and dancing—and not religious traditions per se, although the churches are the principal forces behind the events. By helping the young to identify themselves ethnically by placing before them tangible evidence of their own history and culture, the Syrians expected that they will identify with one of the churches and hopefully seek a Syrian marriage partner.

In order that it be comprehensible and nonoffensive, the content of the cultural heritage presented at these functions is highly limited and rather specific. In Danbury, it is generally acknowledged that without the American and Americanized Arabic entertainment, it would be very difficult to draw so many young people. And the young do attend; over 60 percent of the attendance at these affairs consists of single people below the age of thirty-five. While it seems that most of the people there genuinely enjoy the Arabic entertainment, it also appears that the young are more limited and very selective about the type of Arabic music they respond to.

As a result, a new musical form, "Ameraba," has arisen which while Eastern in inspiration, is essentially Western and often played on Western instruments. It allows the listeners to participate actively by providing them with *debke* (circle dancing) music. The *debke* is actually a Lebanese folk dance primarily intended for weddings and has been refined and learned by all Arabic-speaking Americans. While it originated in Mount Lebanon, it is presently performed extensively by Syrians. However, the Syrians from Aleppo and Damascus had to learn it from the "Lebanese" after they arrived in the United States. The dance is hardly performed in modern Lebanon anymore and visitors from the Orient are amazed at its survival and the enthusiasm with which it is performed here. Undoubtedly, they miss the symbolic and emotional value of the dance.

At Syrian *Haflis* (dances), where most of the participants are older Syrians, there is considerable ambivalence toward this mountain dance since its performance interferes with the older people's desire to listen to music. This is a continuation of their traditional sense of urban decorum. The younger generation, nonetheless, uses the dance as a symbol of its secular-culture identity. Though it shows how adaptive the Syrian-Lebanese are, it also indicates the level and depth of their ethnic content. Somehow, it is felt that gathering together once or twice a year with other Syrians to eat "Arabic" food and do the *Debke* means that "Arabic culture" is being kept alive in America for posterity's sake.

While they help keep some sense of cultural ethnicity alive, functions like these primarily serve as meeting places for eligible unmarried Syrians. While statistical evidence of this is lacking, it seems quite evident to observers that the motivating force for participation in these functions is the increased probability of ethnic in-group marriage. A *modus vivendi* is thus reached which brings together the younger generation in a setting that is ethnic and religious at the same time. The primary work of the churches and the social clubs of the community becomes bringing the American born together.

In time, formal institutional form was given to these secular Syrianisms in several local community organizations and functions. The Arabic-American press, for example, publishes calendars listing the Arabic social events in each city for the upcoming month. As Berger accurately notes:

> Much of the space in the American-Syrian press is devoted to the reporting of achievements in various fields, to personal news, and to organizational affairs. This is more characteristic of the English language than of the Arabic-language publications. . . . The trend is toward increasing triviality and mediocrity. A recent addition to the English language magazines is cutely "wholesome" and vigorously "American"—a "family" publication with fiction stories of the Arab past, sports articles, children's stories, receipes for Syrian dishes, all spiced with Arabic phrases.[20]

More important than the press in assisting the community are the activities of the National Federation of Syrian-Lebanese American clubs. Both the federation and the *mahrajan* reflect the contemporary situation and position of the collectivity vis-à-vis American society and the Syrians' desire for a separate social existence.

The National Federation is a semiformal organization divided into four regional groups each of which has its own social life. The strongest group is the Midwestern, which has a large but dispersed Arabic-speaking population in places like Wisconsin, South Dakota, and New Mexico, without benefit of churches. In the New York region, one rarely if ever hears of the activity of the federation. Perhaps the competition with the churches and other Arab-American groups keeps the federation's influence at a minimum there.

The federation operates independently of the churches and relies solely on ethnicity and culture for its festivities, which usually last over a three-day weekend. Attendance and enthusiasm vary, but the regional activities usually draw spontaneous and capacity crowds from all over the United States. The attendance at the National Federation Convention in Las Vegas in 1969 was 6,500. The purpose of the convention was twofold: to "unite all the children of Arab-Americans in a common bond of appreciation for their culture and heritage," and to pay honor and recognition to all "our brothers and sisters of Arabic parentage who have contributed through the fields of their professions . . . and endeavors for the benefit and very existence of mankind."[21]

The convention awarded the Arabic National Achievement Awards to Dr. Michael DeBakey, Najaeb Halaby, Ralph Nader, Danny Thomas, Lieutenant Governor Elias Francis (New Mexico) and several others. As usual, the American Syrians and Lebanese claimed possession of outstanding individuals after they reached national fame while doing little as a group to help them along. Numerous interviews with "leaders" in the community support this contention. "If we were like the Jews who help their own, we would not be as disadvantaged as we are," is a commonly expressed attitude.

Another, less formal attempt to keep ethnicity and community life prospering is found in the ecological patterns and geographic mobility that various Syrian communities have exhibited. If a Syrian-American family wishes to maintain some tie to a Syrian community, it had to be physically accessible to other members of the community with like interests. In attempting to counteract the problem of small numbers and dispersal, the Syrians have created numerous techniques to help them. For example, many communities literally transplant themselves—almost in their entirety—to summer resorts which they dominate.

Some members of the Brooklyn community, for example, frequently use only certain sections of Jacob Riis Park in Queens while others vacation in Tannersville, New York, or the Pocono Mountains. The Syrian Jews of Brooklyn collectively vacation at Bradley Beach and Deal, New Jersey. The Paterson community descends *en masse* to the Jersey shore, especially Asbury Park and Point Pleasant, while the Syrians of Pennsylvania prefer Atlantic City. In both cities, they stay at "Syrian hotels" and create an active Syrian social life. The various communities in Massachusetts convene on Cape Cod, and at one time the Boston community had a summer camp established for its children. The Syrians hope to increase, by the use of such indirect methods, the probability that their children will meet and marry other Syrians.

Interestingly, when Syrians change residence they tend to replace themselves almost wholly in some other community. We have already noted the migrations to Miami from Paterson and to California from Brooklyn, but more important, similar movements are noticeable within these and other cities. Most of the newly formed families of Paterson, New Jersey, for example, are settling in Wayne, New Jersey, while those of Boston have moved from the South End to West Roxbury and the Roslindale district. Quite simply, they do not move at random but follow specific patterns.

By far the most interesting residential patterns are those of the Brooklyn collectivity. Originally housed on Atlantic Avenue and environs (Brooklyn Heights-Cobble Hill), the group moved, between the two world wars, to the prestigious Park Slope area of Brooklyn. Today, it is located mainly in Bay Ridge and more specifically on and near Shore Road.

Marriage Patterns

One would suspect that an ethnic group that went through so much difficulty to ensure in-marriage would be successful. Data collected in 1970 indicate that the Syrians have in fact failed to stem the tide of out-marriage. Indeed, if we can assume that assimilation is usually considered complete when intermarriage takes place on an extensive scale, then the Syrian community has a dubious future and is virtually on its last legs. As Milton Gordon has observed:

> If large scale intermarriage is to have taken place, then obviously the immigrants must have entered the cliques, clubs, other primary groups and institutions of the host society and in addition, placed their own impress upon these social structures to some extent.[22]

Moreover, intermarriage is also a good indicator not only of degree of assimilation but also of group cohesion, i.e., the higher the number of mixed marriages, the weaker is the group's solidarity. Among other explanations, the occurrence of high out-marriage rates has been attributed to mobility goals, to the lack of cultural solidarity, and to the numerical size theory—that numerically small groups must of necessity intermarry. Syrian out-marriage is related to all these factors and indicates as well the subjugation of religious identity to ethnic identity since their marriage patterns complement those found among other Catholic ethnic groups.

The following data draw a distinction between marriages between two Arabs (homogeneous) and those which involve only a Melkite boy or Melkite girl.

Since Melkites are Syrians, the data might also reflect marriage trends among the non-Melkite Christian Syrian population since they would constitute the Arab population the Melkites married into when in a homogeneous union.

The data reveal a striking tendency for Catholic Syrians to marry other Catholics across nationality boundaries. Syrian out-marriages (at least among the Melkites) have been high for nearly three decades. Data collected for a 1964-65 study reveal that only seventeen couples (less than 15 percent) married in the Melkite Church were both of Arabic-speaking origin. In 1953, only five marriages out of fifteen in Saint Ann's Melkite Church, Paterson, New Jersey, were homogeneous. By 1968, only one marriage out of thirty-five was between two Syrians.[23]

The Syrian-American community loses its children through intermarriage even in those areas where a complete social life exists. Moreover, those Syrians who out-married would probably

TABLE III

Comparative Table of Intermarriages in the Melkite Parishes of Boston, Massachusetts; Brooklyn, New York; Central Falls, Rhode Island; Cleveland, Ohio; Danbury, Connecticut; Lawrence, Massachusetts; New London, Connecticut; Paterson, New Jersey; Worcester, Massachusetts.

	1954				*1957*				*1961*			
	T.	*Ho.*	*Hu.*	*W.*	*T.*	*Ho.*	*Hu.*	*W.*	*T.*	*Ho.*	*Hu.*	*W.*
Boston	7	3	3	1	8	4	3	1	9	6	0	3
Brklyn.	24	14	6	4	27	10	14	3	24	8	14	2
C. Falls	—	—	—	—	—	—	—	—	13	2	5	6
Clvlnd.	2	2	0	0	13	6	4	3	4	1	2	1
Danbury	3	2	1	0	2	1	0	1	5	0	5	0
Lawrence	10	2	6	2	6	2	4	0	9	2	5	2
N. London	—	—	—	—	—	—	—	—	1	0	0	1
Paterson	19	3	8	8	15	3	8	4	13	2	5	6
Worcester	4	2	1	1	4	2	1	1	1	0	0	1
TOTALS:	69	28	25	16	75	28	34	13	79	21	36	22
PERCENT:		40%				37%				26%		

	1963				*1964*				*1968*			
	T.	*Ho.*	*Hu.*	*W.*	*T.*	*Ho.*	*Hu.*	*W.*	*T.*	*Ho.*	*Hu.*	*W.*
Boston	12	6	1	5	12	2	5	5	17	2	4	11
Brklyn.	20	6	10	4	29	7	18	4	22	4	14	4
C. Falls	11	3	2	6	9	1	5	3	—	—	—	—
Clvlnd.	7	3	3	1	8	2	4	2	7	3	3	1
Danbury	9	2	6	1	2	0	1	1	—	—	—	—
Lawrence	6	0	4	2	12	2	7	3	19	3	10	6
N. London	3	0	1	2	5	0	3	2	—	—	—	—
Paterson	15	3	5	7	22	3	11	8	25	1	13	11
Worcester	3	0	3	0	8	0	4	4	—	—	—	—
TOTALS:	86	23	35	28	107	17	58	32	90	13	44	33
PERCENT:		26%				15%				14%		

T.—Total Marriages
Ho.—Homogeneous (Both are of Arabic speaking Origin)
Hu.—Husband only (is of Arabic Speaking Origin)
W.—Wife only (is of Arabic Speaking Origin)
Percent—Percentage of Homogeneous marriages compared to the total of marriages registered in the Church

have severed all ties to the community and its churches had no "modernization" taken place. The churches would have only the in-married population affiliated with them if they had not latinized and Americanized themselves. Yet this same Syrian population would be too small to reproduce itself by in-marriage. Latinization allowed the out-married couple, then, to at least affiliate with the churches and Americanization allowed them to do so in nonethnic terms. Thus, a substantial portion of any Syrian Catholic parish today is actually composed of non-Syrians.

It would seem improbable that the "American" partner in the mixed marriage would be interested in maintaining ethnic continuity. It can also be argued that latinization also encouraged out-marrying by reducing social distance between the ethnics and the host society. In either case, ethnic communal solidarity has been substantially and irrevocably weakened.

CHAPTER XII

Ethnicity and Religion— The Syrian-American Future

THE CHANGES IN AND ELIMINATION OF THE ETHNIC AND religious content of the Syrian-American community can be best explained by reference to the demographic and ecological variables discussed in the previous chapters. However, something must also be said about the overall social irrelevance of maintaining an ethnic identity in a highly urbanized society. As we have suggested, a middle-class group like the Syrians cannot succeed in establishing in-group ethnic solidarity unless it can create both institutions dedicated to the cause of sustaining group cohesion and convincing ideology for doing so. The Syrians were especially deficient in the latter since the possibility, logic, and value of maintaining a separate social life because of certain historical and cultural antecedent, when their newer values varied minimally from those of other Americans, were questionable.

Under such conditions, not only did the arguments for social separateness become weak and less plausible, but the reason for identification with the community weakened with each generation as well. Some identified with the community because they needed self-aggrandizement, others for historical reasons, and still others for very personal ones. Thus, every generation of Syrian-Americans including the present has had its maintainers, its "arabophiles," its workers, and its detractors.

From the sociological point of view, the community has not been successful in ordering and organizing (and hence achieving) its objectives. Language maintenance was sporadically and half-heartedly attempted, appreciation of the cultural heritage was barely achieved, and internal religious differences were never really subdued or replaced by a commitment to Arab history, culture, and nationalism. Consequently, they lacked an overall framework within which a separate social life would be meaningful. Mokarzel, the *Al-Hoda* publisher, in founding an Arabic magazine devoted to solving this problem,

> defended the instinctive desire to cling to life in their own settlements when people show a preference for their music or foods or customs "obtained in the mother land." The idea, he asserted, was to develop an atmosphere which in itself could not be considered objectionable. He recognized at the same time the rise of a state of embarrassment and consciousness on the part of those born here. The urgent need, he felt, was one to correct misconceptions and insufficient knowledge on their part relative to their racial traits which contributed to a lack of sympathy with their parents.[1]

As a remedy for the "ignorance," the Syrian press proposed first to offer a description of life in America and through literary works to reflect that life. Its secondary objective was to present a comprehensive analysis of Syrian political and economic affairs and achievements in the fields of art, the sciences, and literature. "Their commercial attainments," said Mokarzel, "reached stupendous proportions practically throughout the world and which bid fair to gain for them a position of eminence which was once their forefathers, the Phoenicians." Mokarzel wanted to publish interesting and illuminating bits of history that would give Lebanese and Syrian youth a broader vision of their heritage.[2] This knowledge in itself, he asserted, would in the end make them more valuable to the country of their birth.

It is our opinion, however, that one of the main reasons that Syrian youth looked outside their group for identity and meaning was the institutional incompleteness of their own group. This concept was developed by Raymond Breton, who writes that "institutional completeness would be at its extreme whenever the ethnic community could perform all the services required by its members . . . who," he continues, "would never have to make use of native institutions for the satisfaction of any of their needs, such as education, work, food and clothing, medical care or social assistance."[3] Nearly all generations of Syrians had to leave the ethnic group to attain those ends that were not purely social. This fact plus their pro-Americanism probably accounts for more "rejection" and "ignorance" than could any particular disdain for the ethnic heritage.

Those Syrians, then, who did identify with and draw upon their ethnic heritage were highly motivated to do so and thus created a delicate symbiotic relationship between their group and their churches which became responsible for maintaining their ethnicity. Even now these churches are viewed primarily as the witness of ethnicity and the "Syrian way of life." Thus, those who had no difficulty identifying with an ethnic group found the churches quite agreeable since they were continuations of the ethnic past. In speaking of the role of immigrant churches in an ethnic community, Breton offers the following insight, which is applicable in its entirety to the Syrians.

> The weight of the religious institutions can be attributed to the dominant role they hold in the community. Churches are very frequently the center of a number of activities; associations are formed and collective activities are organized under their influence and support. Also, the national sentiments of the immigrant find support in having experiences in church very similar to those in the country of origin—the language is the same; its images used in preaching are the same; the saints worshipped are also those the immigrant has known from early childhood. Moreover, religious leaders frequently become advocates and preachers of a national ideology, providing a raison d'être for the ethnic community and a motivation for identification with it.[4]

So the Syrian churches cater to the "Arab identified" and "in-group oriented," since they are its main supporters. To alienate these people is to destroy the only link the Church has with canonical Easterners. But doing this alienates those whose sights are on the outside world as well as its own "intellectuals" who believe religion and nationalism should be separated.

That the church and people have come to this continued reliance on religion as supportive of ethnicity and then on ethnicity as supportive of rite is the consequence of their assimilation experience here, their lack of knowledge of themselves and their own past and traditions as a unique socioreligious group, and the unwillingness of an immigrant clergy to do other than support this situation. It is conceivable that one day all Syrian Catholics in America will disappear into the dominant Latin rite and Catholic culture of that society. Their churches may either become museums or be rejuvenated under the direction of non-Arab Americans who find these same Eastern churches spiritually rich and satisfying when they are liturgically pure and de-ethnicized.

Since the second Vatican Council, however, some young, American-born Melkites have undergone a serious reexamination of the relationship among rite, culture, and ethnicity in an attempt to ward off a total desertion of rite by canonical Melkites. They focused upon the question and problem of identification, especially that of the young, with a church organization that was inherently ethnic and yet greatly latinized. At a workshop at the eighth annual convention of the Melkite Association of North America in Danbury, Connecticut, the following observation was made on the "problem" of latinization:

> Children tend to imitate their parents. When they see them genuflecting in church, blessing themselves with open hand, praying the rosary, following the liturgy with a Roman missal, and striking their breasts when the bells are rung, the youth are baffled. Then they look around the church and see other inconsistencies, i.e., statues, bells, stations of the cross, no icons or iconastasis, and the Melkite priest is wearing Latin vestments. So the youth has a choice: either accept the status quo as his parents have, or he can ask the priest why his church isn't as Byzantine as it should be. The priest answers that we had to prove we were a Catholic church, not Orthodox, and that's why we adopted Latin customs.[5]

The fully acculturated third generation with no inferiority complex about its religious inheritance began to rediscover and positively restress their religious origins. When they found them so latinized because of the effort to adapt, many began to reject them for the very same reasons that their parents associated themselves with them—they were culturally ghetto-oriented and religiously nondistinctive. Many, of course, attempted to de-latinize them. Other factors in the demise of Eastern Catholicism in America are its lack of parochial education, an ineffective and petty clergy, its subjugation to the discretions or indiscretions of the Latin hierarchy there, the continuation of the inferiority complex begun in the Middle East, and finally, and most important, its continued reliance on ethnicity for relevance rather than its own independent liturgical and theological tradition.

As we hinted, the problem became especially acute for those who could conceptualize the Eastern rites as separate from their immigrant cultures but who could not get the institutional church to do so. It was also a strain on the intellectuals of the community, who found the interaction of the nonethnic social environment with its emphasis on creativity, individuality, and common interests a more stimulating experience than just being related and confined to a particular, unchosen historical past. Other third- and fourth-generation "Syrians" found the title "Syrian" a symbol of a truncated reality since it was essentially devoid of any meaningful and differential content.

Finally, "rejection" of the identification with Syrian ethnicity is undoubtedly related to continuous economic mobility, which tended to negate the usefulness of using generational differences as the sole criterion for judging levels of assimilation. The Syrians were not only consistently mobile but because of their small size and dispersal were in unavoidable contact with non-Arab society. In their work and living arrangements, and especially in school, Syrians developed ties with higher status social groups. This also helped them to assimilate.

Consequently, their "secular mobility" became reflected in their transference of allegiance from the Eastern-rite church to the Latin Catholic Church. Basically, it is mobile to be non-Eastern identified, and this becomes especially true of Melkites and Maronites who viewed Latin Catholicism as the host culture to which they must relate. In a word, when they now substitute "class" for "ethnicity" they substitute the Latin rite for the Eastern.

As our previous data indicated, the Syrian community has been losing adherents every generation and a crisis is imminent. Had no accommodation been reached, the community would have disappeared earlier—before it had even made a collective impression on American society. Since the churches are the primary institutions of the collectivity, when they die so too will the Syrian-American community. The only thing remaining will be Americans of Syrian ancestry with no common life together or ties to each other.

The possibility of the Syrian Catholic churches (and of necessity, the ethnic community as well) being emptied in this decade is evidenced and compounded by the following data. In the first place, rite in Roman Catholic Church law descends only through the father. So the only families added to a parish register are those that are founded by Melkite fathers. More significantly, however, the presence of a non-Melkite mother (even if she is of Arab origin) probably leads to a weakening of ties to the rite itself. Melkite priest Fr. Elya is of the opinion that this situation works generally "against the Melkites whenever the mother is a non-Melkite, but does not work equally in favor of the rite when the mother is Melkite inside a non-Melkite family."[6] Her Eastern rite is inconsequential in adding a new family to the parish and if she is Latin, Fr. Elya believes that as the main "socializer," she will transmit attachment to the Latin rite rather than to her husband's. He summarizes:

> . . . Melkites in America, who are a small minority and who, for the most part, do not know much about their rite . . . feel obliged to keep it usually because of external authority or internal sense of faithfulness. We may expect that whenever they are confronted with the Latin rite inside their own family, there is a great chance that they will lean toward it. Although definitive statistical data about this fact are not presently available, however, the daily experience of many Melkite pastors witness to it.[7]

Also, the survival and growth of the Eastern rites in the United States becomes doubtful when viewed demographically. In addition to intermarriage, which is quite frequent, there is the question of adequate fertility rates, which have been calculated for Melkites as four times less than the national norm.[8] Not only are they reproducing less frequently, but the status of their daughters as Eastern Catholics depends, in terms of duration and permanency, on their marriage to Eastern husbands.

The total Eastern-rite Catholic population of the United States is slightly over 800,000. This includes, of course, Syrian, Ukranian, and Slavic Catholic groups. The Eastern rites collectively had a gross increase of 7,000 members in 1967, i.e., an increase of about one member for every 114 believers. Melkites had a gross increase of only 401 members during the same year: 384 of them were infant baptisms and 17 were converts. However, 112 Melkites died during the same period, leaving a net increase of 289 members. In terms of gross increase, Melkites received one new member for every 137 of their faithful.[9]

Furthermore, there are 46.6 million Roman-rite faithful in the

United States with a total of 60,000 priests. The Roman-rite population increases yearly by about 1.25 million members, a ratio of one new member for every 35 of the Roman-rite faithful.

Generally speaking, the Eastern rites, especially those of the Syrians, have a function that transcends the purely theological. In the first place, they represent the most important institutions of the Syrian community. Second, their religious traditions are the most unusual and controversial aspect of the sociocultural heritage Syrians brought with them to America.

It may be in the religious sphere, therefore, that the Syrians can make some collective contribution to American society. America has a pluralistic society and the principal institutional dimension of the various ethnic subcultures that are socially acceptable to most Americans and legally protected is the religious. By opening their religious faith and practice to America, the Syrians would be giving their very bloodline to their host society. Of course, in opening their traditions to the American public they would be, in effect, crippling their own future as an ethnic community.

On the other hand, they have no real choice. What other legacy could they possibly offer America? Culturally, they have given the country very little beyond some of their specialty foods like yogurt, Syrian bread (Pita) and cheeses, chomos, shish kebab, and assorted lamb dishes. Politically, they have never collectively contributed to any single party so that politicians generally remain unresponsive to them. Economically, they are dispersed throughout the spectrum of occupations and have only a small reputation as rug merchants—a profession dominated by their cousins, the Armenians. Their warmth and style in household matters the general American public cannot be aware of or absorb except through personal encounters, and their small numbers make this impractical and inconsequential to the overall operation of American society.

The religious sphere, which has always been their preoccupation and their forte, is qualitatively different from other forms of social contact and for their survival must continue as the focal point of their relations with American society. This is so because the resolution of the religious question and conflict will ultimately determine what will become of them in the United States. As we have suggested, Melkite-rite Syrian-Americans (and by analogy, Maronites as well) have become only marginally related to the spiritual and liturgical rites of their own Church. For all practical purposes, the only group left structurally supporting the collectivity is the Syrian-Orthodox.

Ironically, however, this religious group has had to "Americanize" the most in order to save Orthodoxy in the Western world. But, unlike their brother Melkites, they have kept their rite intact and merely altered the language and general decorum of the services. Everything done was in line with Eastern theological thought and tradition. At the present time, they are cooperating with other Eastern Orthodox groups in the formation of an indigenous American Orthodox Church which will be devoid of ethnicity completely. The Orthodox Syrians have also come to stress rite over ethnicity. Hence the community has no real sociocultural structural supports except those that are found in purely ethnic clubs.

A substantial majority of the Catholic Syrians prefer affiliation with the dominant Latin rite because it better complements their present level of acculturation. Furthermore, since they were not trained in their own tradition, they are generally more aware of the religious customs and mentality of the Latin Catholic faithful. Such a situation genuinely threatens their desire for a separate communal and social life and the community itself seems to be unaware of the risk involved in being so strongly affiliated with the institutional life of American Catholicism through attachment either to its school system or to its parish organization.

The situation becomes more critical because of the lack of informed leadership within the group itself. The lay "elite" seem to be somewhat concerned with introducing changes into the status quo. But even if successful, they may not be able to circumscribe the traditional levels of social consciousness the Syrians have of themselves as Melkites or Aleppians, et cetera. In fact, they are generally ill-equipped to do this since their positions are based on essentially irrelevant criteria.

The Syrian Catholic clergy, on the other hand, are confronted with the dilemma of an uninformed and misinformed laity that they helped create. Yet, they seem to be generally pleased with the condition of their parishes and communities. Even when the desire for change is present, it is rarely if ever implemented.

With congregations split between the traditionalists—who hold most of the power—and the more Americanized third generation, and with the probability that the local Latin bishop is a conservative hierarch who does not understand, or care to understand, his Eastern Catholic faithful, most Melkite and Maronite pastors would not allow changes that would be deemed too radical—even when authentically Eastern.

For these reasons, the Syrian Eastern Catholics in America have reached a situation of almost total absorption into the triple melting pot of religion without having made a collective impression on either American society in general or American religious traditions. They haven't realized that failure to do so would ultimately undo them. Even the establishment of an independent hierarchy for them under their own bishops has not been effective in altering their generally impotent disposition.

It is for these reasons that the future of the Syrian Catholic churches is in serious doubt. Indeed, in light of the evidence, it is not unreasonable to state that virtually all Eastern-rite parishes and communities are facing a crisis in identity, commitment, and relevance. The ethnic community simply reflects these tensions. No longer can the churches rely on the ethnic foundations that the informal social life and primary contacts of the family and neighborhood offered them. Though the ethnic subculture gave them some formal and informal primary group support and "reinforcement" by supplying a network of culture and activity, this is no longer the case.

Because of their small numbers, relative dispersion, orientation, and level of assimilation, the churches can no longer base their relevance on service to an ethnic community. It is becoming increasingly evident that if the ethnic community disappears, then the churches which are a part of it and which support it are also likely to disappear.

It comes as no surprise, therefore, that there is a struggle within most Melkite and Maronite parishes in the United States over the direction the rite should take. Several schools of thought have arisen and vary along a continuum from total immersion in ethnicity (supported by the immigrant remnant and their clergy) to complete disregard for it (the American born). On the one hand, we have the traditionalists, who are tied to the church primarily for ethnic considerations and who see no reason and no possible way of separating the ethnic identity from the religious. On the other, we have an American-born clergy—often not Syrian in origin—serving an ethnically mixed congregation.

The questions and problems here are of concern to all generations of Syrians. More properly they are related to a crisis in identity. For many, to be Melkite is ipso facto to be Syrian since "all real Melkites are Syrian." The possibility of any other arrangement has never been fully conceptualized and made popular until the recent Vatican Council, on which the Eastern Catholic Church made a strong impression, and the subsequent publication of the quarterly *Melkite Digest* (proposed, controlled, and edited by educated Melkite lay people).

Since that time, those parishes and communities that were served by an American-born clergy began to examine their origins in both religious and ethnic terms. This led to a new "Americanization," which began with an inwardly directed search for liturgical purity upon which legitimate modifications could be placed. Though some rejected the latinized Eastern rites outright, others attempted to "re-Byzantinize" them since it wasn't their Eastern origins that were irrelevant and confusing, but rather the bastardization that developed in the United States. In searching for a new *modus vivendi* with American society, it became increasingly evident that one need not be a "Syrian" to be a Melkite or Maronite.

In other words, no rite (Latin, Melkite, Maronite, et cetera) can be restricted either to preterritorial boundaries—Melkites belong in Syria and in America they should conform to the dominant Latin rite—or to a particular people or culture. In the words of the recent Vatican Council: "These churches enjoy the same rights and are under the same obligations, even with respect to preaching the gospel to the whole world."[10]

The implementation of this or any other directives would require, at the very least, a commitment and awareness that this should be so and an organization capable of forcing adherence to it and carrying out the stated objectives. Without vigorous and creative executive leadership it seems improbable that the Melkites and Maronites will be able to survive in America. Their general inability to separate ideas from the personality of their bearers makes it difficult for them to objectively respond to the real threat of extinction. If the American-born laity and clergy endure during this transitional period, then there might be an Eastern Catholic rite possible in the United States after all. But they are up against very unfavorable odds.

The Eastern Catholics' small numbers mean that they will always find it difficult to create new parishes and communities or a strong religious communal life. The canon laws preventing Easterners from becoming Latins are ineffective since Melkites and Maronites can do so informally (by not letting their real rites be known) and because they have not always established parishes where they are living. On the other hand, the laws are effective in preventing wholesale formal abandoning of the rite. These external constraints, however, are hardly conducive to the development of a lively sense of faith.

It is also possible that the Eastern churches will move into a missionary relationship with those Americans who are not attracted by Latin-rite Christianity. Since two equal rites and churches will then be operating in American society (the Eastern and the Western), it would seem that canon law will have to change to allow for the free choice of rites among all Christians. Right now, it is implicitly felt that people living in the Western world should belong only to the Western or Latin rite. While a free choice of rites might be harmful at first to the Melkite and Maronite Churches (canonical Easterners might actually opt out of the rite), in the long run it will be more beneficial, as it will allow for the formation of a more dedicated, committed, and concerned laity.

While such a situation may increase the numerical strength of their churches, it would not necessarily mean that the Syrian community would be strengthened. It would be far from a cure-all for its many problems or its greatest problems, which are the need for a raison d'être and an integrated institutional system to support and maintain them once this is found. Bringing in non-Easterners to pray and support the churches might help keep these institutions alive, but this new constituency can hardly be expected to make a commitment to Arabic culture as well.

Ironically, the Syrian community might have to "destroy" itself to "save" itself! If it does not reform its primary institutional network (churches), it will lose the third and fourth generations. If its churches modernize without latinizing, if they open their doors to the American public, they will weaken their Arab cultural inheritance and the general community will suffer. But, it is possible that the ethnic community as such can develop new secular institutions to keep alive the cultural patrimony. The churches would be free to develop as they see fit and the community, which now has other culturally oriented organizations, would be free to relate to them as Americans participating in an American Church that just happens to have an Arab past.

CHAPTER XIII

Israel and Syrian-American Consciousness

THE ISRAELI-ARAB CONTROVERSY ERUPTED WITH FULL VIGOR on the American sociopolitical scene at a time when the second and third generations of Syrian-Lebanese in America were settled in stable and relatively affluent communities. Unfortunately for the Arab cause, the Syrian-Americans have not generally been active politically, and hence could effectively influence neither the news coverage of the conflict nor the orientation of the American political establishment. Coming from a tradition that was apolitical on the individual level, the Syrians simply had no political clout in a society run by powerful religious and ethnic interest groups. Instead, their cultural attitude inhibited dissent. Ultimately fatalistic, they believe that "politicking" can lead only to involvement, insecurity, and further problems rather than resolution and peace.

The Disinterest in Politics

As has been mentioned, the Syrians never collectively belonged to one political party. In spite of the usually comfortable economic situation in which most find themselves, many vote Democratic with the businessmen among them voting Republican. Their small numbers in any given area make politicians unaware of and/or unresponsive to their presence. In New York, for example, Pee tells us

> the Syrians were lost in a cloud of immigrant groups which Tammany Hall, concerned mostly with the Irish, Jewish, and Italian groups, largely ignored. Thus, during the 1932 election campaign a Democratic club of

Syrians, Greeks, and Armenians went Republican because Tammany refused them "recognition."[1]

More important, the Syrians, not really interested in self-government or broader political questions, were never financial contributors to political campaigns. They simply never became object oriented, i.e., participating in the world of ideas and events that have nothing directly to do with their families and religious affiliation. They simply do not understand the operation of the American political process or feel obligated to participate fully in it. They do not believe in it in a concrete, day-to-day fashion. Theoretically, the American political system is participatory. As an abstraction they can give it their support, but personal involvement is minimal.

This is not to say that no children of these Arab-Americans are in political positions in this country. Individually speaking and in proportion to their numbers, they seem to have done rather well. Typically, though, they have rarely been elected to office from districts that have relatively large Arabic-speaking populations. We cite here the most recent example of Arab-American indifference as interpreted by a 1972 Arab-American tabloid:

> Mr. Joseph Barakat of Detroit, Michigan, ran for Congress from a Congressional District heavily populated by Arabs and Arab sympathizers. Yet, he was unable to succeed during the primaries. . . . The basic reason for his failure was the lack of adequate financial support. Of course, he received many compliments and good wishes which were completely worthless. Some 3,200 letters were sent to the community on his behalf soliciting financial support to aid the candidate in his campaign. Only 15 letters of reply were received with a grand total of $160.00 which did not even cover the cost of the mailing, in excess of $300. "The support was less than minimal," said Barakat's campaign manager, Dr. Elie Khoury. We are not of the opinion that members of the community should necessarily support an Arab candidate. We do not believe in tribalism and we have condemned attitudes based on tribal relationship many a time. However, Joseph L. Barakat had proven himself as a competent man and the failure of the community in Detroit to support his candidacy speaks poorly of the social and political consciousness of the community.[2]

Small towns in Massachusettes and upstate New York have mayors with Christian Arab last names. Several important judgeships are held by Syrian-Lebanese. The lieutenant governor of

New Mexico is a Lebanese-American and the lower house of Congress has several congressmen who are Syrian and Lebanese. Again, however, they are usually from the Midwest and not the Northeast where most Arabic-speaking Americans reside. For the first time in American history, a Lebanese-American, James Abourezk of South Dakota, was elected to the United States Senate. In April, 1973, he told the Senate that the United States should reexamine its policy in the Middle East and he urged the nation to take a much more active peacemaking role in the area. In addition to supporting the candidacy of pro-Arabist J. William Fulbright, chairman of the Senate Foreign Relations Committee, for re-election, he also headed a delegation meeting with Attorney General William Saxby to discuss what could be done about the violations of the civil rights of Americans of Arab heritage.[3] These activities will most probably make him the leading Arab-American spokesman on the Middle East.

Surprisingly, a group of prominent Arabic-speaking Americans had established a "Non-Partisan Committee for the election of Congressman Abourezk to the United States Senate," reports *Action*, an Arab-American paper.[4] With headquarters in the nation's capital, the committee under the chairmanship of attorney Richard C. Shadyac appealed to Americans of Arabic-speaking background for financial contributions.

Political Consciousness Develops

As we indicated in the beginning, the Syrian-American experience has reflected and continued the traditions of the Arab East. Thus, their reluctance to get involved in international Arab affairs is only one facet of their general lack of interest in politics. This feeling of remoteness from political life of any kind poses serious difficulties for Syrian organizations seeking to raise money even for the relief of Arab refugees and other needy groups in the Arab world. "Philanthropic agencies," notes Berger, "have a tough assignment . . . in seeking to raise money here for general purposes" back home in Syria. For one thing, they run into the old Christian suspicion of the Moslems. For another, "some Syrian businessmen are said to be apprehensive lest their contributions to Arab causes antagonize Jewish businessmen on whose trade they depend."[5]

This means that Arabic-speaking Americans will continue to

fluctuate in their reactions and relationships to the present Middle East crisis—a situation that will certainly affect the direction and identity that their communities will have in the United States. For example, the creation of the myth that there is a unified Arab "nationality" out to destroy Jews certainly forces Arabic-speaking people everywhere to either identify with or dissociate themselves completely from the social reality "Arab."

In light of the Munich incident in 1972 where several Israeli Olympic athletes were massacred, this belief was generally accepted. Since this tragedy, which was initiated by Palestinian commandos—a desperate faction and not the Arab population at large—the Arabic-speaking people as a whole have been depicted as bloodhounds, flesh mongers, a species with an unquenchable appetite for bloodletting. Ambassador Abdullah Bishara, permanent representative of Kuwait to the United Nations, criticized this view, saying:

> A great nation with a traditional sense of fairness like America should not be caught in the web of the hysteria directed against the Arabs in the wake of Munich. The Arabs are by nature, tradition, religion and civilization against bloodshed. The Prophet Mohammed's axiom, "Man is the brother of man, whether he likes it or not," has an immeasurable impact upon the Arabs' concept of fraternity and brotherhood. Islamic teachings of tolerance, benevolence and forgiveness have been the cornerstone of Arab psychology.[6]

Assuming the accuracy of this dimension of Arabic civilization, the campaign of disparagement and malevolence initiated in the Western press is considered unjustifiably cruel and injudicious by the Syrians. The ambassador continues: "It is, indeed, an act of terror to portray all the Arabs as a nation that revels in blood-licking."[7]

As recently as June 3, 1973, the American mass media played up the Arabs' supposed sadism. A film entitled "Golda Meir Profile," shown on WSPD-TV 13 NBC in Toledo, was vigorously interpreted by the Arab-American community as a "masterpiece of deception and falsehood and another Israeli attempt to further brainwash the American people."[8] Spokesmen for the community accused the makers and promoters of the film of outright deception since the film, they said, was not only far from being a portrait of the personal life of Mrs. Meir, but was also treacherous propaganda for the Zionist movement and the Jewish State and a slanderous attack on the integrity of the Arabs. Despite protest, the station elected to show the film. A month later an Arab response was permitted.

Although more Americans are becoming aware that notions of malice, genocide, or extirpation of a people are as loathsome to the Arabs as they are to other civilized nations, Syrians and Lebanese in the United States are now being wrongly considered Arabs in the Palestinian sense and being reacted to as such. It should again be noted that in their earlier history here, Arabic-speaking Americans did not even think of themselves as Arabs, and, according to Morroe Berger, "although Arab nationalism has already emerged as a strong ideology in the Middle East, it has not yet penetrated the largely Christian groups here who still remember their inferior status under the Moslem Turks and their uneasy relations with the Moslems in general."[9] Moreover, the Zionist movement has consistently presented the issue as a Jewish-Arab encounter and the American Syrian-Lebanese consequently have no choice but to argue their position from within this framework.

Despite this, Arabic-speaking Americans themselves have continued to differentiate between the Israeli state as representative of a political ideology and Jews as members of a revered and respected religious faith. In fact, the old-time Syrian-Lebanese can recall with favor their pleasant and continuous relationship with the American Jewish community and the Syrian-Jewish community in particular. Indeed, they emigrated to America together and often supported each other's cultural events. Even today, one of the most popular Arab entertainers at Syrian-Jewish social events in Bradley Beach, New Jersey, is a Lebanese Christian from Brooklyn.

Pro-Israeli factions in America have been successful in downgrading this relationship and supporting the belief that the Arabs are the aggressors and that they are so full of hatred for the "Jews" (not just for Zionism or Israel) that if it were within their power they would throw the Jews into the sea. The false picture of total genocide, as depicted, for example, in *If Israel Lost The War*,[10] is designed to bring to mind the painful memory of the Nazi atrocities against Jews.

Yet because of this bifurcation into Arab versus Jew, and as the

Arabs of the Middle East achieve greater unity in their position against Israel and the Western powers, the Syrian-Lebanese American community might find itself, as a community, identifying positively with the Palestinian cause. Evidence of this possibility was first noted in 1958 by Berger:

> The Syrian community in America, by now composed mainly of the second and third generations for whom the "old squabbles" were not so important, began to think more of Arab independence of the West, the removal of the remains of Western domination in the now independent states of Lebanon and Syria, and the support of the Arabs as a whole against Zionism. Moreover, such attitudes, Syrians felt, were in accord with traditional American anti-colonial policy (at least outside of Latin America). The United States, indeed, supported England against France in favoring independence for Lebanon and Syria during World War II.[11]

Berger continues to point out, however, that there is really only a broad and vaguely defined unity for Arab causes in the Middle East and that religious affiliation usually determines the Syrians' attitude toward the relations of the Arab states with Israel and with the Western powers. The analysis becomes more complicated by virtue of the introduction of so many other variables related directly to the question of whether culture or nationality will or should emerge over religious identity as the focus of interest and commitment.

Indeed, Christianity in the Middle East is suffering, according to the Melkite Catholic patriarch, a crisis in identity and continuity, and this will have repercussions throughout the West.

Many of the Palestinian refugees are, in fact, Melkites under the patriarch's jurisdiction. The ultimate fear is that there will be no Christians left in the Holy Land. Since the now famous Six Day War in June of 1967, the Christians in all of the Holy Land are fewer than 90,000 (of whom 30,000 are Melkites) or not quite 2.2 percent of the total population of more than 4,000,000 people. Of these, more than one and one-half million are Moslem.

The Christians of Israel, furthermore, have a minority complex and generally prefer leaving the Holy Land for countries where religion or race has less influence on ordinary life. Emigration, indeed, is becoming the trend today, especially among the better-educated younger generation which is emigrating to the United States, Canada, and Australia. According to the Patriarch,

Many holy places are already empty of Christians; Ain-Karim, the village of John the Baptist and the Visitation, has no Christians today anymore . . . and its beautiful and large cathedrals are only open when pilgrims come for a visit. Bethlehem in the last ten years has seen more than half of its Christian population emigrate and we can assume if there is no change in this trend, that in 10 or 15 years there will be no Christians in the Land of Christ! And when our Arab Christians have gone they will not be replaced, no other Christians from outside being allowed to settle permanently in the Holy Land.[12]

The American Syrian-Lebanese are thus brought into the controversy as Christians with a responsibility to their historic past and religious inheritance as well as to the thousands of refugees dependent on the charity of the West for their daily existence. Whether Arabic-speaking nationals or Christians, they will inevitably react to the Middle East crisis. Israel's forays into Lebanon and Syria may arouse them even on the level of national, sociocultural identity. Whether it will or not remains to be seen. We are speaking now of a third and fourth generation of non-Arabic-speaking Americans considerably intermarried and essentially uninvolved in the politics of liberation. But there is evidence that they are responding. Project Ryaiat (Loving Care), a program to aid needy Palestinian children, was launched from Indiana in January, 1969, by a group of private citizens in response to the aftermath of the 1967 war in the Near East. It is a sponsorship program designed to render some financial aid to needy and war-victimized Arab families living in Palestine—Christian and Muslim alike. The hope is that such families will then find it easier to resist the various pressures and temptations to leave their homes and join the refugee camps outside Palestine, thus compounding the catastrophe of need, fatherlessness, and widowhood with possible permanent exile. The project received the official backing of the American Arabic Association in Boston (AMARA) and the support of a number of chapters of the Syrian-Orthodox Youth Organization (SOYO).

The AMARA organization has also made generous donations of funds to such organizations as American Middle East Rehabilitation Inc; Action Committee on American Arab Relations; and the Arab Anti-Defamation League. It has also worked closely with the Arab-American University Graduates Association and several church groups interested in developing a more balanced perspective on the Middle East crisis. AMARA is chiefly composed of the descendants of the early Christian Syrian-Lebanese immigration and draws its strength from the numerous yet scattered communities of New England.

The governments of the Middle East often miss the opportunity to capitalize on the potential support of Christian American Arabs. To do so, they would have to overcome the centuries of suspicion that has developed between the Moslem and Christian populations of the regions. On February 25, 1973, the *New York Times* reported that circulation of a proposed new Syrian constitution specifying freedom of religion produced serious disorders led by Islamic traditionalists in both Damascus and Aleppo, Syria —the cities from which most American Syrians have come. "In Damascus, 23 Moslem religious leaders circulated a declaration that called for inclusion in the new charter which is being described as an 'Arab Socialist' constitution, of an article declaring 'Islam is the religion of the Syrian state.' "[13]

The situation does not sit well with the Syrian-Lebanese Christian population in America. For these people to identify with the Palestinian struggle on the level of Arab nationalism requires that they identify themselves with Arabic culture and history. Yet when this tradition insists on being biased in favor of Islam, their affinity with it deteriorates. This says nothing of the fact that five decades of living in the United States have made them partial to a free economic system and that the communist-oriented governments of Syria and Egypt are especially anathema to them.

Regardless of the differences in reaction among the various religious groups in America, however, all Arabic-speaking Christians can respond to the religious issues generated by the conflict with Israel. Consequently, the appeal by the Christian religious leaders of Syria in 1971 did not fall on deaf ears. The plea urged response to the status of Jerusalem. According to a statement released by virtually all the Catholic and Orthodox patriarchs of Syria and Lebanon, the events that are currently taking place in the city of Jerusalem are so grave that their dimensions and implications go beyond the merely political and military local aspects. The patriarchs state:

> The process of expelling the Christian and Moslem inhabitants of the city, their physical liquidation and their replacement by Jews—this process, in addition to being tragic and brutal, exceeds the political and

demographic aspects of the subject. Palestine, and more specifically Jerusalem, was the cradle of civilization in its human and divine sides; spirit was once incarnated in it and thereby gave its land a unique place in history. For centuries the Jews, as a group, lived in this land with other communities and religious groups. There were centuries of peace and amity. Indeed, the Holy City was, and still is, the place in which the tradition of Abraham—the source of the three monotheistic religions—developed and from which it spread its light to the world. The civilization of the spirit thus replaced barbarism; man entered history and came to know the Lord of History.[14]

For the Christian patriarchs, Palestine and more specifically Jerusalem was not only the cradle of civilization but also the source of life, since God was made "man" there. Christian civilization, which they call "The Civilization," grew there, and the events of the 1960's represent to them a complete and radical distortion of its human and spiritual significance. They write:

For the goal of Zionism—implicitly or explicitly stated—is to destroy this human and spiritual heritage in merging it in a fanatical racist State. It claims that a haven is being founded for the Jews, but the whole world knows that this is being done at the expense of the Arabs. The farther goal of Zionism is even worse and much more serious; to uproot Civilization. For Abraham was not a founder of a race or a state. Real and true civilization emanated from a covenant, a genuine covenant between God and Abraham. . . . What the world is witnessing today—knowingly or unknowingly—is an abrogation of this covenant, the covenant of truth and freedom. . . . That proves decisively that Zionism, when its logic is carried to its very limits, has in it the seeds of a new barbarism, or to use more modern terminology, the seeds of an anti-revolution. In its political aspects, the conflict is one concerning a land and a people who have been uprooted and replaced by aliens. But the farther goal of Zionism is in fact to destroy a civilization which is The Civilization.[15]

Rather heady language, needless to say, but as a result all the Eastern Christian religious groups of Arabic extraction in the United States have adopted resolutions on the Middle East. The most outspoken of them is the Antiochian (Syrian) Orthodox Church, which went on record urging Secretary General U Thant to convene the United Nations Security Council to scrutinize breaches in the 1967 General Assembly resolution on Israel.[16]

The resolution protested the annexation of the Arab section of Jerusalem by Israel, an annexation they feel was forced and in unilateral defiance of world opinion and moral law. They especially condemned the current physical changes being made in East Jerusalem by Israeli occupation forces, allegedly arbitrarily and without regard for the wishes of the indigenous inhabitants or for their legal and spiritual rights.

In June of 1972, Dr. Frank Maria, chairman of the department of Near East and Arab refugee problems of the Antiochian Orthodox Christian Church, appeared before the Executive Committee of the National Council of Churches to present the Christian Arab perspective on the Middle East crisis. His concern was over the reluctance of the American Christian establishment to tackle the controversy head on:

> At stake in the Middle East . . . for American Christians are: the future of Christianity, the relationship between the 3 great monotheistic religions (Judaism, Christianity and Islam), the geopolitical interests of the United States, the integrity of the United States as a democracy and as a Christian nation, the peace of the world and possibly even the survival of mankind.[18]

After Israel's shooting down of a Libyan airliner in 1973, she was condemned by Syrian Eastern Christian clerics in many cities in the United States. The most unified action to take place among the American Syrian-Lebanese, however, was in response to the bombing of the Lebanese consulate in Los Angeles. Claiming to represent some 60,000 American Arabs living in Southern California, every Moslem and Syrian Christian leader living there sent telegrams indicating their shock and dismay to Samuel Yorty, mayor of Los Angeles, the district attorney and the chief of police.

In other instances, the new emerging attitude of Arabic-speaking Americans is reflected in the official position of the National Association of Federated Syrian-Lebanese American Clubs. Combining a statement of loyalty to the United States with support for the position of the Arab League on the Palestinian question, the association points out that it is an American organization devoted to the best interests of all the American people. Because its members are of Arab descent, Berger feels that "it can and has served as an effective link between America and the Arab World. . . . However . . . it has not and does not interfere in the internal affairs of these Middle Eastern nations."[19] The association refers to the responsibility of American citizens to make their views known on foreign policy: "Because its membership has close cultural ties and intimate knowledge of the Arab World, the National Association has a special responsibility to make recommendations regarding foreign policy in the Middle East." Guiding itself "solely by the dictates of the genuine interest of all the American people," the association urges the United States to insist upon the implementation of all the United Nations resolutions on the Palestinian question as a means of bringing "peace and justice" to the area.[29]

It must also be stressed that the memory of the immigrants themselves is rooted in the awareness that the Middle East was socially discriminatory to them and residence there an economic liability. America was the land of better opportunity so the phenomenon of Jews or Palestinians who deliberately go back there to live actually amazes many of the old-timers. This is true likewise of the general impression that most Syrian-Americans have of their homeland. The American press has continued the image of a desolate and backward Arab Middle East that the Jews turned into a fertile land.

While no one can disparage the industrial and general economic growth that Israel has fostered in Palestine, it is still somewhat of a historical inaccuracy to imply that the Middle East lacked a civilization and responsible economy until the creation of the Western-style state of Israel. Lebanon, Egypt, and Palestine itself have ancient and flourishing cultures and Lebanon, noted throughout the world as the "Switzerland of the East," is a thriving, free, constitutional democracy.

Lebanon has been the most successful in conveying her progressive image to the West. Consequently, the idea of a return home for a visit by many of the third- and fourth-generation American Syrian-Lebanese actually means going directly to Lebanon for the primary visit and then making a side trip to Syria. Lebanon enjoys an enormously popular reputation among all the Arabic-speaking people in the United States regardless of their specific nationalities. Many Syrian Christian Americans look to it now as their homeland because their patriarchates, that is, the seat of their church governments, are all located there.

Primarily for religious and social reasons, most of the Christians have left Syria for Lebanon and the New World and consequently their religious leaders have had to relocate in Lebanon.

Unity and the Present Syrian-Lebanese View of the Middle East Crisis

The fate of Lebanon in the Middle East crisis will be the key determinant of the reaction that most Christian Arab-Americans will collectively exhibit. The Lebanese in America today do in fact constitute the largest Arabic-speaking population here. Lebanon is considered to be the last best hope of embattled Christendom in the Middle East and many Syrian-Americans actually call themselves Lebanese simply because it implies being Western, French-educated, and democratic. It is also financially more profitable to be identified as a neutral Lebanese than as a hostile Syrian.

It is possible that Israel's forays into Lebanon will increase the anger of the Arabic-speaking Americans and might serve to unite all of them around a common cause. Today, there are nearly one million Americans of some Arabic ancestry who could be mobilized into a political force. While it is true that a majority of them, being American born, have no great emotional commitment to Arabic history and culture, it is also true that they have no inhibitions about crossing the social boundaries (religion, rite, home town) that traditionally controlled their ancestors' lives. They are also better educated and more willing to be identified as Arabs. Younger Syrians are also more willing to refer to their cultural tradition as Arab.[21]

Of course, the question still remains as to whether all these factors can unify the Christian Syrian-Lebanese Americans with their Arab Moslem compatriots and the new core of Arabists developing among the educated and growing American Palestinian population. Overcoming their historical dislike and mistrust of "outsiders," i.e., those outside of the same town and religion, is a formidable task. Even if they succeed, they may not be able to concretize their new consciousness and intentions in the real world of American politics. "Many Arab-Americans," writes Berger, "often can be heard saying 'After all, we're Americans. What have we got to do with those people over there? Let's forget those old ties and realize we're here to stay.' " Individual philanthropy is traditionally unknown in the Middle East except as it may be associated with religion, and as Berger again notes, "both foreign born and native American Syrians share a preoccupation with family, church and career, which . . . seems to exclude political interests."[22] Also, when they are politically active, they tend to be conservative. This judgment was first made in 1924 by Professor Hitti and it still stands today. "Radicalism," he wrote, "has no votaries among these people. . . . Very few of them interest themselves in politics or aspire to office."[23]

It is our belief that Americanization, education, and the need to respond to the mass media's image of them as hostile and aggressive "Arabs" will lead to at least a temporary awakening of the Syrian-Americans' international political consciousness. Indeed, a half century of existence in the United States has already altered the Syrians' general lack of interest in broad political and ideological issues and it seems more likely that they can now, more than ever before, respond effectively to the new call for Arab-American solidarity. For example, it has been suggested that they generally vote Republican today because it was the Truman administration that recognized the state of Israel (even though this same government recognized Lebanese and Syrian independence).[24] If this is the case, then we must assume some increased consciousness and political identification with the countries of the Arab East whence they came.

More significant in the cultivation of the new consciousness among the American-born Syrian-Lebanese is the presence now of vocal and committed leaders. Indeed, the present decade alone has witnessed "an additional 100,000 professionals coming to the states,"[25] from the Arab countries. Modest estimates indicate that almost 30,000 Arab intellectuals have left Egypt, Syria, and Iraq for America since late 1967. Some 70,000 preceded them between 1957 and 1967. Not unexpectedly, these immigrants have demographic characteristics that are quite different from those of the early Arabic-speaking pioneers. These differences may prove crucial in the development of Arab-American consciousness, and the outcome will depend on the interplay of the variables outlined here.

To begin with, about 90 percent of the Arab pioneers were Christians. Almost 70 percent of the late arrivals are Muslim. The pioneers were almost illiterate and were forced for their very survival to concentrate in ethnic communities where they built churches to perpetuate their traditional values. The recent arrivals, on the other hand, are actually the intellectual elite of Arab society and are highly educated and skilled. Nearly 75 percent were educated in the United States or Europe.

In spite of the quota restrictions on the Arab countries, most of the new arrivals entered the United States in the third and sixth immigrant preference categories, and Elkholy writes that

> the fifth immigration preference created by the new immigration law of July 1, 1968, helped many naturalized Americans to bring to the States, as immigrants, their immediate relatives. It takes the educated or skilled Arab no more than three months to acquire his immigration papers to enter the States, off quota. While the great majority of the pioneers married Arabs, around 68% of the late arrivals are married to Americans or Europeans.[26]

Ironically, the economic and military stranglehold that Israel has created in the Middle East has caused the Arab intelligentsia to demand basic structural changes in Arab society to allow for both the involvement of the educated in the political life of their countries and the redistribution of wealth. The Arabs in the Middle East need this population, but they have deserted the region in ever-increasing numbers. It is not that they do not wish to return, for they certainly do. It is just that certain fundamental changes will have to take place before they can become reintegrated in the mainstream of their old societies.

In the New World, Elkholy tells us, the "creation of a better Arab society is the goal of the 100,000 Arab professionals now resident in America."[27] He claims that they "feel sympathy with the Arab masses who are the victims of internal military leadership and external Zionism. The majority are active nationalists. They will become more active in the Arab cause as they enlist in organizations which can mobilize their massive knowledge, skill and talents toward the goal of restoring to their people that which they have lost."[28]

With these objectives in mind, the Association of Arab-American University Graduates (AAUG) was formed and has attracted the leading Arabic-speaking American scholars to its ranks. An evaluation of its membership, which is open to all

American citizens of Arab ancestry and to "anyone interested in Arab society and culture and in fostering understanding between Arabs and Americans," indicates that a substantial proportion of its one thousand members are children of the original Christian Syrian-Lebanese settlers. The association aims at promoting knowledge and understanding of cultural, scientific, and educational matters between the Arab and American peoples. It attempts to educate the American public, and the Arab-American public in particular, to the realities and conditions of the Middle East situation. Several books have been published by the association, conventions have been held, and direct political pressure has begun to be exerted.

Interestingly, the AAUG is a scholarly endeavor that demands an intellectual understanding and commitment to the Arab cause. Perhaps for this reason it can attract the thousands of Syrian-Lebanese Americans who are so Americanized that they could not relate to the Middle East situation in any way other than as interested and concerned Americans. Of course, all Arab-Americans can look to the association for guidance, direction, and leadership. However, they cannot be expected to identify completely with either its methods, purpose, or activities.

It may be that the only variable that will unite the Syrian-Lebanese population in the United States will be an out-and-out invasion of Lebanon. This is the one reality that most of the American Syrian-Lebanese can relate to. For either ethnic or religious reasons, most of them identify to some degree with Lebanon, and an Israeli attack might in fact supply them with an issue around which they could all unite.

Surveys recently taken in several Arab-American communities support the position that the key to Arab-American consciousness raising lies not only in the fate of Lebanon but also in the rise to positions of power in the community of educated American-born Arabs. In November, 1970, the *New York Daily News* ran a two-part series on "The Other New Yorkers" which treated the less-known ethnic enclaves of the city. It began: "Among those immigrants who brought their dreams of a better life to Ellis Island in the late 19th and early 20th century were a number of Arabs."[29] It then confusingly describes these "Arabs" as fully Americanized yet Syrian and/or Lebanese and/or Christian or

Moslem. Seemingly, these "Arabs" are all of these things at the same time!

Unknowingly, the writers set up a typology of "Arab-Americans" ranging from the nonassimilated through the semi and fully assimilated. The first group is purely Palestinian, heavily Moslem, and newly arrived. The second is Christian, American born, conscious of some culturally distinct past, educated in the United States, and at least marginally aware of the Palestinian crisis. At least, the *News* implies, they are not hostile to the Arab cause. The third group is fully Americanized with little or no interest in the affairs "of the old country." Surviving in the American business world is of paramount importance. "I never want to talk about fighting. I just want everyone to eat and be happy," says a Syrian restaurant owner.[30]

The report also notes that in 1970, the focus of the Maronite-dominated *Al-Hoda* press was solely on Lebanon, and "the publication is not wont to get involved in the Palestinian problem." "The *Lebanese-American Journal*," the *News* continues, "carries even less national and international news, concentrating primarily on social and cultural affairs in the tight-knit Arab community."[31] For the *News*, the best summary statement of the feelings of the typical Syrian-Lebanese American of 1970 can be found in the words of the president of the Salaam (Peace) Club, which consists of Syrian-Lebanese businessmen and professionals. "Our members don't want to get involved in the Middle East wars. As a matter of fact, as president, I've been trying to broaden our programs away from purely Arab subjects."[32] The speaker is an American-born Brooklyn Melkite Catholic from one of the most prosperous and popular Syrian Catholic families in the country.

However, the *News* survey also notes that there is a new group of Arab-Americans who "dismiss the business-as-usual form of American politics." They find their heroes "not here but abroad: Yasir Arafat, leader of Al-Fatah, the largest guerrilla group; George Habash, who masterminded the recent hijackings; and Leila Khaled, the woman hijacker."[33]

In a preliminary study of the "Arab" American community on Atlantic Avenue done in 1967 and entitled "Shishkabob, Pastrami and Peace in Brooklyn Heights,"[34] the *News* noted that in spite of the so-called Six Day War, Arabs and Jews "have lived peacefully side by side in Brooklyn Heights" for at least three generations. The owner of a Middle Eastern restaurant is quoted as saying: "We're mostly second and third generation Americans. There's a kind of detached feeling among Jews and Arabs in the neighborhood about the war. Besides, I don't allow any trouble. I'm not running a political play-group here." This feeling, notes the *News*, is typical along the main business street of the Arab community. "Most of the Jews around here have cultural backgrounds in Arab and Syrian culture," says a young, college-educated Arab businessman. It seems that the idea that Arabs and Jews should be fighting is a wishful imagining of the American mass media.

Unfortunately, the *News* and other surveyors only tapped the opinion of the conservative Syrian-Lebanese merchants who have a stake in keeping harmony with their many Jewish customers. While these people are involved in the community, they represent only a segment of it. "But ask Syrian and Lebanese working men," another respondent proffers, "not the rich, how they feel and you will find they agree too" with the Arab point of view. The *News* chose not to interview this population.

It must also be remembered that up until 1970 Lebanon had not been fully brought into the picture. The recent military expeditions into Lebanon, as well as the altered immigration law letting more and better-educated Palestinians into the United States, aroused public interest in the New York Arab population and forced the community out of its self-imposed cultural and political isolation. The Palestinians, for example, are less inclined to be mesmerized by the politically bland Syrian-American past and more inclined to immerse themselves in international politics.

To be an American of Middle Eastern ancestry—especially if it is Syrian—is to suffer, in the words of the *New York Times*, "the tug of an anguishing conflict."[35] The old-timers seem almost incapable of identifying fully with the Arab East. Apparently, doing so brings out a world of hostile feelings and inferiority complexes. On the other hand, forgetting the past creates enormous guilt and weakens the fabric of community life. Morroe Berger first noted this dilemma in 1955 when he wrote of the Syrian-Americans:

> Their relation to the Arab states thus lies within a narrower and less emotion-laden range than that of American Jews to Israel. This is not to say that Syrians avoid contact with representatives of the Arab governments here. They usually hold a banquet for newly arrived delegates from the Arab states or to honor them when they leave. They also welcome talks by speakers sent out by the Arab Information Center in New

York, which is supported by the Arab governments. . . . Syrian Americans, however, are circumspect in dealing with the Arab Information Center. When they ask for speakers, many clubs think it advisable to emphasize their American character, and the fact that they are requesting some services or other "as Americans."[36]

This fear of and reaction to being identified as Arab stems to an extent from the oppressive milieu that existed at the time of the anti-immigrant Dillingham Commission, which drafted the discriminatory Immigration Law of 1924. Indeed, the first text on Syrian Americans authored by Hitti,[37] must be understood against this background. He seems to go out of his way to de-Arabize his population—most likely to speed their acceptance and prevent wholesale legal discrimination against them. The Syrians themselves picked this ethos up and learned to Americanize themselves for acceptance. Accordingly, every complaint raised against immigrants in general was countered specifically by the author and one receives the impression that the Syrians were flawless immigrants who should have been happily and gracefully accepted by everyone. The price paid for acceptance obviously has been great.

As fate would have it, the attacks on Lebanon have actually reversed this general shame in and aversion to being identified as Arab. In the past, there was a tendency for Arabic-speaking people to bury their heads after each defeat by Israel, but there are now feelings of pride and concern as evidenced after the October, 1973, war. What the disparate Arab-American communities seem to share, notes the *New York Times*, "is a sense of being aggrieved. All deny, at least to strangers, being anti-Jewish, but all complain that the Arab side of the Mideast conflict is unfairly presented here."[38]

Following is an excerpt from a commentary made on March 7, 1973, by Robert Pierpoint, CBS White House news correspondent, on his program, *First Line Report.* It seems to support the suspicions of most Arab-Americans:

During this period of its emotion over a series of tragedies in the troubled Middle East, the United States appears to have lost its sense of fair play and justice and seems to be operating on a double standard. . . . The Israeli's have and utilize a formidable political and propaganda force in this country in the form of six million Jews. The Arabs, with only slightly less than a million descendents in America, are just beginning to organize a nationwide counterforce. Perhaps this will help bring balance. In the meantime, the rest of us might apply more studied balance and fair play to the difficult problems of the Middle East.[39]

His text was based on a comparison of the American reaction (including that from the White House) to Israeli raids in Lebanon and the shooting down of the Libyan airliner to that expressed after the Munich massacre.

Regardless of the official reaction of the American people, more and more Arabic-speaking Americans are feeling that the Palestinians are becoming desperate because they realize it is their fight. "They're here because they got thrown out of their country. Our Lebanese now they feel they've been let down. They felt the United States wouldn't let Lebanon get into the war. Now they're afraid because the invasions by the Israelis seem to negate this."[40]

Whatever the motivations or the specific issue, Arabic-speaking Americans are becoming more vocal and assertive. According to a recent report in the *Christian Science Monitor,* "Arab-Americans are beginning to press more vigorously and vocally their deep concern about United States policy in the Middle East." To begin with, they are calling on senators and congressmen with greater frequency. They are speaking on college compuses, and recently a small group met with former Secretary of State William P. Rogers. While this is "just a modest beginning," the *Monitor* reports that it is a trend "welcomed privately by many State Department officials, who feel that the American public, exposed primarily to pro-Israeli propaganda, is not adequately informed about Arab attitudes and problems and the pros and cons of American policy in the Middle East."[41]

A little over a year ago a group of concerned Americans of Arabic heritage met in Washington, D.C., to discuss the United States' posture toward the Middle East. It was determined that a lack of political action on the part of Americans of Arabic descent was very evident. Since that time, discussions with officials of various U.S. government agencies, including the Departments of State and Defense, and the National Security Council at the White House, have not only verified this deficiency, but reiterated the need for a national body.

The National Association of Arab Americans was incorporated in April, 1972, to fill this gap. One of the prime objectives of the

NAAA is to provide moral, financial, and political support to those Americans of Arabic heritage who seek political or public office, regardless of party affiliation. Another objective is to seek a more "balanced" U.S. policy in the Middle East. Members of the association have met with and maintain a continuous dialogue with senior officials at the Department of State, Department of Defense, the White House, members of Congress, and the press to discuss pertinent and timely issues. The founder of the organization, attorney Richard C. Shadyac of Washington, notes that "we do not seek the destruction of Israel, but we believe there should be an evenhanded policy in the Middle East. The energy (oil) problem and trade deficit are of prime concern to Americans and we feel the U.S. now is not acting in its best interests."[42]

Toward this end, Attorney Shadyac and a group of prominent American business and professional men met with Acting Secretary of State James Sisco on June 18, 1974 to express their concern over peace in the Middle East. A major portion of the meeting centered around the legitimate rights of the Palestinian people for a homeland. A month before, Frank Maria, chairman of the Political Action and Government Liaison Committee of the NAAA was a guest on the Mike Douglas Show during the recent energy crisis. His interview was a response to Senator Henry Jackson's remarks on the energy crisis and on defamatory comments and jokes by certain Jewish comedians who had appeared on the Mike Douglas Show since 1967. In brief, Maria argued that the Arabs are not solely to blame for the energy crisis. American support for Zionist expansion in Arab lands must also be considered.[43]

The *Monitor* also points out that the extent to which pro-Zionist pressure in Congress influences U.S. policies is felt by Arab-Americans to be alarming. It is noted, for example, that various trade bills have been held up over an amendment linking trade concessions to the Soviet Union with the issue of Jewish emigration. Thus, members of the association have been trying to impress on lawmakers, especially those who do not have Jewish constituencies, that changes in Washington's Middle East policy are imperative. "They say they have had an 'amazing' reception on Capitol Hill, indicating that legislators want to hear other sides of the question."[44]

Meanwhile, there are other small indications that Americans

may be in more of a mood these days to hear the Arab side of the case on the whole Middle East question. State Department officials, for example, report that more letters critical of Israel and U.S. policy toward it were received in the first few months of 1973 than in the previous three years mainly as a result of the Libyan airliner incident.

CHAPTER XIV

Conclusion

WHAT ALL THIS MEANS FOR THE FUTURE OF THE SYRIAN-Lebanese American community and its disposition toward the Middle East situation is difficult to ascertain at this time. On the one hand, events in the Middle East have raised the consciousness of Arab-Americans in areas never before tapped. As both a religious and ethnic minority they have always underplayed their overall cultural inheritance. Thus, the Middle East crisis may possibly supply them, as it is supplying American Jews, with a new focal point around which they can build some communal enterprises.

Moreover, they are now permitted to be ethnics in terms acceptable to American society in general. They can relate to the Middle East situation as concerned Americans whose cultural ancestry happens merely by accident to be Arab. They can fuse their ethnicity with their patriotism and emerge as fully American with no dual loyalties. In simple terms, they are popularizing the idea that what is good for Israel is not necessarily good for America and that one's loyalty to the United States should come first and is not actually related to support for the Zionist position on the Palestine question.

On the other hand, they are in fact only romantically involved with their historical past. Both socially and religiously, they have become only marginally and selectively involved in the institutions of their ethnic community. This is due to a great extent to the institutional incompleteness of their community and the irrelevance of their primary institutions (churches) to their present socioeconomic status and objectives. It is also because of the change in generations wherein the transmission and maintenance of ethnic identities became irrelevant and unnecessary in today's urban society. Ethnicity is, in the final analysis, a social fabrication that simply presupposes—usually for analytical and historical purposes—that a specific ethnic (national) community does in fact exist and that people dynamically identify themselves in ethnic terms and still live in a "peculiar" cultural fashion. This explains our skepticism in using the category "Arab" or even "Syrian" to describe Americans of Arabic-speaking ancestry.

Moreover, Syrian-Americans come in two varieties. One type carries the implication that they have "risen" *out* of a certain national or ethnic past while the other describes Syrians as participating in and identifying with the institutions and history of that past. As we have demonstrated, most Syrians belong in the first category, and for that reason, we can assume that they will eventually abandon completely the cultural style and social life that characterize their ethnic history.

Ultimately, the fate of those Syrians who identify with and support the community will be determined by the outcome of the assimilation process experienced by the primary institutional components of their community—their churches. Unfortunately for the Arabists among them, even these institutions have had to Americanize in order to attract and keep new members both from within and without the ethnic framework. The community, as has been demonstrated, has been decidedly unable or organizationally unwilling to create a commitment to its institutions among the young, and when it has succeeded, has been unable to sustain it.

Consequently, all the institutions of the Syrian-American community are actually speeding up the dissolution process because of their unwillingness to recognize the needs of a fully Americanized third and fourth English-speaking generation. It is for this reason that the churches of the Syrian-Lebanese Americans will die or become altered beyond recognition, signalling the end of the Syrian-Lebanese community as we now know it.

Also, in spite of its current vogue, the ability of the Middle East conflict to sustain interest in and commitment to the Arab world and its cultural past, short of the destruction of Lebanon by Israel, may not increase with time. Even now the issue is becoming defined more in terms of purely "national" interests, not ethnic ones. Their assumption now is that all Americans, regardless of ethnicity, can and should learn more about the Middle East and the present conflict with the State of Israel.

Notes and References

PREFACE

1. The entire July-August, 1974 issue of the *Center Magazine* (Vol. VII, 4), was dedicated to the question of ethnicity in American life.

2. This same theme is extensively developed in Michael Novak, *The Rise of the Unmeltable Ethnics* (New York: Herder and Herder, 1971).

3. This is the thesis of Will Herberg as stated in *Protestant, Catholic, Jew* (New York: Doubleday, 1960) and forms the basic conceptual framework used in this text.

4. June, 1974 issue of the *Newsletter* of the Association of Arab-American University Graduates (Vol. VII, #2).

CHAPTER I

1. Lewis Gaston Leary, *Syria: The Land of Lebanon* (New York: McBride, Nast & Co., 1913), p. 9.

2. There are several other Catholic Eastern rite groups living in the Middle East and in Eastern Europe. In Syria and Lebanon we have Syriac, Chaldean and Armenian rite Catholics. In Egypt, Copts, and in Eastern Europe Ukranians, Ruthenians. Collectively, they are often referred to as "Uniates."

3. Yves Congar, *After Nine Hundred Years* (New York: Fordham University, 1957).

4. Werner Cahnman, "Religion and Nationality," *American Journal of Sociology* 49:6 (May, 1944), p. 526.

5. Philip K. Hitti, *Lebanon in History* (New York: Macmillan Co., 1957), p. 320.

6. Yves Congar, *After Nine Hundred Years* (New York: Fordham Univ. Press, 1957), pp. 34-36.

7. E Jurji, *The Middle East: Its Religion and Culture* (Philadelphia: Westminster Press, 1956), pp. 59-60.

8. Hitti, *op. cit.*, p. 322.

9. Philip K. Hitti, *Syrians in America* (New York: Doran Co., 1924), p. 38.

10. John Badeau, *The Land Between* (New York: Friendship Press, 1958), p. 36.

11. Hitti, *Syrians in America*, p. 113.

12. Robert L. Daniel, "American Influence in the Near East before 1861," American Quarterly, XVI:I (Spring, 1964), p. 77.

CHAPTER II

1. A complete review of the early Arab pioneers can be found in Dr. Adele Younis's summary article, "The Arabs Who Followed Columbus," *Yearbook, 1965-1966* (New York: The Action Committee on American Arab Relations, 1966).

2. Philip K. Hitti, *Syrians in America*, p. 23.

3. A. H. Hourani, *Syria and Lebanon* (London: Oxford Univ. Press, 1946), pp. 60-61.

4. Abdo A. Elkholy, *The Arab Moslems in the United States* (New Haven, Conn.: College & University Press, 1966), p. 22.

5. *Ibid.*, pp. 22-25. For a further discussion see Philip Kayal, Estimating the Arab-American Population, *Migration Today*, Vol. 2 No. 5 (Sept. 1974) 3.

6. Christians also live in Israel and belong to several sects and rites. 85 percent of them live in Galilee, 60 percent in cities, 25 percent in villages. Among the Catholics there are some 25 thousand Latins, 20 thousand Melkites, 3 thousand Maronites and a few hundred Armenians, Syrians, Chaldeans, Copts and Ruthenians. Among the Orthodox (some 40 thousand in all) about half are Greek Orthodox and half Russian (emigration) Orthodox. Among the Monophysites (five thousand in all) one finds Armenians, Copts, Ethiopians and Syrians. While among the rest one finds Protestants, Anglicans, and about twenty tiny sects—six thousand believers in all.

7. "Christians In the Arab East," *The Link*, Nov./Dec., 1973, p. 1.

8. *Ibid.*, pp. 1-2.

9. Merlin Swartz, "The Position of News in Arab Lands Following the Rise of Islam," *The Muslim World*, LX, 1, 1970, p. 8.

10. *Ibid.*, pp. 1-10.

11. Swartz, *op. cit.* p. 9.

12. A. H. Hourani, *op cit.*, pp. 70-71.

13. Charles H. Malik, "The Near East," in Miner Searle Baten and Wilhelm Pauck, *The Prospects of Christianity Throughout the World* (New York: Charles Scribner & Sons, 1964) p. 88.

14. Hitti, *Syrians in America*, p. 49.

15. Documented throughout in Dr. Adele Younis, "The Coming of the Arabic-Speaking People to the United States," unpublished Ph.D. dissertation, Boston University, 1961.

CHAPTER III

1. Henry Jessup, *Fifty-Three Years in Syria* (New York: Revelle Co., 1910), p. 157.

2. Prominent sociologist Morris Zelditch dealt almost singularly with the Syrian American community when it was just forming here. His data

are available in an unpublished Master's dissertation. Morris Zelditch, "The Syrians in Pittsburgh," University of Pittsburgh, 1936.

3. Quoted in Zelditch, "The Syrians in Pittsburgh," p. 10.

4. See Earl of Cromer, *Modern Egypt I* (New York, 1900), p. 216; British Admiralty, *A Handbook of Syria* (London, 1936), p. 186; Hitti, *Lebanon in History*, p. 450.

5. Cromer, *op. cit.*, p. 218.

6. Sir G. A. Smith, *Syria and the Holy Land* (New York: Doran Co., 1908), p. 35.

7. E. J. Dillon, "Turkey's Plight," *The Contemporary Review*, July, 1913, pp. 123 and 128.

8. Hitti, *Lebanon in History*, p. 485.

9. Norman Duncan, "A People from the East," *Harper's Magazine*, March, 1903, p. 554.

10. Morris Zelditch, *op. cit.*, p. 19.

11. *Ibid.*, p. 39.

CHAPTER IV

1. "The People of New York," *Life*, February 17, 1947, pp. 89-96.

2. "Their First Impression of New York," *World Outlook*, June, 1918, p. 14.

3. Edward Rose, *The Old World and The New* (New York: Century Co., 1914), p. 168.

4. *United States Industrial Commission Reports*, 1900-1916 (Washington, D.C.: U.S. Government Printing Office, 1916), Vol. XV, p. 444.

5. Rev. Cyril Anid, *I Grew With Them* (Jounieh, Lebanon: Paulist Press), 1967, p. 18.

6. Morroe Berger, "America's Syrian Community," *Commentary*, 25:4 (April, 1958), p. 314.

7. Philip K. Hitti, *Lebanon in History*, p. 476.

8. *The Story of Lebanon and Its Emigrants Taken from the Newspaper Al-Hoda*, (New York: Al-Hoda Press, 1968), pp. 85-86.

9. Outlined in John P. Allhoff, "Analysis of the Role of St. Raymond's Maronite Church As an Agent in the Assimilation of Lebanese Families in St. Louis," unpublished Master's dissertation, University of Missouri, 1969, pp. 30-34.

10. *United States Industrial Commission Reports, 1900-1916*, Vol. XV, p. 442.

11. Dr. Peter Roberts, *Immigrant Races in North America* (New York: Y.M.C.A. Press, 1910), p. 74.

12. "Syrians In the United States," *Literary Digest*, May, 3, 1919, p. 43.

13. Quoted in Philip K. Hitti, *Syrians in America*, p. 69.

14. Francis Brown and Joseph Roucik, *One America* (New York: Prentice-Hall, 1952).

15. Habib Katibah, "Syrian Americans," in Brown and Roucik, *op. cit.*, p. 284.
16. Philip K. Hitti, *Syrians in America*, pp. 62-67.
17. William I. Cole, *Immigrant Races in Massachusetts* (Pamphlet, Mass. Dept. of Education, 1921).
18. Mrs. Louise Houghton, "Syrians in the United States," *The Survey*, Part I, July 1, 1911, p. 488.
19. Katibah, *op. cit.*, p. 284.
20. Estimates here are summarized in Hitti, *Syrians in America*, pp. 62-66; and Morris Zelditch, "The Syrians in Pittsburgh," unpublished Master's dissertation, Univ. of Pittsburgh, 1936, pp. 16-20; Morroe Berger, *op. cit.*, p. 314.
21. Berger, *op. cit.*, p. 314.
22. Hitti, *Syrians in America*, p. 65.
23. Cf: Barbara Aswad, ed., *Arabic Speaking Communities in American Cities* (New York: C.M.S. Publications, 1972). A draft study by the Arab-American Media Institute of Columbus, Ohio shows that there were 1,662,000 Americans of Arabic cultural heritage in 1970, of whom 1,080,000 were over the voting age of 18, and 108,000 over the age of 25 holding college degrees. Arab-Americans would then constitute about one percent of the U. S. population in over 270 metropolitan areas.
24. *Reports of the Industrial Commission of Immigration*, Vol. XV, p. 442.
25. Dr. Adele Younis, "The Coming of the Arabic-Speaking People to the United States," p. 224.
26. Analysis found in Zelditch, *op. cit.*, p. 19.
27. Hitti, *Syrians in America*, p. 67.
28. *Literary Digest, op. cit.*, p. 43.
29. Younis, *op. cit.*, p. 239.
30. Dr. Adele Younis, "The Growth of Arabic-Speaking Settlements in the United States," in Elaine Hagopian and Ann Paden, eds., *The Arab-Americans: Studies in Assimilation* (Wilmette, Illinois: The Medina University Press International, 1969), pp. 106-107.
31. Lucius Hopkins Miller, *Our Syrian Population: A Study of the Syrian Population of Greater New York*. (Columbia University Library, New York, and New York Public Library; Widener Collection, Harvard University, 1904).
32. Younis, "The Growth of Arabic-Speaking Settlements in the United States," p. 106.

Chapter V

1. *New York Herald*, October 29, 1905. See also *New York Times*, May 27, 1902, pp. 2, 5, 27; *New York Times*, October 24, 1905.
2. *Reports of the Industrial Commission*, Vol. XV, p. 443.

3. *Ibid.*, p. 445.
4. *Ibid.*, p. 443.
5. Herman Feldman, *Radical Factors in American Industry* (New York: Harper Brothers, 1931), p. 154.
6. *Ibid.*
7. Recounted in Dr. Adele Younis, "The Coming of the Arabic-Speaking People To the United States," p. 299.
8. *Ibid.*, pp. 303–304.
9. Edith Stein, "Some Near Eastern Immigrant Groups in Chicago," unpublished Master's dissertation, Univ. of Chicago, 1922, pp. 71-72.
10. Louise Houghton, "Syrians in the United States," *The Survey*, Part III, Sept. 2, 1911, p. 787.
11. Abstract of the Fifteenth Census, Tables 141, 27, pp. 278 and 1317 respectively; analysis found in Morris Zelditch, "The Syrians in Pittsburgh," p. 36.
12. Philip K. Hitti, *Syrians in America*, p. 91.
13. Edward Wakin, The Lebanese and Syrians In America (Chicago: Claretian Press, 1971), p. 21.
14. Recounted in Wakin, *ibid.*
15. Morroe Berger, "America's Syrian Community," *Commentary*, 25:4 (April, 1958), p. 316.
16. Bengough, "The Syrian Colony," *Harper's Weekly*, XXXIX (August 3, 1895), p. 746.
17. Houghton, *op. cit.*, 26 (Park I, p. 493; Part II, pp. 653, 654, 663, 664).
18. Philip K. Hitti, *Lebanon in History*, pp. 474-475; and Hitti, *Syrians in America*, p. vii.
19. Benedicto Chuaqui, "Arabs in Chile," *Americas*, 4:12 (December, 1952), p. 18.
20. Habib Katibah, "Syrian Americans," in Brown and Rocek, *One America*, pp. 286-287.
21. Dr. Adele Younis, "The Growth of Arabic-Speaking Settlements in the United States," in Hagopian and Paden, ed., *The Arab-Americans: Studies in Assimilation*, p. 108.
22. Berger, *op. cit.*, pp. 315-316.
23. Younis, "The Growth of Arabic-Speaking Settlements," p. 108.
24. Hitti, *Syrians in America*, p. 69.
25. Edward Corsi, *The Shadow of Liberty* (New York: Macmillan Co., 1935), pp. 261-266.
26. Younis, "The Growth of Arabic-Speaking Settlements," p. 108.
27. *Ibid.*, p. 109.
28. *Ibid.*
29. Houghton, *op. cit.*, Part II, pp. 650-654.

30. S. Mokarzel, "History of the Syrians in New York," *New York American*, October 3, 1927.

31. *United States Industrial Commission Report*, Vol. XV, 1901, pp. 30-36.

32. Cecyle S. Neidle, *The New Americans* (New York: Twayne Publishers, 1967), pp. 248-253.

33. Recounted in Wakin, *ibid.*, p. 25.

34. J. K. David, "The Near East Settlers of Jacksonville and Duvall County," paper read at the Jacksonville Historical Society annual meeting May 12, 1954, p. 9.

35. Safia F. Haddad, "The Women's Role in Socialization of Syrian-Americans In Chicago," in Hagopian and Paden, *op. cit.*, p. 94.

36. *Ibid.*

37. Houghton, *op. cit.*, Part II, p. 648.

38. *Ibid.*, p. 650

39. Lucius Hopkins Miller, *A Study of the Syrian Population of Greater New York* (Columbia Univ. Library, New York, 1904), p. 29.

40. Hitti, *Syrians in America*, pp. 93-94.

41. Wakin, *ibid.*, p. 37.

42. Houghton, *op. cit.*, Part II.

43. John F. Allhoff, "Analysis of the Role of St. Raymond's Maronite Church As an Agent in the Assimilation of Lebanese Families in St. Louis," p. 70.

44. Norman Dlin, "Some Cultural and Geographical Aspects of the Christian Lebanese in Metropolitan Los Angeles," unpublished Master's dissertation, Univ. of California, 1961, p. 21.

45. Naseer Aruri, "The Arab-American Community of Springfield, Mass.," in Hagopian and Paden, *op. cit.*, pp. 6-10.

46. *Ibid.*

47. *Ibid.*

48. Berger, *op. cit.*, p. 316.

49. Chuaqui, *op. cit.*, p. 18.

50. B. Abu-Laban, "The Arab-Canadian Community," in Hagopian and Paden, *op. cit.*, pp. 18-36.

CHAPTER VI

1. Many researchers who have attempted to do historical-sociological studies of Syrians in the Americas have mentioned the difficulties they encountered in trying to secure information from their subjects. It seems that the Syrians equated the "data collectors" with their Turkish oppressors and other enemies who used such information, once secured, against them.

2. Rev. Abraham Rihbany, *A Far Journey* (Boston: Houghton, Mifflin Co., 1914), p. 55.

3. The election of Congressman James Abourezk of South Dakota in

1973 to the United States Senate represents, as shall be demonstrated, something of a departure from this pattern.

4. William I. Cole, *Immigrant Races in Massachusetts*, p. 4.

5. Dept. of the Army, *United States Area Handbook of Syria* (Washington, D.C.: American University, 1965), p. 88.

6. Philip K. Hitti, *Syrians in America*, Part IV. Chapter deals with the social and economic conditions of Syrians and pages 83-85 deal with his "crime" rates in particular.

7. Louise Houghton, "Syrians In the United States," *The Survey*, Part II, August 5, 1911, p. 663.

8. Morris Zelditch, "The Syrians in Pittsburgh," p. 57.

9. Hitti, *Syrians in America*, p. 87.

10. Reported *ibid.*, p. 54.

11. *Ibid.*, p. 67.

Chapter VII

1. Mary Bosworth Treudley, "The Ethnic Group as a Collectivity," *Social Forces,* 31:3 (March, 1953), p. 261.

2. V. Nahirny and J. Fishman, "American Immigrant Groups: Ethnic Identification and the Problem of Generation," *The Sociological Review,* 13:3 (Nov., 1965), pp. 311-25.

3. Daniel Glaser, "Dynamics of Ethnic Identification," *American Sociological Review,* 23:1 (Feb., 1958), p. 31.

4. Nahirny and Fishman, *op. cit.*, p. 314.

5. Dr. Adele Younis, "The Coming of the Arabic-Speaking People to the United States," p. 287.

6. Rev. Thomas J. McMahon, "The Glory of Lebanon Shall Come Unto Three," *Lebanese-American Journal,* January 9, 1966, p. S-11.

7. Editorial, *Lebanese-American Journal*, January 2, 1969, p. 1.

8. Morroe Berger, "America's Syrian Community," *Commentary*, 25:4 (April, 1958), p. 317.

9. *The Story of Lebanon and Its Emigrants* (New York: Al-Hoda Press, 1969), p. 54.

10. "Brazil: Sons of the Phoenicians," *Newsweek*, January 8, 1968, p. 40.

11. Treudley, *op. cit.*, p. 261.

12. Naseer Aruri, "The Arab-American Community of Springfield, Mass.," in Hagopian and Paden, eds., *Arab-Americans: Studies in Assimilation,* p. 54.

13. Donald Attwater, *Catholic Eastern Churches* (Wisconsin: Bruce, 1935), p. 18.

14. Archbishop Joseph Raya, "Message of Galilee" (monograph), Nazareth, February, 2, 1969.

15. *Ibid.*

16. Younis, "The Coming of the Arabic-Speaking People," p. 218.

Chapter VIII

1. Rev. Alan Maloof, "Catholics of the Byzantine-Melkite Rite in the U.S.A.," *Eastern Churches Quarterly,* IX: 5 (Winter, 1951), p. 265.

2. See Oona Sullivan, "Metropolitan Anthony," *Jubilee*, Jan., 1962, 9:9 pp. 39-44, for further data on the Syrian Orthodox in this country.

3. Y. J. Chyz and L. Read, "Agencies Organized by Nationality Groups in the United States," *The Annals of the American Academy of Political and Social Science,* 262 (March, 1949), pp. 148-58.

4. Raymond Breton, "Institutional Completeness of Ethnic Communities and the Personal Relations of Immigrants," *American Journal of Sociology,* 70:2 (Sept., 1964), p. 193.

5. Breton, *op. cit.*, p. 200.

6. Oscar Handlin, *The Uprooted* (Boston: Little Brown, 1951), p. 135.

7. Nathan Glazer and Patrick Moynihan, *Beyond the Melting Pot* (Boston: M.I.T. Press, 1961), p. 235.

8. Oscar Handlin, *The American People* (Cambridge: Harvard University Press, 1954), p. 92.

9. Thomas Harte and C. J. Nuesse, *The Sociology of the Parish* (Milwaukee: Bruce, 1951), p. 166.

10. Lloyd Warner and Leo Srole, *The Social Systems of American Ethnic Groups* (New Haven: Yale Univ. Press, 1945), p. 176.

11. Interview with Fr. Robert Lewis, October 21, 1968.

12. Kennedy, *Official Catholic Directory* (1968).

13. Philip M. Kayal, "The Churches of the Catholic Syrians and Their Role in the Assimilation Process," unpublished Ph.D. dissertation, Fordham University, 1970.

14. Will Herberg, *Protestant Catholic, Jew* (New York: Doubleday, 1960).

15. Rev. Alan Maloof, "Catholics of the Byzantine Rite," *op. cit.*, Part II, p. 238.

16. Philip Hitti, *Syrians in America*, p. viii.

17. Hitti, *Lebanon in History*, p. 176.

Chapter IX

1. Oscar Handlin, *Immigration as a Factor in American History* (Englewood Cliffs: Prentice-Hall, 1959), p. 771.

2. Rev. Alan Maloof, "Catholics of the Byzantine-Melkite Rite in the United States," *Eastern Churches Quarterly,* 9:4-7, Part I, p. 197.

3. Outlined further in Afif Tannous, "Acculturation of an Arab-Syrian Community in the Deep South," *American Sociological Review,* 8:3 (June, 1943), pp. 364–71.

4. Hitti puts it this way: "Of all the immigrant races, the Syrians seem to be the most jealous of those of their number who aspire to leadership and are consequently most leaderless. Intensely individualistic with a history and geography that militate against cooperative effort the modern

Syrian has come to look upon organization with suspicion and contempt." *Syrians in America*, p. 94.

5. Habib Katibah, unpublished manuscript quoted in Morris Zelditch, "The Syrians In Pittsburgh," p. 47.

6. H. Richard Niebuhr, *The Social Sources of Denominationalism* (New York: World Publishing Co., 1929), Ch. VII.

7. Patriarch Maximos Hakim, "On the Melkites in the United States," *Melkite Digest*, IV:3 (June-July, 1968), p. 5.

8. King did not mean to imply that the Maronites have become the only latinized Eastern church. Indeed, the Melkites, by their insertion of the "filioque clause" in the creed, their adoption of the Western calendar, the introduction of the low or private mass, as well as the external cultus of the Blessed Sacrament and the feast of Corpus Christi, can hardly consider themselves unlatinized. Archdale King, *The Rites of Eastern Christendom* (Rome: Catholic Book Agency, 1947-48), p. 102.

CHAPTER X

1. Cf: Will Herberg, *Protestant, Catholic, Jew.*

2. Marshal Sklare, "The Function of Ethnic Churches: Judaism in the United States," In J. M. Yinger, *Religion, Society and the Individual* (New York: Macmillan, 1957), p. 461.

3. Mary B. Treudley, "The Ethnic Group as a Collectivity," *Social Forces*, 31:3 (March, 1953), p. 261.

4. Oscar Handlin, *The Uprooted*, p. 187.

5. Philip K. Hitti, *Syrians in America*, p. 34.

6. Cf: Florian Znaniecki, *Modern Nationalities* (Urbana: Univ. of Illinois, 1952).

7. Treudley, *op. cit.*, p. 263.

8. Hitti, *Syrians in America*, p. 87.

9. Treudley, *op. cit.*, p. 261.

10. Rev. John Elya, "The Accommodation of a Socio-Religious Sub-System: The Melkite Catholics in the United States," unpublished term report, Boston College, 1965, p. 10.

11. Oscar Handlin, "Historical Perspectives on the American Ethnic Group," *Daedalus* (Spring, 1961), p. 225.

12. Naseer Aruri, "The Arab-American Community of Springfield, Mass.," in Hagopian and Paden, eds., *The Arab-Americans: Studies in Assimilation*, p. 53.

13. Morroe Berger, "America's Syrian Community," *Commentary*, 25:4 (April, 1958), p. 316.

14. Afif Tannous, "Acculturation of an Arab-Syrian Community in the Deep South," *American Sociological Review*, 8:3 (June, 1943), p. 268.

15. Rev. Constantine Volaitis, "The Orthodox Church in the United States as Viewed from the Social Sciences," *St. Vladimir's Seminary Quarterly*, 5:1, 2 (1961), p. 72.

16. Elaine Hagopian, "The Institutional Development of the Arab-American Community of Boston: A Sketch," in Hagopian and Paden, *op. cit.*, p. 69.

17. Adele Younis, "The Coming of the Arabic-Speaking People to the United States," p. 325.

18. Louise Houghton, "Syrians in the United States: Business Activities," *The Survey*, Part II, Aug. 5, 1911, pp. 798-99.

19. Donald Cole, *Immigrant City: Lawrence, Mass., 1845-1921* (Chapel Hill: University of North Crolina Press, 1963), pp. 160-61.

20. Treudley, *op. cit.*, p. 262.

21. *Ibid.*, p. 263.

22. A complete review of the data collected and referred to herein can be found in the doctoral dissertation of the author: Philip M. Kayal, "The Churches of the Catholic Syrians and Their Role in the Assimilation Process." See especially Chapter X.

23. *Ibid.*, p. 400.

24. Cf: Herberg, *op. cit.*

25. Fr. Raymond Shashasty, "Rochester Youth News," *Melkite Newsletter*, 1:7 (Dec., 1965), p. 7.

26. T. Witterman and Irving Kraus, "Structural and Social World," *Sociology and Social Research*, 48:3 (April 1964), p. 348.

27. Interview, Sept. 10, 1969.

28. Interview, June 10, 1969.

CHAPTER XI

1. These values are reviewed in Robin Williams, *American Society* (New York: Alfred Knopf, 1952) and John Gillin, "National and Regional Cultural Values in the United States," *Social Forces*, 34:2 (Dec., 1955), pp. 107-13.

2. Quoted in Francis Brown and J. Roucik, *One America*, p. 285.

3. Andrew Greeley, "Ethnicity as an Influence on Behavior," address delivered at Fordham Univ., June, 1968, pp. 9-10.

4. Amitai Etzioni, "The Ghetto: A Re-evaluation," *Social Forces*, 37:3 (March, 1959), pp. 255-62.

5. Berger, *op. cit.*, p. 316.

6. Naseer H. Aruri, "The Arab-American Community of Springfield, Mass.," in Hagopian and Paden, eds., *The Arab-Americans: Studies in Assimilation*, p. 63.

7. Marcus Hansen, "The Third Generation In America," *Commentary*, XIV (Nov., 1952), pp. 492-500.

8. Cf: P. J. Campisi, "Ethnic Family Patterns: The Italian Family in the United States," *American Journal of Sociology*, 53:6 (May, 1948), pp. 443-50.

9. Abdo A. Elkholy, "The Arab-Americans: Nationalism and Traditional Preservations," in Hagopian and Paden, *op. cit.*, p. 7.

10. Safia F. Haddad, "The Women's Role in Socialization of Syrian-

Americans in Chicago," in Hagopian and Paden, *op. cit.*, p. 86.

11. *Ibid.*, p. 91.

12. Elkholy, *op. cit.*, p. 12. Aruri writes: "Some 66% of our respondents are able to speak Arabic and 23% speak it frequently in their homes. Similarly 25% can read and write Arabic, but only 20% . . . passed the language on to their children. Only 13% of the Catholics passed it on." *Ibid.*, p. 62.

13. Elaine Hagopian, "The Institutional Development of the Arab-American Community of Boston: A Sketch," in Hagopian and Paden, *op. cit.*, pp. 71-72.

14. Aruri, *op. cit.*, p. 56.

15. *Ibid.*

16. Treudley, *op. cit.*, pp. 261-262.

17. Hagopian and Paden, *op. cit.*, p. 82.

18. Philip K. Hitti, *Syrians in America*, p. 94.

19. "Lebanese Festival in Bridgeport," *The Syrian World*, September, 1930, V:I, pp. 52-53.

20. Berger, *op. cit.*, p. 323.

21. *Action*, Sept. 1, 1969, p. 6.

22. Milton Gordon, *Assimilation in American Life* (New York: Oxford Univ., Press, 1964), p. 125.

23. See data found in the unpublished research report of Fr. John Elya entitled "The Accommodation of a Socio-Religious Sub-System: The Melkite Catholics in the United States."

CHAPTER XII

1. Dr. Adele Younis, "The Coming of the Arabic-Speaking People to the United States," p. 311.

2. Quoted in *ibid.*, p. 311.

3. Raymond Breton, "Institutional Completeness of Ethnic Communities and the Personal Relations of Immigrants," *American Journal of Sociology*, 70:2 (Sept., 1964), pp. 193-205.

4. Breton, *op. cit.*, pp. 200-201.

5. *Melkite Digest*, III:4, p. 11.

6. Rev. John Elya, "The Accommodation of a Socio-Religious Sub-System: The Melkite Catholics in the United States," p. 6.

7. *Ibid.*, p. 5.

8. Thomas Bird, "An Elected Bishop in America," *Commonweal*, 89:10 (Dec. 6, 1968), p. 335.

9. *Ibid.* All statistics taken from this source.

10. Patriarch Maximos Hakim, "On the Melkites in the United States," *Melkite Digest*, IV:3 (June-July, 1968), p. 5.

CHAPTER XIII

1. Roy V. Pee, *The Political Clubs of New York City* (New York: 1935), p. 258, 12.

2. Editorial, "Joseph L. Barakat for Congress," *Action*, August 28,

1972, p. 2.

3. "Senator James Abourezk Tells Senate . . ." *Action*, May 7, 1973, p. 1; "Senator Abourezk Supports Senator Fulbright," *Action*, April 22, 1974, p. 1; "Abourezk, NAAA Meet with Attny, General," *Leb. Amer. Jl.*, July 4, 1974, p. 1.

4. "Support Abourezk, Committee Appeals to Community," *Action*, September 25, 1972, p. 1.

5. Morroe Berger, "America's Syrian Community," *Commentary*, 24:4 (April, 1958), p. 319.

6. "Mideast: A Canvass for Fairness," *Action*, September 25, 1972, p. 2.

7. *Ibid.*

8. "Rebuttle of Golda Meir Profile,' " *Action*, July 9, 1973, p. 4.

9. Berger, *op. cit.*, p. 317.

10. This is the title of a book by Richard Chesnoff, Edward Klein, and Robert Littell (New York: Coward-McCann, 1969).

11. Berger, *op. cit.*, p. 317.

12. Patriarch Maximos V. Hakim, "Christians in the Holy Land," *Melkite Digest*, III, 6 (Nov.-Dec., 1967), p. 5.

13. "Religious Freedom in Charter Said to Stir Syrian Disorders," *New York Times*, February 25, 1973, p. 4.

14. "Christian Religious Leaders of Syria Appeal to Christian Conscience," *Action*, III, 2 (June 14, 1971), p. 2.

15. *Ibid.*

16. "Antiochian Orthodox Church Head Urges U.N. To Check Israel," *Action*, III, 6 (July 26, 1971), p. 3.

17. "Antiochian Orthodox Convention Adopts Historic Resolution on Mideast," *Action*, III, 12, p. 1.

18. "American Christians and the Holy Land," *Action*, IV, 4 (June 12, 1972), p. 2.

19. Berger, *op. cit.*, p. 318.

20. *Ibid.*

21. Berger, *Ibid.*, p. 321.

22. Berger, *Idem.*

23. Philip K. Hitti, *Syrians in America* (New York: Doran Co., 1924), p. 90.

24. Berger, *Ibid.*, p. 319-20.

25. Abdo A. Elkholy, "The Arab-Americans: Nationalism and Traditional Preservations," in Hagopian, *Ibid.*, p. 3.

26. Elkholy, *Idem.*

27. *Ibid.*, p. 16.

28. *Ibid.*, p. 17.

29. "The Other New Yorkers: Arabs, Old and New, Face an Ideology Gap," *New York Daily News*, November 9, 1970, p. 46.

30. "A Dream of Palestine Grows in Brooklyn," *New York Daily News*, November 10, 1970, p. 78.
31. *Daily News, Ibid.*, p. 46.
32. *Idem.*
33. *Idem.*
34. "Shishkabob, Pastrami and Peace in Brooklyn Heights," *New York Daily News*, June 8, 1967, Vol. 48, #298, p. 7C.
35. "Mideast Tensions Afflicting the Arab Communities Here," *New York Times*, October 7, 1972, part II, p. 1.
36. Berger, *Ibid.*, p. 318.
37. Hitti, *Ibid.*
38. *New York Times*, October 7, 1972, Part II, p. 1.
39. "Double Standard on Mid East," *Action*, March 12, 1973, p. 1.
40. *New York Times*, October 7, 1972, part II, p. 1.
41. "U. S. Arabs Rap Policy on Mideast," *The Christian Science Monitor*, May 12, 1973, p. 6.
42. *Idem.*
43. *Idem.* "NAAA Meets With Sisco," *Lebanese American Journal*, July 4, 1974, p. 1; "Frank Maria on the Mike Douglas Show," *Action*, May 6, 1974, p. 1.
44. Monitor, *Idem.*

Selected Bibliography

Cataloguing research reports, data, texts and general information on Arab Americans is difficult because of the wide range of peoples and nationalities who are Arabic speaking and resident in this country. The fact that Arab Americans are both Christian and Moslem and immigrants over several decades as well as from a host of countries does not simplify the task any. Researchers, however, might be wise to check the following general sources before they refer to the specific items listed at the end.

To begin with, the histories of Moslem Americans are somewhat easier to locate simply because they are less numerous and the majority are of more recent origin. An excellent source, which is complete with bibliography, is Abdo A. Elkholy's *The Arab Moslems In the United States* (New Haven: College & Univer. Press, 1966). Journals and collections like the *Encylopedia Britannica, The Encylopedia of Islam* and *The Moslem World, The Palestine Digest* and the trade magazines of the various oil companies like *ARAMCO World Magazine* often times carry articles on and by Arabs in the diaspora. They also help clarify terms and concepts which are unique to the Middle East such as 'millet,' rite, Eastern Churches, Sun'ni Moslem, etc.

Good sources of the communities' activities can also be found in such national tabloids as the *Muslim Star*, published by the Federation of Islamic Associations in the U. S. and Canada (headquarters in Detroit), and the *Bulletin*, published by the Islamic Center in Washington, D. C. Also such newspapers as *The Arab-American Message* and *Al Bayan* (both published in Detroit) carry news of the various Moslem communities. For historical information, sometimes local libraries will have copies of past suspended newspapers. For example the Detroit Public Library has some copies of some six suspended tabloids in the Detroit region.

The Arab Christian experience is more complicated because it is diffused throughout several areas and originated in so many different nation-states. Because most of the early migrants were in fact Christians, descriptive and educational religious texts written in this country after 1915 often times have reference to Syrian and/or Lebanese Christian Americans. These immigrants were members of Eastern Christianity which is partially Roman Catholic and partially Eastern Orthodox. The

Catholic segment as indicated is divided into several rites and it is under this rubric, i.e., Eastern Churches or Eastern rites that much material on their religious experiences in this country can be found. For example, *The Eastern Churches Quarterly* and *Diakonia* have several articles on the Maronites of Lebanon in America and the assimilation of American Melkites who are primarily Syrians. The Orthodox experience has been treated in these journals as well as the *St. Vladimir's Seminary Quarterly*. See especially, Constantine Volaitis, "The Orthodox Church in the United States as Viewed from the Social Sciences." *St. Vladimir's Sem. Quart.*, 5:1-2 (1961), pp. 63-87.

Researchers are advised that they must not expect articles on Arab-Americans to be necessarily indexed under that title. The Christian Arab population, for example, is described and analyzed in texts or articles on "national parishes," "Eastern Catholics," or even "Syrian Christians" when in fact the authors usually mean and are describing "Lebanese Catholics." All these categories, therefore, should be searched out thoroughly.

The most important source of histories and biographies of the various Arab communities in this country are found in the *Anniversary Journals* of each independent parish or Mosque as well as those of the larger religious bodies they belong to. For example, each Arab Christian parish has traditionally published a yearly journal depicting its growth, changes and history for its readers. On the national level, it is wise to utilize the Journals of the *Syrian Orthodox Youth Organization* (SOYO), the *Melkite Exarchate* and the *Maronite Eparchy*. One journal, *The Melkite Digest* and a survey text entitled *Melkites In America* (Boston: Melkite Exarchate, 1971) are especially important.

In a similar and related vein are the journals of the local and national Syrian/Lebanese and other Arab social organizations. In particular the journals of the *Haddad Foundation*, the *ALSAC* organization of entertainer Danny Thomas, the publications of the *Association of Arab-American University Graduates* (AAUG), and the *National Federation of Syrian-Lebanese Clubs* as well as their affiliated chapters. More important as preliminary sources are the publications of the *Al-Hoda* press such as *The Syrian World*, (on microfilm at the Library of Congress), *The Syrian Commerce of New York*, *The Syrian-Business Directory (1908-1909)*, *Al-Hoda* (in Arabic as is *Al-Bayan*), the *Lebanese-American Journal*, *Heritage*, and *Action* which appears primarily in English and gives contemporary information on all United States Arab communities. The emerging Egyptian community in North America puts out *Misr* an Arab bi-weekly newspaper. It originates in Jersey City, New Jersey. Another new publication is the *Arabic Tribune* published by the Federation of Arab Immigrants. Toledo, Ohio. Most of these tabloids can be located through the services of *Al-Hoda* or *Action* in New York City.

Another available and useful primary source for information on

Syrian/Lebanese immigration and subsequent assimilation can be found in the autobiographies of the early Christian pioneers. For example, *I Grew With Them* by Rev. Cyril Anid (Jounieh, Lebanon: Paulist Press, 1967) is actually the assimilation story of the Catholic Syrians of Paterson, New Jersey. Similar texts are Rev. Abraham Rihbany, *A Far Journey* (Boston: Houghton, Mifflin Co., 1914), and Salom Rizk, *Syrian Yankee* (Garden City: Doubleday, 1943). A humorous account of growing up Lebanese in the United States is found in William P. Blatty's *Which Way to Mecca, Jack?* (New York: B. Geis Assoc., 1960).

Generally speaking, the classic American texts on immigration barely touch on the Arab-Americans who are variously described as Turks, Asians, or Assyrians. Some useful surveys, however, can be found in *One America* (New York: Prentice-Hall, 1952) by Brown and Roucik; *Around the World in New York* (New York: Century Co., 1924) by Konrad Berovici and William J. Cole's *Immigrant Races in Massachusetts* (Boston: Dept. of Education, 1919).

Two other publications deserve special mention here. The Association of Arab-American University Graduates has published a collection of articles entitled *Arab-Americans: Studies in Assimilation* (Wilmette, Illinois: Medina University Press, 1969) and edited by Elaine Hagopian and Ann Paden. Each contribution is separately listed below. Just recently the AAUG in conjunction with the Center for Migration Studies published *Arabic Speaking Communities in American Cities* (1974) edited by Barbara Aswad of Wayne State University. A doctoral dissertation by Dr. Adele L. Younis is also noteworthy. Entitled *The Coming of the Arabic-Speaking People to the United States* it contains a complete bibliography of all material appearing on Arab Americans up to 1961. Newspaper reports are also catalogued. Currently numerous attempts are being made to collect materials on the various communities before they are lost or thrown away. The AAUG has established an Archives Collection for North America in conjunction with the Center for Immigrant Studies of the University of Minnesota in Minneapolis. Some local AAUG chapters, such as that of Detroit, are also collecting materials for a local collection.

Additional References

ABDAH, MOSHID. *From the Visions of Life: A Group of Stories and Social Articles* (Arabic). Boston: The Syrian Press. 1929.

ABU-LABAN, BAHA. "The Arab-Canadian Community," in Hagopian and Paden, *op. cit.*, pp. 18-36. 1969.

ADDIA, WILLIAM E. and THOMAS ARNOLD. *Christians of Chaldean Rite, A Catholic Directory*. London: Rutledge & Kegan Paul. 1964.

ADENEY, WALTER F. *The Greek and Eastern Churches*. Clifton, New Jersey: Reference Book Publishers. 1965.

AL-HODA. *The Story of Lebanon and Its Emigrants*. New York: Al-Hoda Press. 1968.

ANTEBI, MICHAEL. "The Syrian Sephardim of Bensonhurst," *Jewish Press*, Sept. 23rd. 1960.

ARIDA, NASIB and SABRI ANDREA. *Directory of Syrian Americans in the United States*. New York: Syrian American Printers. 1930.

ASWAD, BARBARA. *Arabic Speaking Communities in American Cities*. New York: Center for Migration Studies, 1974.

BEYNON, E. D. "The Near East in Flint, Michigan: Assyrians and Druze and Their Antecedents," *Geographical Review*, 24 (January), pp. 234-274. 1944.

BARCLAY, HAROLD. "A Lebanese (Moslem) Community in Lac LaBiche, Alberta," *Immigrant Groups*, Jean L. Elliot, ed., Scarborough, Ontario: Prentice-Hall of Canada, Ltd. 1961.

BENGOUGH, W. "The Syrian Colony," *Harpers Weekly*, August 3rd., p. 746. 1895.

BERGER, MORROE. "America's Syrian Community," *Commentary*, 25:4 (April), pp. 314-323. 1958.

———"Americans from the Arab World" in James Kritzeck & R. Bayly Winder (eds.) *The World of Islam*. New York. St. Martins Press. Pp. 351-372. 1959.

CAHNMAN, WERNER. "Religion and Nationality," *American Journal of Sociology*, 49:6 (May), pp. 524-529. 1944.

CHUAQUI, BENEDICTO. "Arabs in Chile," *Americas*, 4:12 (Dec.) pp. 17-29. 1952.

DAVIES, R. P. "Syrian Arabic Kinship Terms," *Southwestern Journal of Anthropology*, 5:3 (Autumn), pp. 244-252. 1949.

DUNCAN, NORMAN. "A People from the East," *Harpers Magazine* (March), pp. 62-65. 1903.

ELKHOLY, ABDO A. "The Arab Americans: Nationalism and Traditional Preservations," in Hagopian and Paden, *op. cit.*, pp. 3-17. 1969.

GOLDBERG, MERLE. "Casbah In Brooklyn," *New York Magazine*, July 14th, pp. 62-65. 1969.

GRIGORIEFF, DIMITRY. "The Historical Background of Orthodoxy in America," *St. Vladimir's Seminary Quarterly*, 5:1,2. pp. 3-53. 1961.

HANNA, MARWAN. "The Lebanese in West Africa," *West Africa*, #2141 (April 26th). 1958.

HADDAD, SAFIA. "The Woman's Role in Socialization of Syrian-Americans in Chicago," in Hagopian and Paden, *op. cit.*, pp. 84-101. 1969.

HAGOPIAN, ELAINE C. "The Institutional Development of the Arab-American Community of Boston: A Sketch," in Hagopian and Paden, *op. cit.*, pp. 67-83. 1969.

HITTI, PHILIP. *Syrians In America*. New York: George Doran. 1924.

HOUGHTON, LOUISE. "Syrians in the United States," *The Survey*. Vol. 26, Part I-July 1; Part II-August 5th; Part III-Sept. 2nd; Part IV-

Oct. 7th. 1911.

"In Santiago Society, No One Cares If Your Name is Carey or De-Yrazaval," *New York Times*, Sept. 14th, p. 84. 1969.

JOSEPH, SUAD. "Where the Twain Shall Meet: The Lebanese in Cortland County," *New York Folklore Quarterly*, 20:3, (Sept.), pp. 175-191. 1964.

KASSES, ASSAD S. "Cross Cultural Comparative Familism of a Christian Arab People," *Jl. of Marriage and the Family*, Vol. 34, #3 (August), pp. 539-544. 1972.

KATIBAH, HABIB I. *Arabic-speaking Americans*. New York: The Institute of Arab-American Affairs. 1946.

KAYAL, PHILIP. "Eastern Catholics See New Role in America," *Melkite Digest* 3:1 (Dec.-Jan.) pp. 5-7. 1966.

———"Eastern Christians in America: Problems in Dialogue," *Diakonia* 2:2, pp. 93-100. 1967.

———"Religion and Assimilation: Catholic 'Syrians' in America," *International Migration Review*, Vol. 7, No. 4 (Winter) pp. 409-426. 1973.

———"Problems in Classification: Estimating the Arab-American Population," *Migration Today*, 2:5. (Sept. 1974) 3.

———"Religion in the Syrian-American Community," in Barnara Aswod, op. cit., pp. 111-136.

KAROUB, MICHAEL (ed.). Golden Jubilee Testimonial Program Honoring Hussein Karoub for Fifty Years to Islam and the American-Arab Communities in the U. S. and Canada. Detroit: Arab-American Printing Co. 1962.

LACKO, MICHAEL. "The Churches of Eastern Rite in North America," *Unitas* 16 (Summer), pp. 89-115. 1964.

LOVELL, EMILY. "A Survey of the Arab-Muslims In the United States and Canada." Muslim World Vol. 43, #2, (April), pp. 139-154. 1973.

MAKDISI, NADIM. "The Maronites in the Americas and in Atlanta," *Golden Jubilee Book, 1962*. Atlanta: Atlanta Maronite Community. 1962.

———"Arab Adventures in the New World," *Yearbook, 1965–66*. New York: The Action Committee on American Arab Relations. 1966.

MALOOF, LOUIS. *The Maronite Heritage Intact and Immaculate. In Defense of the Irish of the East*. Atlanta Maronite Community. 1962.

MILLER, LUCIUS HOPKINS. *Our Syrian Population: A Study of the Syrian Population of Greater New York*. Columbia University Library, N. Y., and N. Y. Public Library, Widener Collection, Harvard University. 1904.

MOKARZEL, SALLOUM. "A Picturesque Colony," *New York Tribune*,

October 2nd; p. 21. 1892.

———"History of the Syrians in New York," *New York American*, October 3rd. 1927.

"The People of New York," *Life*, February 17th; pp. 89-96. 1947.

RICE, JACK. "A Resurgence of a Lebanese Parish in St. Louis." *St. Louis Post Dispatch*, Nov. 27th, pp. 1-3. 1967.

SAFA, ELIE. "Syrians and Arabians In America," *American Review of Reviews*, November; pp. 533-534. 1916.

SENGSTOCK, MARY C. The Corporation and the Ghetto: An Analysis of the Effects of Corporate Retail Grocery Sales on Ghetto Life. *Journal of Urban Law*. 45:673-703. 1968.

———"Telkeif, Baghdad, Detroit-Chaldeans Blend Three Cultures." *Michigan History* 54:29-310. 1970.

SULEIMAN, MICHAEL W. "The New Arab-American Community," in Hagopian and Paden, *op. cit.*, pp. 37-49. 1969.

"Syrians in the United States," *Literary Digest*, May 3rd; p. 43. 1919.

TANNOUS, AFIF. "Social Change in an Arab Village," *American Sociological Review*. 6:5 (October), pp. 650-652. 1941.

———"Emigration as a Force of Social Change in an Arab Village, *Rural Sociology*, 7:1 (March), pp. 62-74. 1942.

———"Acculturation of an Arab-Syrian Community in the Deep South, *American Sociological Review*. 8:3 (June), pp. 264-271.

"Their First Impression of New York," *World Outlook*, (June). 1918.

TREUDLEY, MARY B. "The Ethnic Group As A Collectivity," *Social Forces*, 31:3, (March), pp. 261-265. 1953.

WAKIN, EDWARD. *The Lebanese and Syrians in America*. Chicago: Claretian Publisher. 1974.

WILSON, HOWARD BARRETT. Notes on Syria Folk-Lore Collected in Boston. *Journal of American Folk-Lore* 16:133-147. 1903.

WINDER, R. BAYLY. "The Lebanese Emigration in West Africa," *Comparative Studies In Society and History*, 4:3, pp. 296-333. 1962.

WOLF, C. UMHAU. Muslims in the American Mid-West, *The Muslim World*. Jan: 39-48. 1960.

YAZBEK, MSGR. JOSEPH. "The Syrians," *Catholic Builders of the Nation*. Boston: Continental Press, Inc. 1923.

YOUNIS, DR. ADELE. "The Arabs Who followed Columbus," *Yearbook, 1965-66*. New York: Action Committee on American Arab Relations. 1966.

———"The Growth of Arabic-Speaking Settlements In the United States," in Hagopian and Paden, *op. cit.*, pp. 102-111. 1969.

UNPUBLISHED MATERIAL

AHDAB-YEHIA, MAY. 'Some General Characteristics of the Lebanese Maronite Community in Detroit,' Wayne State University: Unpublished M.A. thesis. 1970.

ALLHOFF, JOHN. 'Analysis of the Role of St. Raymond's Maronite Church as an Agent in the Assimilation of Lebanese Families in St. Louis.' University of Mississippi: Unpublished M.A. dissertation.

AL-TAHIR, ABDUL. 'The Arab Community in the Chicago Area: A Comparative Study of The Christian-Syrians and the Muslim Palestinians,' University of Chicago: Unpublished Ph.D. dissertation. 1952.

AL-NOURI, QAIS NAIM. 'Conflict and Persistence in the Iraqi-Chaldean Acculturation,' University of Washington, Seattle: Unpublished Ph.D. dissertation. 1964.

DAVID, J. K. 'The Near East Settlers of Jacksonville and Duval County.' Paper presented at the annual meeting of the Jacksonville Historical Society, May 12, 1954, Jacksonville, Florida. 1954.

DLIN, NORMAN. 'Some Cultural and Geographic Aspects of the Christian Lebanese in Metropolitan Los Angeles,' University of California at Los Angeles: Unpublished M.A. thesis. 1961.

ELYA, REV. JOHN. "The Accommodation of a Socio-Religious Sub-System: The Melkite Catholics in the United States," Unpublished term report, Boston College. 1965.

GASPERETTI, ELI. 'The Maronites: The Origin and Development of a Theocracy,' Columbia University: Unpublished M.A. thesis. 1948.

KASSEES, ASSAD S. 'The People of Ramallah: A People of Christian Arab Heritage.' Florida State University: Unpublished Ph.D. dissertation. 1970.

KAYAL, PHILIP M. 'The Churches of the Catholic Syrians and Their Role in the Assimilation Process.' Fordham University: Unpublished Ph.D. dissertation. 1970.

KNOWLTON, CLARK S. 'Spatial and Social Mobility of the Syrians and Lebanese in the City of Sao Paulo, Brazil,' Vanderbilt University: Unpublished Ph.D. dissertation. 1955.

MALOOF, LOUIS J. 'A Sociological Study of Arabic Speaking People in Mexico,' University of Florida: Unpublished Ph.D. dissertation. 1958.

SABA, LEILA. 'The Social Assimilation of the Ramallah Community Residing in Detroit,' Wayne State University: Unpublished M.A. thesis. 1971.

SENGSTOCK, MARY C. 'Maintenance of Social Interaction Patterns in an Ethnic Group,' Washington University: Unpublished Ph.D. dissertation. 1967.

STEIN, EDITH. 'Some Near Eastern Immigrant Groups in Chicago,' University of Chicago: Unpublished M.A. thesis. 1922.

SWANSON, JON C. 'Mate Selection and Intermarriage in an American Arab Moslem Community,' University of Iowa: Unpublished M.A. thesis. 1970.

Tannous, Afif. 'Trends of Social and Cultural Change in Bishmizeen,' Cornell University: Unpublished Ph.D. dissertation. 1940.

Wasfi, A. A. 'Dearborn Arab-Moslem Community: A Study of Acculturation.' Ann Arbor, Michigan: Michigan Microfilms. 1970.

Younis, Adele. 'The Coming of the Arabic-Speaking People to the United States,' Boston University: Unpublished Ph.D. dissertation. 1961.

Zelditch, Morris. 'The Syrians in Pittsburgh,' University of Pittsburgh: Unpublished M.A. thesis. 1936.

Index